Beyond All This Fiddle

Beyond All This Fiddle

ESSAYS 1955 – 1967

A. ALVAREZ

Random House / New York

FIRST AMERICAN EDITION

9 8 7 6 5 4 3 2

Published in the United States by Random House, Inc., New York

Library of Congress Catalog Card Number: 69-16460
Manufactured in the United States of America

TO MY MOTHER

I, too, dislike it: there are things that
are important beyond all this fiddle.

MARIANNE MOORE '*Poetry*'

This cosmic order which is the same for all
things has not been created, neither by gods nor
by men; it always was, and is, and will be,
an ever living Fire, flaring up according to
measure, and dying down according to measure.
. . . In its advance, the Fire will judge, seize,
and convict, everything.

HERACLITUS

Criticism cannot therefore be a single
developing theory; it must be partisan and
polemical in order to join art in asserting what
art is to become.

HAROLD ROSENBERG

Contents

Preface

The essays in this book are selected from roughly twelve years' work as a free-lance critic and literary journalist. In 1956, after two spells in America, I decided that English university life was not for me. Since then I have suffered, with more or less intensity, from what C. K. Ogden called 'Hand-to-Mouth Disease'.

For a decade I was the regular poetry reviewer of *The Observer*, whose literary editor, Terry Kilmartin, has been uncomplaining to the point of saintliness. Though most of these *Observer* reviews were round-ups of several poets in a short space, there was a chance, every so often, to write at greater length and in greater detail about a single poet. I have selected a few of these longer pieces to make a Verse Chronicle.

Out of this long involvement with contemporary poetry certain themes have emerged, which are the subject of the opening section on 'Modernism'. It began, while I was still at Oxford, as dissatisfaction with the conformities and programmed hopelessness of the Movement style, then all the rage. That, with progressive impatience, is the theme of the two earlier essays, 'The Fate of the Platypus' and 'Beyond the Gentility Principle'. It has ended in the theory of what I now call Extremist poetry. I have outlined that in the long title essay which stands at the beginning of this book and was written in the hope of providing a basis for everything that follows, of pulling it all together and setting a tone. I suppose I also thought of it as the end of a certain style of work for me, a kind of farewell to arms.

The other essays were originally written as introductions to Penguin, Signet and World's Classics editions, as lead reviews in *The*

Spectator and *New Statesman*, and as contributions to *The New York Review of Books*, *Commentary*, *The Hudson Review*, *The Kenyon Review*, *The American Scholar*, *The Times Literary Supplement*, *The Listener*, *The Twentieth Century*, *The Review*, *Tri-Quarterly* and *The Climbers' Club Journal*. Four have appeared in the following anthologies: *Hardy: a Collection of Critical Essays*, *The American Scholar Reader*, *Master Poems of the English Language*, *The Mountaineer's Companion*. My thanks to all the editors concerned for their permission to reprint the essays here.

During the last twelve years I have done a number of odd literary jobs, some odder than others: for two disastrous and improbable years, for example, I was the *New Statesman*'s theatre critic. I have also written a good deal on three of my passions: films, mountaineering and travel. But from all this I have reprinted here only four general essays. I have also left out all those close textual analyses which I developed a taste for at Oxford. That particular form of long-winded criticism now seems to me a pointless occupation for anyone not professionally involved in teaching. So what follows is a selection, from literally hundreds of articles and reviews, of some of the longer pieces which, I hope, will stand on their own.

I owe a debt of gratitude to Ian Hamilton for his pertinent and detailed comments on the opening essay, and above all to my wife, Anne, who cheerfully, encouragingly, and with patience, has slogged through it all.

A.A., 1967

1

MODERNISM

Beyond All This Fiddle

We are using our skins for wallpaper and we cannot win.

JOHN BERRYMAN

During the first thirty-odd years of this century the arts were sustained by a vague but optimistic feeling that a specifically Modernist style was emerging. What precisely it was to be was never agreed, though the theoretical shapes and possibilities were clear enough. It would certainly be anti-traditional, breaking with the old conventions, old rules, old gods; yet at the same time it would be concerned, in a worried way, with the breakdown of traditions, and so prone to nostalgia for a lost classical culture – as in early Pound and Eliot. It would also be highly, self-consciously intellectual – as in Cubism or the Jesuit Cubist language of James Joyce, or in the whole movement to reinstate the title 'Metaphysical Poet' as a fighting term. It would make use of the newly popularized insights of psychoanalysis (Kafka, the Surrealists), and yet somehow be attuned to the Marxist vision of reality (Mayakovsky, Attila József). And so on. If the details were imprecise, the hopes were considerable. Whatever else, the Modernist style would be freer and more strenuous than anything before: difficult, disciplined, complex, aware, elliptical and unprecedented, as was appropriate for the bewildering and bewildered society that had emerged.

Even the least optimistic agreed that certain advances were being made from which there was no going back. Where, say, Eliot or Pound led others would follow. Given *New Bearings in English Poetry*, the line of march was assured even if the destination wasn't. Yet it didn't finally turn out that way. In England a relatively inert traditionalism gradually reasserted itself until, by the end of the 1950s, poetry was more or less back at the place where the Moderns had left it in 1914. Even in the U.S.A., where most of the Modernist writers originated, the movement also backtracked into another kind of nostalgia: instead of returning to traditional forms, the poets resurrected traditional experiments. Hence the odd phenomenon of the latest *avant-garde* being largely a rewrite of that of fifty years ago. Hence, too, the even odder phenomenon of no one being bothered that Pound looms behind Charles Olson's shoulder and William Carlos Williams towers over Robert Creeley's. The stuff is felt to *be* modern simply because it *looks* modern. The *avant-garde* is acceptable because it is essentially reactionary, harmless.

I think there are two reasons for this. First, the revolutionary spirit that motivates every genuinely new movement in the arts – the desire to have done with the old clichés, and make it new – in this instance is a revolution of the academy, not of the market place. In the fifties the accepted Academic–Modern style – the style that would help a struggling poet to a comfortable university job – was the Pound–Eliot–Wallace Stevens line. That has now been replaced by the Pound–Williams–Cummings line. That is, the cosmopolitan bias in American poetry has been abandoned in favour of something altogether more chauvinistic. Hence the theoretical, almost antiquarian attitude to experiment in so many of the *avant-garde* poets, as though their iconoclasm involved nothing more than the principles on which a seminar in Creative Writing should be run. The second reason is implicit in this: I mean the deeply aesthetic attitude of these writers towards the least flicker of their sensibilities. It is not so much an aestheticism of the surface of their art – the perfect word in the perfect place – as of their surface responses, an aestheticism of the Muse. The whole theory of Projective verse, where the form is tailored to the pulse-rate and breathing of the poet, seems to me to ensure only a kind of psychic myopia. The poet becomes so rapt with whatever is immediately at his nerve-ends that he has no time to attend to anything else or to respond at any depth. He is also so unwilling to tamper with his Muse that he ends by tolerating dross, wastage, irrelevance, obscurity, all in the paradoxical name of the aesthetic purity of his inspiration – as who should say, 'My poems are so messy because they are so pure'.

It may be that all this is inevitable, since the academy is arguably the only place left for the traditional arts. I will come back to this. It may also be that this kind of aestheticism is the only valid defence the artists have against the pressures they are subjected to; which being so, they deserve their triviality. But it may also be that the need merely to *look* modern and experimental, no matter how tired the clichés you are dealing in, is a symptom of a general anxiety in the arts, an anxiety in which experiment itself becomes a style.

Certainly, for the past forty years or more, the history of the arts could be written in terms of the continual and continually accelerating change from one style to another. The machinery of communications and publicity is now so efficient that we go through styles in the arts as quickly as we go through socks; so quickly, indeed, that there seem no longer any real styles at all. Instead, there are fashions, idiosyncrasies, group mannerisms and obsessions. But all these are different from genuine style, which in the past has always been an expression of a certain fundamental coherence, an agreement about the ways random experience can be made sense of. When you talk of 'the Romantic style', you don't imply that Wordsworth, Keats, Byron, Coleridge and Shelley all wrote alike; simply that there are certain elements common to them all. Style, in short, is bound up with belief of one kind or another.

Clearly, any modern artist starts from premises more dispersed, empirical and ad-libbed than that, and also more democratic, in de Tocqueville's sense of the term:

> Men are no longer bound together by ideas, but by interests; and it would seem as if human opinions were reduced to a sort of intellectual dust, scattered on all sides, unable to collect, unable to cohere.

In terms of the contemporary arts, this means that there are as many viable styles as there are good artists. Perhaps that is what is meant by all the grandiose talk about 'the crisis in the arts'. It is not a crisis of style, it's a crisis of no-style, a crisis of nerve. For where there is no style in the overarching sense, but only fashions controlled by the middlemen of art – the critics, gallery-owners, big collectors and culturally ambitious chairmen of university departments; in short, by all those whose relationship to the artist is that of the big industrial concern to the inventor, a matter of production, promotion, marketing and cash – then a great strain is put on the artist. For where nothing is given, everything begins and ends with him, and his job becomes proportionately more difficult, tentative, compromising, risky. The reason is simple: where anything goes, a major test of originality is not a question of form but of psychic exploration, not of artifact but of the artist's identity. There is no longer any clear distinction between a critical and an existential judgement.

In these circumstances it follows that aestheticism is, almost by definition, square. This is another reason why so many 'way-out' experiments seem old-fashioned. It's not a matter of skill but of priorities. The really significant modern poets, I mean, take their technical originality for granted. They may have achieved it by hard labour, sweat and great concentration – consider, for example, the sheer formal tension of John Berryman's *Dream Songs*, the tension of an instrument tuned almost to breaking-point – but it is no longer their prime concern. Their technical innovations are a necessary background for their real pioneering in areas not previously explored by the arts.

The assumption that every serious artist, to be worth his salt, must create his own world and style from scratch, for himself and from himself, with no common values to lean on, is often used as evidence of his 'alienation' from society. This seems to me to be misleading in at least two ways. First, 'alienation' is a curious word for the financially profitable situation most artists now enjoy. Success of a kind has probably never been so easily come by. There are a multitude of prizes and foundations, publishing advances, television interviews, and a whole elaborate network of public relations and publicity, all poised for the least sign of talent. In New York and London the hardest thing for a man with any gifts to achieve is failure. Granted, all this may promote in a few artists only a certain uneasiness; they regard all that cash and publicity as a kind of consolation prize for not being taken seriously. The arts, they argue, are richly rewarded not because they have real influence but because they are relegated to a sub-division of the entertainment industry; in Saul Bellow's words, 'people are looking for something to goose the new middle-class with'. Therefore *avant-garde* writing, B-movies, television serials, surfing, sky-diving, spectator sports and the rest are all contained within the same bracket: useful outlets for fantasies and aggressions otherwise suppressed by society. So 'alienation' becomes a term to describe the serious artist's anxiety about his impotence when faced with a permissive, absorbent, utterly immovable audience, which pays back the most impassioned vituperation with hard cash and applause.

But 'alienation' is also a political term thick with thirties left-wing associations. That is, it is used not only to define the artist's situation but also to criticize bourgeois capitalist society. The fact that the artist is not a going member of it is thought to be a measure of society's failure. Eventually, it is implied, the set-up will be changed so that the artist, the worker and the administrator will all function fruitfully and to each other's mutual benefit; meanwhile the artist remains a critical and also rather tragic outsider. Political optimism apart, this seems to me peculiarly misleading. An outsider, by definition, must have at least some sense of what he is outside. It is precisely the lack of even this that has created the peculiar strain of Modernism. The artist is not 'alienated', he is simply lost. He lacks altogether the four traditional supports upon which every previous generation has been able, in one degree or another, to rely: religion, politics, national cultural tradition, reason. Yet although this ideological void creates a radically new situation for the arts, it makes the situation of the artist himself in no way special. On the contrary, the averagely-intelligent reader of any new work takes for granted not merely that the author will be committed to no ideology but also that, if he is committed, his work is somehow suspect, not serious.

In short, we take for granted only the proposition that we can take nothing for granted. By this token, we think of religion as a kind of mannerism, like Yeats's Neo-Platonism, or as a gesture of social solidarity: for example, when W. H. Auden goes on record as believing in all XXXIX Articles he seems less to be defining his beliefs than the role of the slightly fuddy-duddy Christian English gentleman which he adopted soon after he became an American citizen. T. S. Eliot was the only major modern artist whose Christian orthodoxy deeply influenced his work, and it now seems that this is precisely the element that gets in the way of contemporary readers and has contributed to the decline of his influence.* If there is any religious tone at all in the modern arts, it is a certain Jewishness. I mean Judaism not as a narrow orthodoxy but as a force working perennially on the side of sanity. It is, after all, the one great secular religion, a religion with no belief in the after-life, and founded on a social ethic of respect, responsibility and family piety. Hence it is empirical in its attitude to experience, pragmatic and hard-minded. Since these seem to be the qualities most valued and demanded now the writer becomes, almost of necessity, either a real or, in John

* Boris Pasternak's Christianity, from an orthodox standpoint, is strictly revisionist; that is, belief seems to matter less than charity, suffering and whatever Christian virtues can be most forcibly contrasted with Stalinism.

Berryman's words, an 'imaginary' Jew. He is concerned, that is, not with beliefs but with sceptical, non-idealistic survival.

Much the same anti-idealistic bias prevails whenever the arts now tangle with politics. This total revulsion from ideology is presumably connected with the curious way in which, in this century, all political idealism – of the left and of the right – ends sooner or later in totalitarianism. It is as though whenever a political principle were amplified on to a scale large enough and loud enough to be effective in a vast, statistical modern society it undergoes a double change: first it ceases to be a principle and becomes merely a slogan – exchanging whatever moral overtones it may have had for something cruder and more rousing; then it gradually becomes an instigation of national paranoia – as Maoism has been used to justify the genuinely psychotic behaviour of the Red Guards. And as the radical ideologies slide towards psychosis, so the democratic centre hardens into cynicism: since the differences between Labour and Conservative, Democrat and Republican, are now so marginal, the test of a party's value is precisely *not* its values but its skill in manipulating the machinery of power. Thus the average citizen tends to maintain a strictly agnostic attitude towards his government; he may believe in the parliamentary processes but not in political ideals. Correspondingly, when writers turn to political themes, as they have increasingly in the past few years, the politics they promote are those of privacy and protest. Against the bland and impervious clichés of the professional politicians, they set the personal gesture, though a personal gesture made in as public a manner as possible. Allen Ginsberg, for instance, is often very close in tone and emphasis to the radical poets of the thirties. The difference is that, instead of Marxism, he campaigns on a platform made up of two planks: drugs and homosexuality. He may be perfectly justified, since neither the protesters nor those protested against have ever showed much willingness to distinguish between political and sexual deviation. Hence the odd, quasi-political urgency in the arguments about pornography, perversion and drugs. Opiates, it seems, have at last become the opiate of the intellectuals. Or, as Leslie Fiedler put it, 'Just as certainly as liberalism is the LSD of the ageing, LSD is the radicalism of the young'.

Yet if the artist was denied the more obvious forms of belief, there was always art itself which became, in an Arnoldian way, increasingly a focus of all values. An English writer, in theory, could draw strength from an artistic–moral tradition that reached from *Gawaine* and Chaucer to Lawrence and Eliot. Yet somehow even this argument no longer works. The Great Tradition may go down to Eliot but it doesn't go beyond him, at least not in terms of any work that Dr Leavis finds significant. This in itself casts doubt on the Leavisite values, making them seem somehow irrelevant. They not only centre most eloquently and convincingly on D. H. Lawrence but also on a tradition of which he, apparently, was the last and finest flowering. Yet although Lawrence's insights into a submerged, a-social world of instincts, physical knowledge and subtle emotional undertows have profoundly influenced the literature and the sensibility of our time, he developed them in spite and in the teeth of modern urban society. In one way or another, he himself often and bitterly lamented that the basis of his values had been eroded by the Industrial Revolution and wholly destroyed by the First World War. If they lasted through the period between the two wars, it was only as a memory of something precious that had been lost. Not even that memory meant much after 1945. However excellent the social and moral values that had gone, they were gone irredeemably. The technological society which has taken the place of what Lawrence used to call 'the old England' may be utterly lacking in all the sense of community and natural order and moral awareness which the old tradition was supposed to have had, but it is, after all, the only society we have left. It is also the only one most of us have ever known. To be nostalgic for values and ideals wholly outside your experience is, in the end, a form of snobbery; it also effectively cuts you off from whatever strength and excellence there may be in the situation as it is.*

I suspect that T. S. Eliot, for all his emphasis on tradition, helped create the discontinuous culture which is the antithesis of Leavis's values. The cosmopolitan flair that enabled him to be influenced as equally by French and Italian poets as by English, was at one with the curiously international spirit of the Modernist movement in its great days. Harold Rosenberg has remarked that in Paris between the wars the artist was free from 'national folklore, national politics, national careers'. It was, he said, 'the only spot where . . . it was possible to shake up such "modern" doses as Viennese psychology, African sculpture, American detective stories, Russian music, neo-Catholicism, German technique, Italian desperation'. Modernism,

* See the essay on Miroslav Holub, p. 140.

in short, is synonymous with internationalism. Abstract painting and sculpture, functional architecture, electronic music and free verse – which in casting off traditional metres also becomes easier to translate – all serve to break down regional and national differences. Granted, there has been a swing against abstraction recently. Pop art and the related cults of the comic strip and television are attempts to create a kind of folk art out of the everyday props of the technological society. But as every technological society approaches, or aspires to, the condition of America, so pop art itself becomes international, global and, in the final analysis, abstract. Those cans of beer and soup, those strip-cartoon Supermen and Supergirls celebrated by the pop artists are so clearly objects that have been rolled off a production line that they seem utterly without individuality, extendable, repeatable to infinity. If there is a certain abstraction about the arts even when they are most concerned with things, it is because they are products of what Karl Popper calls an 'abstract or de-personalized society'.

This shadow of moral doubt and uncertainty has extended finally to reason itself. It is as though it, too, were no longer wholly adequate. Oddly enough, the source of this suspicion is the rationalists, the scientists themselves. Their message to the outside world is much like the message of the arts: the neat, logical, rather formal world of Newtonian science has vanished as utterly as the classical conventions of prosody, piety and perspective. In its place is something so complex and variable that the exact sciences themselves begin to seem inexact – relative, unpredictable, provisional. Hence Herbert Marshall McLuhan's brave new space-time of instantaneous electronic communication by TV and computer. He promotes this vision in a style which is half-oracle, half-advertisement because his business is to create a kind of metaphysic of technology. If he is often impenetrable, this is because, as he says, 'the medium is the message'; and the message is that the world of computers and space machinery is wholly baffling, frustrating and magical for the non-specialist. Modern scientific *practice* is now so sophisticated that it is as far beyond the uninitiated as scientific *theory* used to be. Meanwhile theory itself has gone into orbit; it deals with material as complex and changeable as the human psyche itself. Literally so, since advanced physics seems now to proceed on much the same assumptions and in much the same tentative, provisional way as a behavioural science. The only modern science whose elements can be more or less grasped by the layman is psychoanalysis; and from that he learns, above all, to recognize and accept the irrational as the basis of his being. Science and reason, in short, no longer offer a tidy, impersonal world as a consoling alternative to chaos. Instead, they seem merely like the private world writ large – shifting and confusing. 'How can one expect to reason with some generality,' complained Valéry, 'when the first elements of solid reasoning are not there?'

With no firm area of common belief or agreement, styles come and go like neon signs, since they do no more than satisfy a temporary need. Yet this is not necessarily crippling or destructive. Artists usually talk of their alienation in a world without values with a sob in their throats. This seems to me as inappropriate as the tone of those protest songs about nuclear weapons, where the singer invariably manages to imply that the H-bomb has been invented solely to get at *him*. As I see it, the failure of all traditions and beliefs is not an excuse for the failure of the arts, it is their greatest challenge or irritant. It simply entails a new emphasis. The artist's need to create his own style and language for himself and from scratch means that he is deliberately *using* his art, using it to create his own identity. Hence that sense of strain and extra-aesthetic urgency in so much of the best contemporary work. Hence, too, the relative failure of so much British literature since the war to produce anything significantly new. In spite of all the skill and subtlety, there is a weary insistence on a class system and traditional pieties, on cults of niceness and understatement, and a whole world of charm and nostalgia, which no longer seems relevant to anything. There are moments when the last twenty years of British writing seem like some great illusionist's trick, confidently and wishfully creating a society which no longer exists. Despite all the cleverness and skill, the final effect is of something oddly muffled and unreal. The reason is not that the social realities have altered but that they are no longer particularly *real*; certainly, they seem a good deal less urgent and reliable than the psychic realities. It is as though the revolution started by the abstract artists had finally been achieved: abstraction is no longer a theory, nor even a style; it is the defining condition of the arts.

The quality common to most *avant-garde* writing is a certain substancelessness. Beckett's plays take place in limbo, in a land without geography and among blank figures without history or even characteristics. Robert Lowell's New York and New England landscapes dissolve poem by poem into so many hells inside his own head. When Sylvia Plath writes a poem about riding a horse – 'Ariel' – the animal exists only as a reflection of internal violence contained and then released. Even Saul Bellow's *Herzog* which seems, as you read it, to include the whole of American society in its vision, never really gets out into that society, never really gives you a sense of an outer world that goes on despite Herzog and his obsessions; the people, the scenes, the comedy exist only as facets of his internal reality, as provokers of ideas, as excuses for those brilliant, nutty letters. Granted, the novel is about a man having a breakdown, so the indifference and dislocation might have been deliberately written into it as symptoms of the hero's near-psychosis. Yet the book doesn't give that impression; on the contrary, Bellow seems to make great efforts to justify Herzog and his sanity. It is as though the creative undertaking itself resisted him. 'You must aim the imagination', says Herzog, 'also at yourself, point blank.' This is the one unavoidable directive for any artist who is trying to make it new; yet when he follows it he invariably seems to end facing a state which borders, however knowingly, on psychosis.

I have tried to show elsewhere* that the modern movement, despite all the talk of a new classicism which heralded it fifty years ago, is simply an extension of Romanticism in new terms. The intense subjectivity of the Romantics remains at the centre of the modern arts, but it persists there as detached, almost clinical material. For the first Romantics the right to respond in their own way, unfettered by Augustan conventions, was a quasi-political ideal, the aesthetic equivalent of the revolutionary creed of Liberty, Equality and Fraternity. There was a firm, though subterranean connection between universal suffrage and universal suffering, between one man, one vote, and one man, one grief. That particular form of emotional democracy is now taken for granted, and the modern descendant of the Romantics is faced with the responsibilities of freedom and independence. That is, he is involved not simply in his emotions but in their sources, in his hidden motives and compulsions, in his own internal power politics and the roots of his own violence. His clinical awareness of all this has been created by his growing intimacy with psychoanalysis; so, too, has his cool, analytic attitude

* *Under Pressure* (Harmondsworth: Penguin, 1965), pp. 184 ff.

to his own distress. But he shares this cool with his audience; so the more ruthless he is with himself, the more unshockable the audience becomes. This pushes the artist into what I would call Extremism. He pursues his insights to the edge of breakdown and then beyond it, until mania, depression, paranoia and the hallucinations that come in psychosis or are induced by drugs become as urgent and as commonplace as Beauty, Truth, Nature and the Soul were to the Romantics.

If all this sounds modish and self-indulgent, the fault is not in the work but in my description of it. Clearly, it takes a highly disciplined and informed art to probe dispassionately and successfully into the extremes of inner space. So it is appropriate that the poet from whom the whole movement towards Extremism derives should be Robert Lowell, who is not only the most brilliant and assured technician now writing but is also – in background, preoccupations and intellectual tone – most naturally the heir to T. S. Eliot. Lowell began by exploring the rhetorical possibilities of Eliot's legacy, adapting it to a nervous system palpably rawer and less protected. From the start he had an unwavering command of language and a knack of stamping every line with his own, utterly individual rhythm. This rhetorical brilliance matched the willed, convert's intensity of his Roman Catholicism. It was as though virtuosity and religion were his own special, serious brand of magic, a conjuring trick by which he controlled forces which might otherwise have been insupportable. Yet the real measure of Lowell's creative power was not in his rhetoric but the way in which he was able to break out of the limits of his technical gifts. The turning-point came when, after a long silence, he published *Life Studies*. The American edition of the book was in four parts, which together represented a whole cycle of poetic evolution. The first contained four poems more or less in the old style: tense, thick-languaged, agonized. Then following a long prose section – omitted for no obvious reason from the English edition – about his parents and his childhood. This, too, was tense, though in a different way: it was elegant, careful, ironic, as though he were anxious not to be trapped in any easy emotion. Yet this effort to face his past, however warily, seemed to clear the air, leaving him free to go on to something quite new. The two parts that followed – Part Three contained poems about writers, Part Four comprised the 'Life Studies' themselves – were written in a manner far looser, easier, less stretched, and much closer to his natural speaking voice than anything he had done before. The poems were not less concentrated, they were simply concentrated in another way and for a different purpose. In the fourth part in particular the whole effort was to re-create certain key situations – with parents or relatives, wife or child – in all their strain and conflict, leaving nothing out, taking no easy exit and employing no technical, rhetorical or theological evasion, however brilliant or seductive.

Though the subject-matter was largely the kind of material that is dug up in psychoanalysis, the poems were in no vulgar sense confessional – neither self-gratifying nor overweeningly self-absorbed. Instead, all his skill was concentrated on making them witty, tender and intensely serious without affectations. Reading them and his subsequent volumes – *Imitations*, *For the Union Dead* – you feel you are in the presence of a powerful and eloquent *person*, whereas in his earlier work the power had always seemed a by-product of his technical accomplishment, an artifact rather than an attribute. Where the earlier work is compressed and opaque, the poems since *Life Studies* have gained a kind of transparency: you look through them to see the man as he is, a man of great contradictions, tenderness and violence, a man obsessed equally by his own crack-ups and by the symptoms of crack-up in the society around him. The skill, intelligence and discipline never falter, but they are all in the service of an insistent directness. The raw material of the poems is, precisely, raw and the poet refuses all aesthetic subterfuges to disguise the fact. Instead, he concentrates his technique on stating the case as it is, without nagging or hysteria.

The peculiar transparency of his work obviously puts a great personal responsibility on Lowell. A poem succeeds or fails by virtue of the balance and subtlety of the man himself. Perhaps this is why he began to write in this way only when he reached his full maturity as an artist. Before that he could scarcely have brought to bear on such intimate themes resources that would have been full enough, poised enough, detached enough to allow the poems to survive as art.

Just how difficult the process is becomes clear when you compare Lowell's work with that of a gifted disciple like Anne Sexton. Her subjects are much the same as his – nervous breakdown, the strains of marriage, the pervasive instability of things – but she lacks his critical assurance. So her work veers between good and terrible almost indiscriminately. It is not a question of her writing bad poems from time to time, like everybody else; she also prints them cheek by jowl with her purest work. The reason, I suppose, is that the bad poems are bad in much the same way as her good ones are good: in their head-on intimacy and their persistence in exploring whatever is most painful to the author. Her temptation is to leave the effect to the material, as though whatever were sufficiently naked and overwhelming couldn't fail. Yet the obvious truth is that the more subjectively exposed the theme, the more delicate the artistic control needed to handle it.

Perhaps the basic misunderstanding encouraged by Extremist art is that the artist's experience on the outer edge of whatever is tolerable is somehow a substitute for creativity. In fact, the opposite is true; in order to make art out of deprivation and despair the artist needs proportionately rich internal resources. Contrary to current belief, there is no short cut to creative ability, not even through the psychiatric ward of the most progressive mental hospital. However rigidly his experience is internalized, the genuine artist does not simply project his own nervous system as a pattern for reality. He is what he is because his inner world is more substantial, variable and self-renewing than that of ordinary people, so that even in his deepest isolation he is left with something more sustaining than mere narcissism. In this, of course, the modern artist is like every other creative figure in history: he knows what he knows, he has his own vision steady within him, and every new work is an attempt to reveal a little more of it. What sets the contemporary artist apart from his predecessors is his lack of external standards by which to judge his reality. He not only has to launch his craft and control it, he also has to make his own compass.

Just how necessary this inner wealth is to him, as he moves towards the extreme limits of what he can bear, can be seen in Sylvia Plath's last poems. In an interview for the British Council shortly before her death, she went on record as saying that the 'peculiar private and taboo subjects' explored by Lowell in his poems about nervous breakdown had set her free to go in the direction she wanted. But, she added,

> I must say I cannot sympathize with these cries from the heart that are informed by nothing except a needle or a knife or whatever it is. I believe that one should be able to control and manipulate experiences, even the most terrifying . . ., with an informed and intelligent mind. I think that personal experience shouldn't be a kind of shut box and a

mirror-looking narcissistic experience. I believe it should be generally relevant, to such things as Hiroshima and Dachau, and so on.

Clearly, this kind of feeling is not going to be made 'generally relevant' by any vague, vote-catching appeal to the camps or the bomb. When a writer tries to hitch a ride from these themes, he usually ends only by exposing the triviality of his responses. What is needed is that extreme tension and concentration which creates a kind of silence of shock and calm around the images:

I have done it again.
One year in every ten
I manage it –

A sort of walking miracle, my skin
Bright as a Nazi lampshade,
My right foot

A paperweight,
My face a featureless, fine
Jew linen.

Consider how the penultimate line-ending is cannily used to create a pause before the epithet 'Jew'. The effect is two-fold: first shock, then an odd detachment. The image is unspeakable, yet the poet's use of it is calm, almost elegant. And this, perhaps, is the only way of handling such despair: objectively, accurately, and with a certain contempt.

This is typical of Sylvia Plath's procedure in these last poems. The more desperate she is, the more image thickens into image, dividing and multiplying like fertilized cells; the tighter, too, is her rhythmical control, varying between a chopped, savage, American throw-away and a weirdly jaunty nursery-rhyme bounce. A wealth of image-breeding creativity and the whole book of technique is thrown at situations and feelings that otherwise seem to overbear all technique. It is an art like that of a racing driver drifting a car: the art of keeping precise control over something which, to the outsider, seems utterly beyond all control.

Whether her involvement with suicide, like Lowell's with nervous breakdown, was real or imaginary is beside the point so far as her art is concerned. All that matters is that the poetry should make a convincing imaginative reality. No doubt she and Lowell handle their themes so coolly, with such little regard for mere shock, because they have in fact been there before. Thus breakdown and suicide become almost neutral subjects – like God or the weather – because the poets can accept them as wholly normal, even normative. Yet there are other, equally potent factors involved in this kind of writing. Just as Lowell's poetry is an extension of the Romantic Agony into modern, analytic terms, so Sylvia Plath's is a logical extension of Lowell's explorations: she simply went further in the direction he had already taken. For her, it turned out to be a one-way street from which there was no going back. So she went to the extreme, far edge of the bearable and, in the end, slipped over. That is a risk in handling such touchy, violent material. Yet she turned it, too, to advantage: the courage it took to gamble in this way is reflected in the curious sense of creative optimism, of possibilities in the teeth of the impossible, that stirs in her poems like a moving bass.

Art always depends on a principle of natural selection; there are simply too many contenders to allow for anything except the survival of the creatively fittest. Extremism, however, is based on a form of psychic Darwinism that is far beyond the most stringent usual demands of talent. There are many possible reasons for this. The most conventional is to blame the violence and destructiveness of the period. The Australian painter, Sidney Nolan, has a theory that artists act as an Early Warning System for history: what they put in their work is sooner or later acted out on a large scale. By that reckoning, Extremist art becomes a premonition of the holocaust, whilst its slightly schizophrenic detachment from its own anguish corresponds to the split in the environment between violence and cosiness, war and well-being.

Or it may be that the gloomy, dissatisfied determination of most Extremist artists to make things more than usually impossible for themselves is the product of a kind of boredom: they cultivate their psychosis because every more conventional response has been drained dry of significance. Just as a mathematician with a sophisticated computer is no longer interested in simple arithmetic, so the super-sophistication of means in the arts, combined with unshockable, total permissiveness in the audience, has finished by driving the artists, literally, towards distraction.

But perhaps Extremism is also the last, desperate reaction of the traditional arts to an untraditional situation. William James's division of philosophy into the 'tender-minded' and the 'tough-minded' applies also to the arts. Tender-minded meant: 'rationalistic – that is, going by principles – intellectualistic, idealistic, optimistic, religious, free-willist, monistic, dogmatical'. All these epithets might apply to the traditional Romantic and formalist inheritance of the arts, with their 'monistic' belief in a unique formula for experience. Yet the society in which the arts now have to function is insistently tough-minded: 'empiricist – that is, going by facts – sensationalistic, materialistic, pessimistic, irreligious, fatalistic, pluralistic, sceptical'. It follows, then, that different standards will apply. The 'tender-minded' need to impose a style and solution on the wilderness presupposes a certain idealistic innocence. The alternative is what might best be called 'worldliness'. It is a quality which often has little to do with sophistication; it depends, instead, on accepting corrupted reality as being both inescapable and unchangeable. In the arts this means, among other things, accepting new ideas, new forms, new areas of experience, without any illusions as to their ultimate value. In these terms, worldliness is a precondition of survival, which is, as I suggested earlier, a peculiarly Jewish quality.

This brand of worldliness is most potent in that exclusively twentieth-century and dominantly Jewish art-form, the cinema. With television, cinema has all the more gloomy worldly qualities expected in a highly industrialized society. It is:

(*a*) *corporate:* involving many people and intricate commercial organization, since we are suspicious of individualism and believe in collective, democratic effort;

(*b*) *technological:* involving elaborate scientific processes and scores of technicians, since we believe, in a hazy, religiose way, in the power of scientific technology;

(*c*) *commercial:* since the less we believe in minority culture the more we believe in audience-ratings and box-office returns as criteria of excellence;

(*d*) *disposable:* since art, on these terms, is reduced to one product among many designed to occupy the leisure of a consumer society; it must therefore be consumed and replaced in order to maintain the art industry's cycle of production;

(*e*) *cynical:* since in the last analysis we believe in nothing.

Yet the cinema is also worldly in a more profound and healthy way. It remains, that is, inextricably committed to the world as it is.

This is not a question of principle but of a quality inherent in the medium itself. However tightly a director selects, stylizes and controls the image on the screen, he can never entirely obliterate the presence of the world that extends beyond the frame. Simply because the picture moves, it is in a continual, cross-fertilizing relationship with the casual outside world, unredeemed by art and choice. The camera takes in too much for the audience not to be aware of haphazard life going on around the selected action. Thus the camera itself provides a framework of judgement for the action. It creates a visual morality. For example, the art of a master like Luis Buñuel lies in his being not only original and radical but also utterly unobtrusive. He simply uses his camera to look at people, plainly, patiently, mostly in mid-shot, without tricks or illusions or expectations. Like a man whose gift of silence makes other people talk more and more anxiously, Buñuel's camera waits for the characters to reveal themselves – their obsessions, their perversions, their corruptions. The director, meanwhile, defines nothing, asserts nothing; he remains detached, accepting, sardonic. The result is a kind of nihilism of silence, nihilism by observation.*

For the traditional static arts, like poetry and painting, the cinema's peculiar brand of total and unfooled realism presents a considerable problem. Marshall McLuhan has analysed at length the ways in which film and television are new forms expressing a new sensibility, and doing so in defiance of all traditional means. A by-product of this process is that they have also sapped the confidence of the older arts. Pop and op art may be answers to this crisis of nerve: not only attempts to create iconographies for the technological superstates but also ways of changing the artist's role. The op artist functions as an aesthetic technician or crypto-scientist, whilst the pop painter simply chooses among the products of urban society. Since his final standard of excellence is solely that of taste – in his choice of images and handling of paint, etc. – he is reduced to the status of a high-level interior decorator.

Similarly, the pop movement in poetry is more than a reaction against a dead or dying formalism; it is also prompted by the new attitude towards language implicit in cinema and television. McLuhan calls cinema 'a form of statement without language'; that is, words and arguments are merely one means amongst several of

* These arguments are developed in a different way and in more detail in the essay, 'Cinema', pp. 236–42.

nudging the audience in a certain direction. The more literary a script, the less effective it is as cinema. Yet, at the same time, the cinema also communicates more widely and compulsively than any other art form. This spectacle of pop culture effortlessly usurping the power of high culture is, I suspect, behind the fashion for the diluted near-verse designed for mass readings and poetry-and-jazz concerts. With few exceptions, the writing on these occasions is rudimentary. It may well not be rudimentary enough. The lesson to be learnt from film and TV is that language can function in a different way and with utterly different disciplines once it merges with other forms of communication. But the pop poets do nothing more radical than model their verse on the lyrics of pop songs. Which means that they remain tied to the logic of a traditional form at its weariest. Their aim is not to innovate but to popularize, to seduce an audience which is interested in poetry simply as an assertion of Bohemian non-conformity. In its way, this is a largely political project: art is valuable simply as a means of rejecting the square world. So the poet resigns his responsibilities; he becomes less concerned to create a work than to create a public life; what he offers is not poetry but instant protest. Where the pop painter becomes an interior decorator, the pop poet becomes a kind of unacknowledged social worker.

'The trouble with modern theories of behaviourism', Hannah Arendt once wrote, 'is not that they are wrong but that they could become true.' This applies also to Marshall McLuhan's theories of the mass media. If he is right, then the old formal arts are no longer wholly meaningful and the artists are in imminent danger of being made redundant. For the impact of the 'electronic culture' threatens to shatter all the traditional disciplines which are worked so hard for and acquired only slowly and with such difficulty. Suddenly, unexpectedly, they no longer seem much use. To survive and communicate the artist may have to abandon his inheritance, his training, even his habits of mind, and start again from the beginning. Granted, this always happens when there is a fundamental change in the arts; that is why every genuinely new movement is resisted. But this time what is in question is something more radical and thorough-going than a manner of speaking or seeing; those 'new styles of architecture, a change of heart', seem newer, more changed and less hopeful than anyone ever expected. In the face of this threatening transformation, the Extremist style is the most courageous response. It may, after all, have less to do with the prognosis of a nuclear holocaust than with the relatively simple understanding of the fact that the traditional basis of the arts has smashed. Given a situation so precarious, internal confusion transmuted into new kinds of artistic order becomes the only possible form of coherence.

The Times Literary Supplement, 1967

The Literature of the Holocaust

In the twenty years since the war ended the flood of literature on the Nazi atrocities has never slackened; gradually, however, its style has changed and its direction. To the libraries full of documentary material, and the shelf upon shelf of more or less abstract analyses of the madness, a little genuinely creative work is slowly being added. There have, of course, been concentration-camp novels by the hundred, but even setting aside the cheaply sensational, few of them could claim much as literature. With rare exceptions, there are qualities that elude even the best, leaving them in some half-world of art.

The root of the trouble lies in the enormity and the truth of the events they describe. Consider, for example, Josef Bor's *Terezin Requiem** and Elie Wiesel's *Night*,† both serious works by serious men, both well thought of, and both imaginative rehandlings of incidents that really took place. Bor's work is about a performance of Verdi's *Requiem*, conducted by Raphael Schacter in the Theresienstadt ghetto in Czechoslovakia. The sub-title is 'A Narrative of the Human Spirit' – justifiably, for the whole thing was an extraordinary triumph: the organization of a big choir, soloists, and orchestra, constant rehearsals, and a final performance in the teeth of the Nazis, the transports, and the whole chaos of the time. It is, in short, a real-life allegory of art poising itself precariously against destruction.

Night is more personal and very much more painful, less an

* New York: Knopf, 1963.
† New York: Hill and Wang, 1960.

allegory than a scantily fictionalized autobiography. A young boy and his father are transported from a Hungarian ghetto to Auschwitz, where they endure months of degradation, brutality and hunger. Finally, as the Red Army closes in, they are evacuated through the frozen countryside to Buchenwald. There the father dies slowly of dysentery, while his son nurses him fearfully, guiltily, resentfully. It is here, not in the cruelty, that the sense of shock which vibrates so continuously through the book is located:

> I did not weep, and it pained me that I could not weep. But I had no more tears. And, in the depths of my being, in the recesses of my weakened conscience, could I have searched it, I might perhaps have found something like – free at last!

Wiesel's pain lies in the discovery that neither love, filial piety, nor his intense Talmudic training can stand up against extremes of starvation and fear. On the road to survival everything goes, leaving only the most primitive terrors and desires.

As a human document, *Night* is almost unbearably painful, and certainly beyond criticism. But like *The Terezin Requiem* and dozens of other equally sincere, equally distressing books, it is a failure as a work of art. As the passage above shows, when what Wiesel has to say becomes intolerable for him, he falls back on rhetoric. The terror and the failure are stated, but their real potency is never quite expressed. So they become unreal, remote, something out there. Perhaps the answer to that is a massive '*So what?* The atrocities and their exposure are more urgent than art.' I don't believe this, and for reasons beyond the obvious one: that from the fragile, tentative, individual discriminations of art emerge precisely those moral values which, if understood and accepted, would make totalitarian atrocities impossible.

It is partly a question of time. The atrocities have in no way been diminished by their twenty years' distance, but their meaning has changed slightly, and in changing it has become more, rather than less, urgent. In the beginning, the horror of the camps was heightened by a certain relief – 'Thank God it wasn't me' – and this in turn provoked guilt. To judge from their writing, even former inmates seem to have felt obscurely guilty at having survived when friends and family had gone under – as though survival were almost a mark of cowardice, as though it certainly meant, for them, that they had had to compromise with the omnipresent and contagious corruption. For the rest of us, there was the far obscurer guilt of being Jews who had never been exposed to the camps at all. In these circumstances, the rhetoric of so much concentration-camp literature was comforting; it enabled us to feel engaged while in reality preserving our safe distance. Since then the situation has changed. The question of survival is less obvious, but more ubiquitous, more pervasive. I once suggested (in a piece for *The Atlantic Monthly*, December 1962) that one of the reasons why the camps continue to keep such a tight hold on our imaginations is that we see in them a small-scale trial run for a nuclear war. Between 1940 and 1945, four-and-a-half-million people died in Auschwitz; the same number would die in minutes if a hydrogen bomb landed on London or New York. Then there are those other curious, upside-down similarities: the use of modern industrial processes for the mass production of corpses, with all the attendant paraphernalia of efficiency, meticulous paperwork and bureaucratic organization; the deliberate annihilation not merely of lives but of identities, as in some paranoid vision of a mass culture. And so on. It adds up to a perverted, lunatic parody of our own engulfing but otherwise comfortable technological societies. So the literature of the camps has become, insidiously and unanswerably, our own under-literature. Its connections with our lives, our despairs, our fantasies are subterranean but constant and powerful. When the façade of our bright, jazzy, careless affluence rifts, and our well-conditioned domestic psyches explode, what oozes out is the same sour destructiveness – passive or active, the need to destroy or be destroyed – as once, for some years, contaminated almost the whole of European morality. If our century has invented unprecedented ways of making life easier, it has also provided us with multitudinous, sophisticated, and equally unprecedented means of annihilation. The camps are a proof of that, and a working model. In them the language of our sickness was created.

All this is more or less cliché, more or less accepted. The problem is to know to what extent the acceptance implies understanding, and the understanding affects our behaviour:

> Probably, we shall never be able to determine the psychic havoc of the concentration camps and the atom bomb upon the unconscious mind of almost everyone alive in these years. For the first time in civilized history, perhaps for the first time in all of history, we have been forced

to live with the suppressed knowledge that the smallest facets of our personality or the most minor projection of our ideas, or indeed the absence of ideas and the absence of personality could mean equally well that we might still be doomed to die as a cipher in some vast statistical operation in which our teeth would be counted, and our hair would be saved, but our death itself would be unknown, unhonoured, and unremarked, a death which could not follow with dignity as a possible consequence to serious actions we had chosen, but rather a death by *deus ex machina* in a gas chamber or a radioactive city. . . . The Second World War presented a mirror to the human condition which blinded anyone who looked into it. For if tens of millions were killed in concentration camps out of the inexorable agonies and contractions of super-states founded upon the always insoluble contradictions of injustice, one was then obliged also to see that no matter how crippled and perverted an image of man was the society he had created, it was nonetheless his creation, his collective creation (at least his collective creation from the past) and if society was so murderous, then who could ignore the more hideous of questions about his own nature?

That is how Norman Mailer began 'The White Negro'. His thesis was that contemporary stresses were so great that psychopathic behaviour had become an existential necessity. But I presume that he was defining something rather closer to himself than hipsterism; rather, he was working out how he could preserve his identity *as a creative artist* against the sheerness, violence and anonymity of his society. The answer he came up with was: By behaving badly. Since the camps and the bomb were also created in our image, then anything goes.

There seems a certain paradoxical sanity in this. The camps are no longer such 'a world apart' as they were when David Rousset wrote his book of that name, and they seem to be getting increasingly closer. Indeed, something like the Eichmann, Dering and Frankfurt Trials should, I think, be continually in progress, not for the sake of revenge – which is a concept scarcely relevant to such obscenities and so many million deaths – nor to humiliate the Germans – which seems, anyway, to be impossible – but simply to remind us of the kind of society we have created, and what we are capable of.

Anyone trying to create imaginative art out of the experience of the concentration camps has to face much the same problems as Mailer defined in 'The White Negro', but in a much more extreme form. He has, in fact, to do the impossible. He must create a coherent artistic world out of one which was the deliberate negation of all values. He must exercise his imagination on situations which, in proved, lived fact, were beyond the imagination, and on circumstances where the imagination, with its power of making things come nervously close, was potentially the most dangerous and destructive of all qualities. He has to take the utterly psychopathic as his norm, and make art out of the forces of anti-art.

It is here that so many of the holocaust novels fail. Wiesel and Bor, for example, both write as though the stories they told were essentially like any other – however much more terrible; as though, that is, they were available to normal human values. If the results seem excessive, even a bit journalistic, that is less because the authors overwrite than because the feelings are so fiercely present in the barest recital of the facts that any attempt to elaborate, underline or explain them seems like wild overstatement. The process by which a child is not merely forced to witness the gradual death of his father, but is also forced to acknowledge that he is glad and relieved when the old man dies – in short, when he psychically becomes his father's murderer – may fit naturally enough into the shorthand of dreams and psychosis; it is, however, beyond the conventional language of guilt and grief and suffering. Similarly, the episode Bor describes is beyond propaganda, even propaganda for the human spirit. The camps, of course, can be used devastatingly for *political* propaganda, as the Israeli and Eastern European governments well know (Poland has a Department of Martyrology specifically for this). But in being so used, they lose a good deal of their inner truth and power; they become, in a way, less important.

The difficulty is to find language for this world without values, with its meticulously controlled lunacy and bureaucracy of suffering. Perhaps the most convincing way is that by which dreams express anguish: by displacement, disguise, and indirection. The most powerful exception is the Pole, Tadeusz Borowski, who alone managed to convey the full force of the concentration camp experience while he was still close to it in time.* His style is curt, icy, and brutally direct; and he assuaged his survivor's guilt by a kind of moral self-destruction: he identified with the evil he described.

* Two of his stories have appeared in translation: 'A Day at Harmenz' is in *The Modern Polish Mind*, ed. Maria Kuncewitz (Boston: Little, Brown and Company, 1962); and 'This Way for the Gas' is in *Commentary*, July 1962. They were originally in collections published in Poland in 1946 and 1948.

Although in reality he is said to have behaved with great courage in Auschwitz, in his stories he transforms and degrades himself. The first-person singular narrator is well up in the prisoners' hierarchy and well in with it; he is a politico, a spiv with a cushy job, egotistical, well-fed, and mostly impervious to the horrors around him. His anger is all for the weakness of those who go under, forcing him into the parallel weakness of being shocked and sickened. Indeed, anger is the dominant, the determining force in these stories. Czeslaw Milosz, writing of Borowski in *The Captive Mind*, called him 'a frustrated lover'. He meant, I take it, that the springs of feeling were poisoned in Borowski by the facts he had to face, leaving only a dry rage that such things should be. So all he could do was present a bare record of how and why love had to fail. Borowski himself has been quoted as describing his work as 'a journey to the utmost limit of a certain kind of morality'. But he eventually took the step beyond that limit. His anger turned increasingly on himself; he gave up his creative work and immersed himself more and more deeply in Stalinist politics. Finally, having escaped the Zyklon B of Auschwitz, he gassed himself at home in 1951.

Borowski's work brings home the full double force of that phrase, *l'univers concentrationnaire*. It refers not only to the closed world without value of the camps, but also to the insupportable concentration of the universe on one man's back. It suggests what happens when a sensitive man experiences so much that he can no longer properly cope with his reactions, and the burden of them becomes intolerable. All that remains to do is to record the bare facts clearly, sharply, and without comment. The judgements are there by omission. Around Borowski's stories there is a kind of moral silence, like the pause which follows a scream.

Something of the same method was used by the brilliant young Polish director, Andrzej Munk, in his recent, though posthumous, film about Auschwitz, *The Passenger*. The main story concerns an ambivalent, deviously Lesbian conflict between a German woman overseer and a Polish prisoner. But it is played out against a background of routine, rather than polemic, horror: children queue docilely for the gas-chamber, while a comfortable, fatherly German soldier sets in order the pellets of Zyklon B; the incinerators belch thick, human smoke, and nobody notices; the whistle of a transport bringing new 'material' interrupts a Bach concert, at which the camp staff sit poker-backed, proper and smilingly absorbed; the camp orchestra tootles away while the corpses are brought in after the day's labour; the S.S. amuse themselves with nightmare sports with naked women and dogs. The brutalities are casual, habitual, anonymous, and to one side. Emotionally, they seem to occur only in one corner of the screen.

Like Borowski, Munk died before his time, killed in a car crash before he could finish *The Passenger*. Considering the minute amount of traffic in Poland, even in 1961, this in itself was almost an achievement. Yet it seems, in a way, to have been inevitable. The concentration camps are a dangerous topic to handle. They stir mud from the bottom, clouding the mind, rousing dormant self-destructiveness. In the last few years I personally have known half-a-dozen suicides or near suicides; and each has prefaced his act with a fierce immersion in the literature of the camps. That is why I suggested that these places, these crimes, have an existential meaning beyond politics or shock or pity. They have become symbols of our own inturned nihilism, which their disproportionately vast scale heightens, even justifies, by making individual suffering seem so insignificant. In his fumbling way, I imagine Arthur Miller was after something like this when he thumbed an emotional lift from Dachau in *After the Fall*. Granted he cheapened all those deaths by using them to say things which were trite, vulgar, and reeking of self-pity. But quality apart, there was a kind of sense in his manoeuvre: the camps have become a focus of contemporary suffering. The worse things get, the closer and more meaningful they become; as in some modern Grail Legend, everyone was wounded by that Dolorous Stroke. So the crime against humanity, as Mailer suggested, becomes also a projection of one's own inner violence and misery. Clearly, it is at this point that the apparently trivial aesthetic question of tone becomes vital.

Borowski's ultimate brutality with himself helped him to take the camps straight and yet make art out of them. More recently, a number of holocaust books have appeared which are surprisingly convincing as novels in their own right. But a great deal of the imaginative effort which went into them is devoted to finding ways round the basic premise: 'I am the man, I suffered, I was there.'

The least evasive, most conventional, and probably earliest (the dates of the original publications are not given in the translations) are the stories of the Czech writer Arnost Lustig, *Night and Hope** and *Diamonds in the Night*.† These have something of Borowski's directness, but they lack almost entirely that sense the Pole gives of the utter decadence and corruption of everyone in the camps, particularly the narrator and his fellow-prisoners. Lustig's figures have the remnants of a certain pathetic loyalty to each other, and a certain pitiable innocence. And for a good reason, which is also the source of the stories' power: his murderous, agile scarecrows, who treat death, starvation and pain as casually as the weather, are all children. It is only when you pause to take this in – Lustig never insists on it, scarcely even bothers to mention it – that the stories become unthinkable.

Herod's Children,‡ a recent novel by an Austrian, Ilse Aichinger, has the same subject – a group of young, mostly Jewish, children in Nazi Vienna – but the treatment is the exact opposite of Lustig's. The style of *Herod's Children* is oblique, poetic and as highly-strung as a racehorse. The young heroine wanders through the book in a kind of hallucinated trance in which sharp impressions, insights, symbols, action and fragments of poetry continually shift and merge. The book has about it an air of slightly transposed high feeling which I don't much like, a sensitivity so acute that it ends by being sensitive only to itself. It is saved from hyperaesthesia only by the harshness of the events it describes, and by a feeling, common to all holocaust literature, of desperation of purpose – as though writing the novel were the author's only hope of survival. The result is something like a dream: full of odd shifts and flights and happenings, and infused with unbearable but continually displaced emotion.

Aichinger's dream of sensitivity in the teeth of horror, and Lustig's tender yet indignant factuality, both manage to present visions of childhoods twisted beyond all possible repair, yet still retaining something of their original alertness and spontaneous generosity. They also represent the two most obvious and accepted solutions for coming to terms with the camps. The Czech's unflickering sense of fact is a way in for a political interpretation; his stories could be (and have been) used as Party documents. In contrast, the Austrian's sensitivity is an oblique insistence on art and personal interpretation as the only possible means of salvation or understanding. But

* New York: Dutton. † New York: Arthur Vanous.
‡ New York: Atheneum, 1963.

both miss something of the adult sense of intolerable violence right under the skin, of the camps exploding *at this instant* in our lives.

It is this quality which is achieved in two of the most complete and original disaster novels, which are also the most recent: Jorge Semprun's *The Long Voyage** and Piotr Rawicz's *Blood from the Sky*.† Both were originally written in French, though neither author is a Frenchman (Semprun was born in Spain, Rawicz in the Ukraine); both have a studiedly Parisian manner, hard, clever, cynical, highly intellectual; both find imaginative ways around the atrocities, so that they tap the reserves of threat and terror without ever quite meeting them head-on. Otherwise they are totally different.

Rawicz never mentions the concentration camps, though he himself was in three of them. He has written a strange portmanteau of a novel, stuffed with fantasies, poems, parables, bits of philosophy and a lunatic humour which is rarely funny but often frightening. The hold-all in which all these notes and queries are packed is the story of a young, wealthy, highly cultivated Ukrainian Jew who, thanks to blond hair, blue eyes and cunning, escapes the camps altogether. He is doomed to live, with an alias and an identity not his own, while his whole society is being exterminated. And he is by no means certain if he has the better bargain. The fantastic thread of the story comes and goes, yet remains compulsive. Oddly enough, the fragments and diversions strengthen it. The sour-mouthed poems, the notes on disgust, weary meditations and mad allegories, all contribute to the same condemnation: the whole world has become murderous, hypocritical, corrupt and moneygrubbing; and the victims are as contaminated as their torturers. The Jews, the Nazis and the Jew-hating, German-hating Poles all swim in the same filth; the effort to keep afloat only provokes in the author weariness and self-disgust. It is an imaginative projection of the dead-end moral nihilism embodied in the camps. If at times the writing is too brittle, the brilliance too 'brilliant', the cynicism too tricksy, these may be necessary defences. Like Dante's *terza rima*, they are a means of preserving a degree of detachment between the artist and the inferno; they insulate the book from the screaming and

* Translated by Richard Seaver (New York: Grove Press, 1964).

† Translated by Peter Wiles (New York: Harcourt, Brace and World, 1964).

outrage in the next room, and also from a pity which could not be handled.

Where Rawicz uses diversionary tactics to convey intensities which he could not otherwise express, Semprun, in a unique way, seems wholly to have assimilated his experience in Buchenwald. Granted, *The Long Voyage* is not quite about his time there; his subject is the journey to the camp and the return, but by using a complicated Proustian time-scheme, he transforms this into a summation of his whole life. The figures from his childhood, his companions in the Resistance, his fellow transportees and camp inmates, the S.S., the guards, the peasants from the neighbouring German village, and the liberators are all seen *sub specie* of the concentration camp. Semprun uses Buchenwald and the knowledge of what happened there in the same way as Matthew Arnold used his literary touchstones. How do people measure up to it as men? How do they react, justify their part in the process, or their refusal to see? What is the mentality of the modern bureaucratic killer, his accomplices and his victims? How do you choose or fail to choose your fate when the conditions become so extreme that you can no longer avoid the responsibility?

Semprun's style is tough – tougher perhaps for being excellently translated into Hemingwayese – but the toughness is not of a muscle-flexing kind. It is, instead, a question of a certain hardness of intelligence, probing away at the complex fate of having an identity. He is also – and this alone would make him unique in the field – genuinely funny at times, with the burnt-out wit of a man who has come through: 'Remember, getting there is half the fun', the narrator remarks to his companion when the going in the transport gets particularly rough. In this poised, questioning setting, the rare details of camp horror – such as a ghastly hunt of Jewish children by the S.S. and their dogs – explode like some shouted obscenity.

What Semprun is doing, in short, is exploring the possibilities of human behaviour in inhuman circumstances. The extreme situation is a catalyst which works in two ways: it either disintegrates a personality or precipitates it. He is trying to demonstrate imaginatively that from the absence itself of morality a morality can emerge. And this seems to have been a part of the experience as it really was. One of the most moving moments of the Dering trial in London came in the testimony of a French woman doctor: soon after she arrived in Auschwitz she asked a colleague, also a woman, whether or not she should cooperate with the S.S. in their experiments. The other doctor replied, in effect, 'We have probably only a few weeks to live. In that time we can at least try to behave like human beings.' Semprun's achievement is to have made this form of bare moral survival into an aesthetic, creative procedure. Instead of taking the easy way out – sensationalism, journalism, hysteria, self-pity – he uses intelligence, humour and pity to make something positive out of hell. The technical accomplishment is an image of the personal achievement involved. If the book was hard to write, it must have been doubly hard to have arrived at the point of being able to write it in that way.

Rawicz's effort, on the other hand, is channelled in the opposite direction; he makes his art out of disintegration. His hero survives by an act of treason to himself and his people, by assuming an identity which is his own turned upside down; the aristocratic Jewish poet comes through by becoming a cloddish, anti-Semitic Ukrainian farm-hand. Inevitably, this betrayal of himself produces guilt, nightmare and the glimmerings of madness. Hence Rawicz's schizophrenic style – a style, that is, dictated by what the psychologists call 'inappropriateness of affect': trivial incidents provoke despair, and horrors make for icy control or manic humour; nowhere is it ever possible wholly to get through to anyone else.

Before Semprun and Rawicz published their novels, the literature of the concentration camps was a specialized subject, a sub-division of the history of an insult to humanity. The real destructive nihilism acted out in the camps was expressed artistically only in works like Beckett's *Endgame* or *Waiting for Godot*, in which the naked unaccommodated man is reduced to the role of helpless, hopeless, impotent comic, who talks and talks and talks in order to postpone for a while the silence of his own desolation. But this was only an abstraction from *l'univers concentrationnaire*, an echo at best of its state of mind. *The Long Voyage* and *Blood from the Sky*, however, provide two opposite ways of coping with the nihilism at the same time as they show it in action; they people hell and describe its geography. By making it potent to the imagination, they make it also relevant to our own, mercifully more humdrum lives. And this, as Rawicz insists in the postscript to his book, is the purpose of the whole operation:

This book is not a historical record.

If the notion of chance (like most other notions) did not strike the author as absurd, he would gladly say that any reference to a particular period, territory, or race is purely coincidental.

The events that he describes could crop up in any place, at any time, in the mind of any man, planet, mineral. . . .

Commentary, 1964

Beyond the Gentility Principle*

In 1932 F. R. Leavis proclaimed that Eliot and Pound had between them brought about a significant reorientation of literature. Twenty years later he took most of it back again, blaming the anti-critical workings of the London literary circuit and the decay of an educated reading public. He may have been perfectly justified in crediting the metropolitan pundits with setting up so many false gods. But the relative failure of talent is another matter entirely. So is the manner in which so much of the talent that has arrived has been misused. The London old-boy circuit may often be stupid, conceited and parasitic but I don't believe that it is in a deliberate conspiracy against good work.

I once suggested† that the experimental techniques of Eliot and the rest never really took on in England because they were an essentially American concern: attempts to forge a distinctively American language for poetry. Certainly, since Eliot removed himself into another, remote sphere of influence by proclaiming himself 'Anglo-Catholic in religion, royalist in politics and classicist in literature', the whole movement of English verse has been to correct the balance experimentation had so unpredictably disturbed. Some time in the twenties Thomas Hardy remarked to Robert Graves that '*vers libre* could come to nothing in England. "All we can do is to write on the old themes in the old styles, but try to do a little better than those who went before us." ' Since about 1930 the machinery of

* Introduction to *The New Poetry* (Harmondsworth: Penguin, 1962); also published in *Commentary*, 1961.

† In *The Shaping Spirit* (London: Chatto and Windus, 1958).

modern English poetry seems to have been controlled by a series of negative feed-backs designed to produce precisely the effect Hardy wanted.

The final justification of experimentalism lay, of course, beyond mere technique. The great moderns experimented not just to make it new formally, but to open poetry up to new areas of experience. The kind of insights which had already been substantiated by the novelists – by Melville, Dostoevsky, Lawrence and even, at times, by Hardy himself – seemed about due to appear in poetry. The negative feed-backs came into action to stop this happening.

The literary historians perhaps would see the process differently. And the English scene is peculiarly amenable to literary history: it is savage with gang-warfare which, at a distance, can be dignified as disagreements between schools of verse. So maybe a little potted, though rather partial, literary history would be in place.

The thirties poets reacted against those of the twenties by asserting that they had no time to be difficult or inward or experimental; the political situation was too urgent. Auden gave them the go-ahead because he combined an extraordinary technical skill in traditional forms with an extraordinary feel for the most contemporary of contemporary idiom. When he began it must really have looked as though he were about to do something quite new in English. In a poem like 'Sir, no man's enemy', for example, he used the new, difficult language of psychology with a concentration that was almost Shakespearian; or even in an unambitious piece like 'O lurcher-loving collier, black as night' he managed triumphantly to re-create a traditional lyric – its ancestor is 'O mistress mine, where art thou roaming' – in terms of the contemporary, unromantic, industrial scene. His trouble was that he was too skilful; he found both the art of verse and the art of success too easy. So he was able to channel his deep neurotic disturbances into light verse – much of it, admittedly, very fine – while his contemporary knowingness, his skill with references, with slang, with the time's immediate worries went into the production of a kind of social, occasional verse, mostly traditional in form, but highly up to date in idiom. His example encouraged a whole swarm of poetasters who believed, apparently, that to be modern was merely a matter of sounding modern; it had precious little to do with originality. (I would exclude from this Louis MacNeice, whose social–political verse was mostly more effective and certainly more deeply felt than Auden's own.) By the end of the thirties experimental verse was out and traditional forms, in a chic contemporary guise, were back in. That was the first negative feed-back.

The reaction to Auden took the form of anti-intellectualism. He was thought to be too clever and not sufficiently emotional for the extreme circumstances of the forties. The war brought with it a taste for high, if obscure, rhetoric. The log-rolling thirties were followed by the drum-rolling forties. The new master, of course, was Dylan Thomas. But Thomas was not only a fine rhetorician, he also, in his early poems, had something rather original to say. Admittedly, he was under constant pressure from the literary public relations officers to continue at all costs less with his poetry than with his act as the blindly inspired poet; which meant that his rhetoric eventually ran on when the reasons for it had faltered. But the talent was there, however self-destructive it eventually became. His followers, however, used his work as an excuse to kiss *all* meaning good-bye. All that mattered was that the verse should sound impressive. This was the second negative feed-back: a blockage against intelligence.

The third stage was yet another reaction: against wild, loose emotion. The name of the reaction was the Movement, and its anthology was Robert Conquest's *New Lines*. Of the nine poets to appear in this, six, at the time, were university teachers, two librarians, and one a civil servant. It was, in short, academic–administrative verse, polite, knowledgeable, efficient, polished, and, in its quiet way, even intelligent. What it had to offer positively was more difficult to describe. Even the editor found he could define it only in negatives:

> It submits to no great systems of theoretical constructs nor agglomerations of unconscious commands. It is free from both mystical and logical compulsions and – like the modern philosophy – is empirical in attitude to all that comes. . . . On the more technical side . . . we see the refusal to abandon a rational structure and comprehensible language. . . . It will be seen at once that these poets do not have as much in common as they would if they were a group of doctrine-saddled writers forming a definite school complete with programme and rules. What they do have in common is, perhaps, at its lowest, little more than a negative determination to avoid bad principles.

Mr Conquest is, I think, exaggerating when he says that his poets have nothing very much in common. For example:

Picture of lover or friend that is not either
Like you or me who, to sustain our pose,
Need wine and conversation, colour and light;
In short, a past that no one now can share,
No matter whose your future; calm and dry,
In sex I do not dither more than either,
Nor should I now swell to halloo the names
Of feelings that no one needs to remember:
The same few dismal properties, the same
Oppressive air of justified unease
Of our imaginations and our beds.
It seems the poet made a bad mistake.

Perhaps the logic seems a little tenuous? The shifts a little hard to follow? The content a little too fine-drawn? They should do. The piece is synthetic; it contains eight of the nine *New Lines* poets. I have omitted D. J. Enright since he rarely sticks to the metrical norms on which the rest insist. Otherwise I have not cheated in compiling the poem. I have taken the poets in the order in which they appear in the anthology, without using more than two lines from any one and without changing the punctuation except, in a minor way, between quotations. Yet though the poem may not be quite comprehensible, it is, I think, unified in tone. Wouldn't the impartial reader be hard put to know where one quotation ended and another began? Wouldn't he find a considerable similarity in the quality both of the language and of the experience? A kind of unity of flatness? The pieties of the Movement were as predictable as the politics of the thirties' poets. They are summed up at the beginning of Philip Larkin's 'Church-going':

Hatless, I take off
My cycle clips in awkward reverence.

This, in concentrated form, is the image of the Welfare State Englishman of the late forties and early fifties: shabby and not concerned with his appearance; poor – he has a bike, not a car; gauche but full of agnostic piety; underfed, underpaid, overtaxed, hopeless, bored, wry. This is the third negative feed-back: an attempt to show that the poet is not a strange creature inspired; on the contrary, he is just like the man next door – in fact, he probably *is* the man next door.

Now, I am wholly in favour of restoring poetry to the realm of common sense. But there is always the delicate question of how common common sense should be. All three negative feed-backs work, in their different ways, to preserve the idea that life in England goes on much as it always has, give or take a few minor changes in the class system. The upper-middle class, or Tory, ideal – presented in its pure crystalline form by John Betjeman – may have given way to the predominantly lower-middle class, or Labour, ideal of the Movement and the Angries, but the concept of gentility still reigns supreme. And gentility is a belief that life is always more or less orderly, people always more or less polite, their emotions and habits more or less decent and more or less controllable; that God, in short, is more or less good.

It is a stance which is becoming increasingly precarious to maintain. That the English have succeeded so long owes a good deal to the fact that England is an island; it is, literally, insulated from the rest of the world. But since the First World War, that insulation has slowly broken down. Robert Graves's *Goodbye to All That*, for example, shows perfectly how powerless the orthodox defences ultimately became under extreme conditions. When the level of misery was normal the defences worked efficiently enough. His childhood at preparatory and public school meant loneliness, philistinism, lewdness, insensitivity and unhappiness. These were all to be expected, and Graves duly countered them in the orthodox ways: games, toughness, asexual love, wit, and a clipped, dry, you-can't-touch-me manner. He developed, in short, a stiff upper lip. This got him through the first two years of the war, then gradually it broke. The horror of the trenches was too great. What he saw and what he went through were beyond the bounds of anything his training had prepared him for. Physically he survived, but emotionally he could no longer properly cope. The result was a kind of shell-shock which, he says himself, stayed with him for ten years. And even then he had to exile himself from England and erect the elaborate barricade of White Goddesses and classicizing through which his genuine poetry has only slowly and painfully filtered.

In the same way, George Orwell felt he had to purge himself of his governing-class upbringing by deliberately plunging into the abjectest poverty and pain partly, at least, because what he saw in Burma gave the lie to the whole ethos in which he had been raised.

The only English writer who was able to face the more uncompromising forces at work in our time was D. H. Lawrence. And he was born in the working class and spent most of his life outside England; so he had almost nothing to do with middle-class gentility. 'In those days', he wrote, 'they were always telling me I had genius as though to console me for not having their own incomparable advantages.'

But these forces I have invoked are beyond mere shell-shock and class guilt. They are general and concern us all. What, I suggest, has happened in the last half century is that we are gradually being made to realize that all our lives, even those of the most genteel and enislanded, are influenced profoundly by forces which have nothing to do with gentility, decency or politeness. Theologians would call these forces evil, psychoanalysts, perhaps, libido. Either way, they are the forces of disintegration which destroy the old standards of civilization. Their public faces are those of two world wars, of the concentration camps, of genocide and the threat of nuclear war.

I do not wish to over-dramatize the situation. War and cruelty have always existed, but those of the twentieth century are different in two ways. First, mass evil (for lack of a better term) has been magnified to match the scale of mass society. We no longer have local wars, we have world wars, which involve the civilians quite as deeply as the military. Where once, at worst, regiments of professional soldiers were wiped out, now whole cities go. Instead of the death of individuals, we have a mass extermination. Instead of individual torture and sadism, we have concentration camps run scientifically as death factories. The disintegration, to put it most mildly, has reached proportions which make it increasingly difficult to ignore. Once upon a time, the English could safely believe that Evil was something that happened on the Continent, or farther off, in the Empire where soldiers were paid to take care of it. To believe this now requires at best an extraordinary single-mindedness, at worst stupidity.

The second, and specifically modern difference in our attitude to the problem is this: the forcible recognition of a mass evil outside us has developed precisely parallel with psychoanalysis; that is, with our recognition of the ways in which the same forces are at work within us. One of the therapeutic purposes, for example, of Bruno Buttelheim's secret psychoanalytic observations when he was in Dachau and Buchenwald was to educate himself into realizing how much of what went on around him expressed what went on inside himself. Another analyst has suggested that the guilt which seems to dog the refugees who escaped from Germany may in part be due to the fact that the Nazis fulfilled the deepest and most primitive drives of the refugees themselves, killing fathers, mothers, brothers, sisters and children. Be this as it may, it is hard to live in an age of psychoanalysis and feel oneself wholly detached from the dominant public savagery. In this way, at least, the makers of horror films are more in tune with contemporary anxiety than most of the English poets.

But as England was not affected by the concentration camps, so it has remained, on the whole, contemptuously impervious to psychoanalysis. Primitivism is only generally acknowledged in this country when it takes a peculiarly British form: the domestic sex murder. Then the gloating is public and universal. Had Freud been born in London instead of Vienna, he would probably have finished in criminology.

I am not suggesting that modern English poetry, to be really modern, must be concerned with psychoanalysis or with the concentration camps or with the hydrogen bomb or with any other of the modern horrors. I am not suggesting, in fact, that it *must* be anything. For poetry that feels it has to cope with predetermined subjects ceases to be poetry and becomes propaganda. I am, however, suggesting that it drop the pretence that life, give or take a few social distinctions, is the same as ever, that gentility, decency and all the other social totems will eventually muddle through.

What poetry needs, in brief, is a new seriousness. I would define this seriousness simply as the poet's ability and willingness to face the full range of his experience with his full intelligence; not to take the easy exits of either the conventional response or choking incoherence. Believe in it or not, psychoanalysis has left its mark on poetry. First, the writer can no longer deny with any assurance the fears and desires he does not wish to face; he knows obscurely that they are there, however skilfully he manages to elude them. Second, having acknowledged their existence, he is no longer absolved from the need to use all his intelligence and skill to make poetic sense of them. Since Freud, the late Romantic dichotomy between emotion and intelligence has become totally meaningless.

This position had, I think, already been partially assumed by T. S. Eliot when he wrote *The Waste Land*. The poem follows, with great precision and delicacy, the movement of a psyche, not just of a society, in the process of disintegration. Eliot's talk of classicism, like his use in the poem of literature and theology, was an elaborate and successful defence which forced impersonality on a deeply personal and painful subject. But during the later twenties and thirties in America, Eliot's technical achievements and the radical revaluation of literary tradition that went with them seemed so bewilderingly impressive that the urgently personal uses this technique was put to were overlooked. A whole school of criticism was developed to prove technically that there was no necessary or even significant connection between art and its roots in the artist's life. During the forties, however, when English poetry was at a nadir, there arose in the States a new generation of poets, the most important of whom were Robert Lowell and John Berryman. They had assimilated the lesson of Eliot and the critical thirties: they assumed that a poet, to earn his title, had to be very skilful, very original and very intelligent. But they were no longer concerned with Eliot's rearguard action against the late Romantics; they were, I mean, no longer adherents of the cult of rigid impersonality. So they were able to write poetry of immense skill and intelligence which coped openly with the quick of their experience, experience sometimes on the edge of disintegration and breakdown. Robert Lowell's latest book *Life Studies*, for example, is a large step forward in this new direction. It may contain no single poem as impressive as the 'Quaker Graveyard in Nantucket', but the total impact of the book as a whole is altogether more powerful. Where once Lowell tried to externalize his disturbances theologically in Catholicism and rhetorically in certain mannerisms of language and rhythm, he is now, I think, trying to cope with them nakedly, and without evasion.

But to walk naked is, of course, no guarantee of achievement in the arts – often the contrary. Several pieces in *Life Studies* fail for appearing more compulsively concerned with the processes of psychoanalysis than with those of poetry. Conversely, with their deliberate common sense and understatement, some of the Movement poets command, at their best, a self-contained strength and a concern for the discipline of verse which is vital if the art is to remain public. The question is the kind of success a style allows. Compare, for instance, Philip Larkin's 'At Grass' with Ted Hughes's 'A Dream of Horses':

AT GRASS

The eye can hardly pick them out
From the cold shade they shelter in,
Till wind distresses tail and mane;
Then one crops grass, and moves about
– The other seeming to look on –
And stands anonymous again.

Yet fifteen years ago, perhaps
Two dozen distances sufficed
To fable them: faint afternoons
Of Cups and Stakes and Handicaps,
Whereby their names were artificed
To inlay faded, classic Junes –

Silks at the start: against the sky
Numbers and parasols: outside,
Squadrons of empty cars, and heat,
And littered grass: then the long cry
Hanging unhushed till it subside
To stop-press columns on the street.

Do memories plague their ears like flies?
They shake their heads. Dusk brims the shadows.
Summer by summer, all stole away,
The starting-gates, the crowds and cries –
All but the unmolesting meadows.
Almanacked, their names live; they

Have slipped their names, and stand at ease,
Or gallop for what must be joy,
And not a fieldglass sees them home,
Or curious stop-watch prophesies:
Only the groom, and the groom's boy,
With bridles in the evening come.

Larkin's poem, elegant and unpretentious and rather beautiful in its gentle way, is a nostalgic re-creation of the Platonic (or *New Yorker*) idea of the English scene, part pastoral, part sporting. His horses are *social* creatures of fashionable race meetings and high style; emotionally, they belong to the world of the R.S.P.C.A. It is more skilful but less urgent than 'A Dream of Horses':

We were born grooms, in stable-straw we sleep still,
All our wealth horse-dung and the combings of horses,
And all we can talk about is what horses ail.

Out of the night that gulfed beyond the palace-gate
There shook hooves and hooves and hooves of horses:
Our horses battered their stalls; their eyes jerked white.

And we ran out, mice in our pockets and straw in our hair,
Into darkness that was avalanching to horses
And a quake of hooves. Our lantern's little orange flare

Made a round mask of our each sleep-dazed face,
Bodiless, or else bodied by horses
That whinnied and bit and cannoned the world from its place.

The tall palace was so white, the moon was so round,
Everything else this plunging of horses
To the rim of our eyes that strove for the shapes of the sound.

We crouched at our lantern, our bodies drank the din,
And we longed for a death trampled by such horses
As every grain of the earth had hooves and mane.

We must have fallen like drunkards into a dream
Of listening, lulled by the thunder of the horses.
We awoke stiff; broad day had come.

Out through the gate the unprinted desert stretched
To stone and scorpion; our stable-horses
Lay in their straw, in a hag-sweat, listless and wretched.

Now let us, tied, be quartered by these poor horses,
If but doomsday's flames be great horses,
The forever itself a circling of the hooves of horses.

The poem, by the standard of Hughes's best writing, is not all that good; it is less controlled than Larkin's and has some of the quasi-medieval trappings of the romantic realm of Gormenghast. But it is unquestionably *about* something; it is a serious attempt to re-create and so clarify, unfalsified and in the strongest imaginative terms possible, a powerful complex of emotions and sensations. Unlike Larkin's, Hughes's horses have a violent, impending presence. But through the sharp details which bring them so threateningly to life, they reach back, as in a dream, into a nexus of fear and sensation. Their brute world is part physical, part state of mind.

They have, of course, their literary antecedents: the strange, savage horses which terrorize Ursula Brangwen at the end of *The Rainbow*. But this is part of their wider significance. Dr Leavis has come, apparently, to believe that D. H. Lawrence and T. S. Eliot represent the two warring and unreconcilable poles of modern literature. The best contemporary English verse, however, shows that their influences can be creatively reconciled. In the seriousness of what I have called the new depth poetry, the openness to experience, the psychological insight and integrity of D. H. Lawrence would, ideally, combine with the technical skill and formal intelligence of T. S. Eliot. If this were to happen we would have contemporary work which, like Coleridge's 'Imagination', would reconcile 'a more than usual state of emotion with more than usual order'.

My own feeling is that a good deal of poetic talent exists in England at the moment. But whether or not it will come to anything largely depends not on the machinations of any literary racket but on the degree to which the poets can remain immune to the disease so often found in English culture: gentility.

1962

Sylvia Plath

Prefatory Note

What follows was originally written as a memorial broadcast which went out on the B.B.C. Third Programme very shortly after Sylvia Plath's death in 1963. It was designed partly as a tribute and partly as an attempt to show how those strange last poems might be read. Clearly, their newness made some kind of explanation, or hints, seem necessary. The British Council had interviewed her and taped her reading some of the last poems not long before she died. I based my broadcast on these tapes, and planned it as little more than a running commentary. So inevitably it lacks the formal poise of a proper essay. And because it was written so close to her death – a time of great turmoil and confusion – it is far rougher than anything I would do today. But perhaps that roughness is a genuine part of the thing; it seems impossible now, without entirely recasting it, to polish it up much or amplify the many points that are made too briefly. I don't even believe that more elegance would be appropriate.

At the time, it seemed more important to try to define the extraordinary originality of her later poems – what they were doing and how they were doing it – than to dwell on the tragic circumstances of her death. I still believe that this is the right priority.

The broadcast was later published in *The Review* and seemed, as a result, to acquire some kind of underground critical currency. But in the process, some of the closing remarks have been misunderstood. So I have added a final note to try to get the emphasis right.

A.A., 1966

She was a tall, spindly girl with waist-length sandy hair, which she usually wore in a bun, and that curious, advertisement-trained, transatlantic air of anxious pleasantness. But this was merely a nervous social manner; under it, she was ruthless about her perceptions, wary and very individual.

She was born in 1932. Her parents were both teachers and both of German origin: her mother Austrian, her father pure Prussian; he died when she was nine. They lived in Boston, Massachusetts: 'I went to public school,' she wrote, 'genuinely public. Everybody went.'* Hers was Wellesley High School. From there she went to Smith College, remorselessly winning all the prizes. In 1955 she got a Fulbright Scholarship to Newnham College, Cambridge. Whilst there she met Ted Hughes, who at that point had published almost nothing; they were married in 1956, on Bloomsday. They went to America, where she taught at Smith for a year. In 1959 they returned to England and settled there for good – first in London, then in Devon. By this time she had become a full-time exile and used to refer to herself as an English poet. In 1960 her first child, Frieda, was born and her first book, *The Colossus*, was published. Two years later she had a son, Nicholas. In the middle of January 1963 she published her first novel, *The Bell Jar*, using a pseudonym, Victoria Lukas, partly, she told me, because she didn't consider it a serious work – though it was more serious and achieved than she admitted, and got good reviews – and partly because she thought too many people would be hurt by it – which was probably true. She died one month later, on 11 February 1963.

Her first poem came out in *The Boston Traveller*, when she was eight-and-a-half. I have no idea what these earliest poems were like, though their subject-matter appears to have been conventional enough: 'Birds, bees, spring, fall', she said in an interview,

> . . . all those subjects which are absolute gifts to the person who doesn't have any interior experience to write about.†

Clearly the poems were very precocious, like everything she did in her school and college days. She seemed effortlessly good at things: she was a prize scholar as well as a prize poet; and later, when she

* From 'The All-Round Image', a talk prepared for the B.B.C. Third Programme.

† From an interview and reading of poems made by her for the British Council.

married, she was good at having children and keeping a house clean, cooking, making honey, even at riding horses. There was a ruthless efficiency in all she did which left no room for mistakes or uncertainties.

Poetry, however, is not made by efficiency – least of all Sylvia Plath's poetry. Instead, her extraordinary general competence was, I think, made necessary by what made her write: an underlying sense of violent unease. It took a great deal of efficiency to cope with that, to keep it in check. And when the efficiency finally failed, her world collapsed.

But she was disciplined in art, as in everything else. For a first volume, by someone still in her twenties, *The Colossus* is exceptionally accomplished. A poem like 'The Ghost's Leave-taking' is fairly typical. It exhibits her broad and flexible range of language, in which the unexpected, right word comes so easily:

> *. . . the waking head rubbishes out of the draggled lot*
> *Of sulphurous landscapes and obscure lunar conundrums*

and her ability to make startling images out of humdrum objects:

> *The oracular ghost who dwindles on pin-legs*
> *To a knot of laundry, with a classic bunch of sheets*
> *Upraised, as a hand, emblematic of farewell.*

But that last line is also typical of the book's weakness: certainly, it's beautiful, but also peculiarly careful, held in check, a bit ornate and rhetorical. Throughout *The Colossus* she is using her art to keep the disturbance, out of which she made her verse, at a distance. It is as though she had not yet come to grips with her subject as an artist. She has Style, but not properly her own style. You can trace the influence of Ted Hughes, and there are also poems which sound like Theodore Roethke's – including the long 'Poem for a Birthday', which stands last in the book and attempts, I think, to deal with a subject which later possessed her: her nervous breakdown and near suicide at the age of nineteen. It was this which also made the climax and main theme of her novel.

Most of the poems in *The Colossus* were written during the first three years of her marriage, from 1956 to 1959. The *real* poems began in 1960, after the birth of her daughter, Frieda. It is as though the child were a proof of her identity, as though it liberated her into her real self. I think this guess is borne out by the fact that her most creative period followed the birth of her son, two years later. This triggered off an extraordinary outburst: for two or three months, right up to her death, she was writing one, or two, sometimes three poems a day, seven days a week. She said, in a note written for the B.B.C.:

> These new poems of mine have one thing in common. They were all written at about four in the morning . . . that still blue, almost eternal hour before the baby's cry, before the glassy music of the milkman, settling his bottles.*

A poem like 'Poppies in October' is simpler, much more direct, than those in *The Colossus*. The unexpectedness is still there, both in the language –

> *a sky palely and flamily igniting its carbon monoxide*

and the images –

> *the woman in the ambulance whose red heart blooms*
> *through her coat so astoundingly.*

But that leaping, arching imagination is no longer baroque, no longer a gesture on the surface of the poem. It is part of what she is actually saying. The poem is about the unexpectedness of the poppies, their gratuitous beauty in her own frozen life.

This change of tone and access of strength is partly, as she said herself, a technical development:

> May I say this: that the ones I've read are very recent, and I have found myself having to read them aloud to myself. Now this is something I didn't do. For example, my first book, *The Colossus* – I can't read any of the poems aloud now. I didn't write them to be read aloud. In fact, they quite privately bore me. Now these very recent ones – I've got to say them. I speak them to myself. Whatever lucidity they may have comes from the fact that I say them aloud.†

The difference, in short, is between finger-count and ear-count; one measures the rhythm by rules, the other catches the movement by the inner disturbance it creates. And she could only 'write poems out loud' when she had discovered her own speaking voice; that is, her own identity.

* From the introductory notes to 'New Poems', a reading prepared for the B.B.C. Third Programme but never broadcast.

† From an interview and reading of poems made by her for the British Council.

The second main difference between this and her earlier verse is in the direct relevance of the experience. In 'The Ghost's Leave-taking' the subject is nominally very personal – it's about the way dreams stay with you when you first wake up – but the effect is predominantly of very brilliant scene-setting. In 'Poppies in October', on the other hand, what starts as a description finishes as a way of defining her own state of mind. This, I think, is the key to the later poems; the more vivid and imaginative the details are, the more resolutely she turns them inwards. The more objective they seem, the more subjective they, in fact, become. Take, for example, a poem about her favourite horse, 'Ariel':

Stasis in darkness.
Then the substanceless blue
Pour of tor and distances.

God's lioness,
How one we grow,
Pivot of heels and knees! – The furrow

Splits and passes, sister to
The brown arc
Of the neck I cannot catch,

Nigger-eye
Berries cast dark
Hooks –

Black sweet blood mouthfuls,
Shadows.
Something else

Hauls me through air –
Thighs, hair;
Flakes from my heels.

White
Godiva, I unpeel –
Dead hands, dead stringencies.

And now I
Foam to wheat, a glitter of seas.
The child's cry

Melts in the wall.
And I
Am the arrow,

The dew that flies
Suicidal, at one with the drive
Into the red

Eye, the cauldron of morning.

The difficulty with this poem lies in separating one element from another. Yet that is also its theme; the rider is one with the horse, the horse is one with the furrowed earth, and the dew on the furrow is one with the rider. The movement of the imagery, like that of the perceptions, is circular. There is also another peculiarity: although the poem is nominally about riding a horse, it is curiously 'substanceless' – to use her own word. You are made to *feel* the horse's physical presence, but not to see it. The detail is all inward. It is as though the horse itself were an emotional state. So the poem is not just about the stallion 'Ariel', it is about what happens when the 'stasis in darkness' ceases to be static, when the potential violence of the animal is unleashed. And also the violence of the rider.

In a way, most of her later poems are about just that: about the unleashing of power, about tapping the roots of her own inner violence. There is, of course, nothing so very extraordinary about that. I think that this, in general, is the direction all the best contemporary poetry is taking. She, certainly, did not claim to be original in the kind of writing she was doing:

I've been very excited by what I feel is the new breakthrough that came with, say, Robert Lowell's *Life Studies*. This intense breakthrough into very serious, very personal emotional experience, which I feel has been partly taboo. Robert Lowell's poems about his experiences in a mental hospital, for example, interest me very much. These peculiar private and taboo subjects I feel have been explored in recent American poetry – I think particularly of the poetess Anne Sexton, who writes also about her experiences as a mother; as a mother who's had a nervous breakdown, as an extremely emotional and feeling young woman. And her poems are wonderfully craftsmanlike poems, and yet they have a kind of emotional and psychological depth which I think is something perhaps quite new and exciting.*

* From an interview and reading of poems made by her for the British Council.

Robert Lowell and Anne Sexton make pretty distinguished company, but I think Sylvia Plath took further than either of them her analysis of the intolerable and the 'taboo'. And she did it in a wholly original way. For example, her poem 'Fever 103°', which she described in this way:

> This poem is about two kinds of fire – the fires of hell, which merely agonize, and the fires of heaven, which purify. During the poem, the first sort of fire suffers itself into the second.*

Reading it for the first time, it sounds as though it were just free association on a theme: the theme that illness and pain are cumbersome and intolerable, but that if they go on long enough they cancel themselves out and the purity of death takes over. But the progress is not in fact haphazard. Death is there from the start: 'dull, fat Cerberus . . . wheezes at the gate' right from the beginning. What the poem does is to work away at this idea of a heavy, mundane death until it is purified of all extraneous matter and only the essential bodilessness remains. At the same time this movement is also that of a personal catharsis. She is clarifying not only an abstract death but also her feelings about it, from the cluttered and insufferable to the pure and acceptable. Her method is to let image breed image until, in some curious way, they also breed statements, conclusions:

They will not rise,
But trundle round the globe
Choking the aged and the meek,
The weak

Hothouse baby in its crib,
The ghastly orchid
Hanging its hanging garden in the air,

Devilish leopard!
Radiation turned it white
And killed it in an hour.

Greasing the bodies of adulterers
Like Hiroshima ash and eating in.
The sin. The sin.

The baby becomes the orchid, the spotted orchid the leopard, the beast of prey the adulteress; by which time the fever has become a

* From the introductory notes to 'New Poems', a reading prepared for the B.B.C. Third Programme but never broadcast.

kind of atomic radiation (perhaps she was remembering the film *Hiroshima mon amour*, where adultery, radiation and expiation were also joined inextricably together). The idea of the individual and the world purged of sin is established, and the poem is free to move on to the realm of purification.

Now, the movement is complicated. Often in these last poems it seems unnecessarily so. The images came so easily to her that sometimes they confuse each other until the poems choke in the obscurity of their own inventiveness. But they never suffer from the final insoluble obscurity of private references – as, say, Pound's do in the *Pisan Cantos*. The reasons for Sylvia Plath's images are always there, though sometimes you have to work hard to find them. She is, in short, always in intelligent control of her feelings. Her work bears out her theories:

> I think my poems come immediately out of the sensuous and emotional experiences I have, but I must say I cannot sympathize with these cries from the heart that are informed by nothing except a needle or a knife or whatever it is. I believe that one should be able to control and manipulate experiences, even the most terrifying – like madness, being tortured, this kind of experience – and one should be able to manipulate these experiences with an informed and intelligent mind. I think that personal experience shouldn't be a kind of shut box and mirror-looking narcissistic experience. I believe it should be generally relevant, to such things as Hiroshima and Dachau, and so on.*

It seems to me that it was only by her determination both to face her most inward and terrifying experiences and to use her intelligence in doing so – so as not to be overwhelmed by them – that she managed to write these extraordinary last poems, which are at once deeply autobiographical and yet detached, generally relevant.

'Lady Lazarus' is a stage further on from 'Fever 103°'; its subject is the total purification of achieved death. It is also far more intimately concerned with the drift of Sylvia Plath's life. The deaths of Lady Lazarus correspond to her own crises: the first just after her father died, the second when she had her nervous breakdown, the third perhaps a presentiment of the death that was shortly to come. Maybe this closeness of the subject helped make the poem so direct. The details don't clog each other: they are swept forward by the current of immediate feeling, marshalled by it and ordered. But

* From an interview and reading of poems made by her for the British Council.

what is remarkable about the poem is the objectivity with which she handles such personal material. She is not just talking about her own private suffering. Instead, it is the very closeness of her pain which gives it a general meaning; through it she assumes the suffering of all the modern victims. Above all, she becomes an imaginary Jew. I think this is a vitally important element in her work. For two reasons. First, because anyone whose subject is suffering has a ready-made modern example of hell on earth in the concentration camps. And what matters in them is not so much the physical torture – since sadism is general and perennial – but the way modern, as it were industrial, techniques can be used to destroy utterly the human identity. Individual suffering can be heroic provided it leaves the person who suffers a sense of his own individuality – provided, that is, there is an illusion of choice remaining to him. But when suffering is mass-produced, men and women become as equal and identity-less as objects on an assembly-line, and nothing remains – certainly no values, no humanity. This anonymity of pain, which makes all dignity impossible, was Sylvia Plath's subject. Second, she seemed convinced, in these last poems, that the root of her suffering was the death of her father, whom she loved, who abandoned her and who dragged her after him into death. And in her fantasies her father was pure German, pure Aryan, pure anti-semite.

It all comes together in the most powerful of her last poems, 'Daddy', about which she wrote the following bleak note:

> The poem is spoken by a girl with an Electra complex. Her father died while she thought he was God. Her case is complicated by the fact that her father was also a Nazi and her mother very possibly part Jewish. In the daughter the two strains marry and paralyse each other – she has to act out the awful little allegory before she is free of it.*

'DADDY'

You do not do, you do not do
Any more, black shoe
In which I have lived like a foot
For thirty years, poor and white,
Barely daring to breathe or Achoo.

* From the introductory notes to 'New Poems', a reading prepared for the B.B.C. Third Programme but never broadcast.

Daddy, I have had to kill you.
You died before I had time –
Marble-heavy, a bag full of God,
Ghastly statue with one grey toe
Big as a Frisco seal

And a head in the freakish Atlantic
Where it pours bean green over blue
In the waters off beautiful Nauset.
I used to pray to recover you.
Ach, du.

In the German tongue, in the Polish town
Scraped flat by the roller
Of wars, wars, wars.
But the name of the town is common.
My Polack friend

Says there are a dozen or two.
So I never could tell where you
Put your foot, your root,
I never could talk to you.
The tongue stuck in my jaw.

It stuck in a barb wire snare.
Ich, ich, ich, ich,
I could hardly speak.
I thought every German was you.
And the language obscene

An engine, an engine
Chuffing me off like a Jew.
A Jew to Dachau, Auschwitz, Belsen.
I began to talk like a Jew.
I think I may well be a Jew.

The snows of the Tyrol, the clear beer of Vienna
Are not very pure or true.
With my gypsy ancestress and my weird luck
And my Taroc pack and my Taroc pack
I may be a bit of a Jew.

I have always been scared of you,
With your Luftwaffe, your gobbledygoo.
And your neat moustache
And your Aryan eye, bright blue.
Panzer-man, panzer-man, O You –

Not God but a swastika
So black no sky could squeak through.
Every woman adores a Fascist,
The boot in the face, the brute
Brute heart of a brute like you.

You stand at the blackboard, daddy,
In the picture I have of you,
A cleft in your chin instead of your foot
But no less a devil for that, no not
Any less the black man who

Bit my pretty red heart in two.
I was ten when they buried you.
At twenty I tried to die
And get back, back, back at you.
I thought even the bones would do.

But they pulled me out of the sack,
And they stuck me together with glue.
And then I knew what to do.
I made a model of you,
A man in black with a Meinkampf look

And a love of the rack and the screw.
And I said I do, I do.
So daddy, I'm finally through.
The black telephone's off at the root,
The voices just can't worm through.

If I've killed one man, I've killed two –
The vampire who said he was you
And drank my blood for a year,
Seven years, if you want to know.
Daddy, you can lie back now.

There's a stake in your fat black heart
And the villagers never liked you.
They are dancing and stamping on you.
They always knew *it was you.*
Daddy, daddy, you bastard, I'm through.

'Lady Lazarus' ends with a final, defensive, desperate assertion of omnipotence:

Out of the ash
I rise with my red hair
And I eat men like air.

Not even that defence is left her in 'Daddy'; instead, she goes right down to the deep spring of her sickness and describes it purely. What comes through most powerfully, I think, is the terrible unforgivingness of her verse, the continual sense not so much of violence – although there is a good deal of that – as of violent resentment that this should have been done to *her*. What she does in the poem is, with a weird detachment, to turn the violence against herself so as to show that she can equal her oppressors with her self-inflicted oppression. And this is the strategy of the concentration camps. When suffering is there whatever you do, by inflicting it upon yourself you achieve your identity, you set yourself free.

Yet the tone of the poem, like its psychological mechanisms, is not single or simple, and she uses a great deal of skill to keep it complex. Basically, her trick is to tell this horror story in a verse form as insistently jaunty and ritualistic as a nursery rhyme. And this helps her to maintain towards all the protagonists – her father, her husband and herself – a note of hard and sardonic anger, as though she were almost amused that her own suffering should be so extreme, so grotesque. The technical psychoanalytic term for this kind of insistent gaiety to protect you from what, if faced nakedly, would be insufferable, is 'manic defence'. But what, in a neurotic, is a means of avoiding reality can become, for an artist, a source of creative strength, a way of handling the unhandleable, and presenting the situation in all its fullness. When she first read me the poem a few days after she wrote it, she called it a piece of 'light verse'. It obviously isn't, yet equally obviously it also isn't the racking personal confession that a mere description or précis of it might make it sound.

Yet neither is it unchangingly vindictive or angry. The whole poem works on one single, returning note and rhyme, echoing from start to finish:

> *You do not do, you do not do . . .*
> *. . . I used to pray to recover you.*
> *Ach, du . . .*

There is a kind of cooing tenderness in this which complicates the other, more savage note of resentment. It brings in an element of pity, less for herself and her own suffering than for the person who made her suffer. Despite everything, 'Daddy' is a love poem.

When Sylvia Plath died I wrote an epitaph on her in *The Observer*, at the end of which I said 'The loss to literature is inestimable'. But someone pointed out to me that this wasn't quite true. The achievement of her final style is to make poetry and death inseparable. The one could not exist without the other. And this is right. In a curious way, the poems read as though they were written posthumously. It needed not only great intelligence and insight to handle the material of them, it also took a kind of bravery. Poetry of this order is a murderous art.

The Review, 1963

Postscript, 1966

These final remarks seem to have caused some confusion. I was *not* in any sense meaning to imply that breakdown or suicide is a validation of what I now call Extremist poetry. No amount of personal horror will make a good poet out of a bad one. Rather, the opposite: to know from evidence outside the poetry that a man has suffered a great deal will throw into high relief just how much he lacks as an artist.

I was also *not* in any sense meaning to imply that a breakdown or suicide is the necessary corollary or result of Extremist work. Obviously, the poet is not obliged to prove in his life that what he writes about is genuine. After all, he is a poet by virtue of his ability to create an imaginative world which has an objective existence apart from him. The poetry is its own proof. Indeed, the chances are that the more hip the art the squarer the life of the artist who creates it. A genuinely hip life leaves little time for art.

But I did mean to imply that this kind of writing involves an element of risk. The Extremist artist sets out deliberately to explore the roots of his emotions, the obscurest springs of his personality, maybe even the sickness he feels himself to be prey to, 'giving himself over to it', as I have written elsewhere, 'for the sake of the range and intensity of his art'.* It is precisely here that the risk lies. I do not personally believe in the classical Freudian argument that art is therapeutic, that the artist is relieved of his fantasies by expressing them. On the contrary, the weird logic of art seems to be that the act of formal expression merely makes the dredged-up material more readily available to the artist. So the result of handling it in his art may well be that he finds himself living it out. Keats is the prime example of this devious mechanism: the poems of his great period – from the second *Hyperion* onwards – are all about death. Apparently, this great creative outburst was triggered off by nursing his brother Tom through his final illness. But if Tom's death were the cause, Keats's own may have been the ultimate effect. He had, that is, pushed death so much to the foreground of his consciousness that it became unavoidable; having written the poems there was nothing left for him to do except die.

I think much the same happened with Sylvia Plath. The very source of her creative energy was, it turned out, her self-destructiveness. But it was, precisely, a source of *living* energy, of her imaginative, creative power. So, though death itself may have been a side-issue, it was also an unavoidable risk in writing her kind of poem. My own impression of the circumstances surrounding her eventual death is that she gambled, not much caring whether she won or lost; and she lost. Had she won, the power of those last poems would have been in no way altered or falsified, and she would have been free to go on to other work. That she didn't is the real tragedy.

* *Under Pressure* (Harmondsworth: Penguin, 1965), p. 185.

Tri Quarterly, 1966

The Fate of the Platypus

Poetry in the middle of the twentieth century is in a paradoxical situation: it is the art at once least and most threatened by mass communications and mass culture. It is least threatened in the same way as the platypus is of all creatures the least threatened by the H-bomb. It has reached that point of minimum survival where almost nothing can make any difference to it; extinction itself is at least a logical, if not an inevitable, step. There is, for example, the question of poetry reviews: the responsible weekly papers and the periodicals continue to publish them, but it is doubtful if more than a tiny proportion of the reading public responds to this piety. And that tiny proportion is, I suggest, made up of, first, the poets immediately involved, and their friends and relations; second, those who hope, sooner or later, to be involved – that is, other poets; and third, specialists whose business is with English literature – that is, critics and teachers. And this third category is, I think, dwindling.

The reading of poetry, in short, is now almost wholly professional. The general educated public, which goes to the reviews of novels, biographies, travel books and the rest in order to find out what it should or should not read, what might or might not interest it, treats poetry as a diversion that is simply no longer its concern. Occasionally, it may prick its ears to the lives and scandals of the poets, but that is something quite different from poetry. The professional classes, the diplomats, lawyers, clergymen, civil servants and politicians, who, in the seventeenth century, *were* the poets and who, in the nineteenth, made Tennyson a best-seller, seem now no longer interested. If poetry, after its long illness, were finally to die of mass culture, there would be precious few mourners. And if, which is more likely, a new genius restores it to health, the educated public will probably continue to be as vitally unconcerned as ever.

No doubt the poets themselves were at first partly to blame for this. The attitude of the founders of the modern movement was that if the public was willing to listen only to tired conventionalities, then the poets would have to ignore popular tastes and write to a standard that would at least satisfy their own artistic consciences. Hence a great deal of modern poetry seems often as specialized as modern science; both require a degree of single-minded preparedness to which the general public is neither willing nor able to attain. But it is also possible that the new arts of mass communication have somehow lowered the standard of intellectual and artistic curiosity. Simply because they are dealing in *mass* communications, the organizers have never been able to assume more than a minimum standard of interest; so they have set out to be easy, appealing and pat in their answers. Now, it appears, the taste for glibness is spreading upwards. In 1957, for example, when the Third Programme was emasculated, the original announcement read: 'More of what is broadcast will be designed for relaxation and entertainment. There will be less talk on the air and more music of every kind.' The tone, in fact, implied that the changes were relieving the public of a great weight of unwanted culture. When a vocal minority replied with protest instead of gratitude the senior officials of the B.B.C. seemed shocked and hurt. This particular horse is now, of course, dead. I am only kicking at it again because in all the fuss last year one aspect of the affair was hardly noticed: that is, the cheerful vulgarity of that first statement, the assumption that things highbrow were at best only a matter of prestige and of no real interest to anyone except specialists. This was not the tone of a few minor bureaucrats but of those senior and presumably responsible administrators who, not so very long ago, would have formed the most influential audience of the arts.

Poetry, in fact, is threatened less by mass communications themselves than by a mass indifference which is spreading up from below. For there is a great difference between popular culture and mass culture. The ballads and Shakespeare's plays were both forms of popular culture and entertainment. But both presumed on a lively individual response and a certain individual attention which made intelligent communication possible. Whereas the skills of mass culture are devoted to flattering a kind of collective inertia. Their purpose is to break down the 'sales resistance' of individual taste so that the public will end by buying whatever product or dogma the controllers of the mass media have to sell.

This predicament has recently been analysed in two brilliant and important studies, Hannah Arendt's *The Human Condition** and Erich Kahler's *The Tower and the Abyss*.† From very different premises both writers conclude that the real enemy of the new, vast, highly organized societies, founded on technology and devoted to it, is, quite simply, the individual:

> The last stage of the labouring society, the society of jobholders [says Miss Arendt] demands of its members a sheer automatic functioning, as though individual life had actually been submerged in the over-all life process of the species and the only active decision still required of the individual were to let go, so to speak, to abandon his individuality, the still individually sensed pain and trouble of living, and acquiesce in a dazed, 'tranquillized', functional type of behaviour. The trouble with modern theories of behaviourism is not that they are wrong but that they could become true. . . .

Obviously, if this movement were ever completed, poetry, that wholly individual statement of 'the pain and trouble of living', would no longer be possible. It would be replaced, if at all, by a kind of State doggerel. And even if society, despite itself, continued to throw up individuals talented enough to write, 'the new insensibility', as Professor Kahler calls it, would deprive them of the interested, informed and critical audience on which all the arts depend if they are to flourish.

All this is still, more or less, in the future. Mass communications, however, are having a more immediate effect on poetry: they are breaking down the ability to read. Poetry is, after all, the one art which depends wholly on concentration. The others will hardly flourish without it but they may at least get by. Painting and sculpture can be treated as mere decoration, music can be turned into a pleasant background noise, and even the novel, apparently, can be read with half an eye: in an American poll on novel-reading habits one housewife confessed that she liked something light which she could read while knitting and watching television. But poetry, because it takes the common language and remoulds it to fit exactly

* Chicago and London: University of Chicago Press, 1958.
† New York: Braziller, 1957.

the writer's sensibility, demands of the reader a great effort of concentration; he has, in a sense, to relearn the language with each new poet. Mass media, on the other hand, begin with the idea that no one is capable of attending properly for more than a few seconds at a time. Hence they have cultivated an empty, flaccid style which relies on two simple devices: first, that of blinding repetition; second, the use of 'loaded' language to elicit automatic, unthinking responses. These, at least, are the staples of the most highly developed and most effective form of mass communication, advertising. The technique depends on a kind of controlled dissipation of thought. Its end is to condition the public to respond in terms of slogans, rather than by its more intricate and unpredictable personal lights. Consequently, the skills of mass communications are working against the habit of attention and the ability to reinterpret language afresh, which are the two basic qualities needed to understand poetry. As for cutting one's losses and taking over into poetry the coarsened, depersonalized, i.e. political language of the mass media: the experiments of the 1930s show how little can come of that.

The least that seems likely to happen, then, is that, because of the great rift between the simplicities of the mass media and the intricacies of art, poetry will cease to be regarded as human, pleasurable activity; instead, it will be taken over, organized and used merely as a discipline for teaching. In the last couple of decades English literature has gone a long way in replacing the classics as the major subject of the Humanities. The real danger is that it might succeed altogether and suffer the same fate. If, for example, one asks a classics teacher what good it is to drum Latin and Greek into unwilling pupils, it is unlikely that he will reply, in effect: 'So that they may understand how some of the most intelligent and sensitive people of two great civilizations thought and felt; hence so they may have some standards by which to compare their own experience.' On the contrary, it is ten to one he will answer flatly: 'It trains the mind.' In the same way, English poetry, because it is concentrated and allusive, will also 'train the mind'. Indeed, recent academic verse on both sides of the Atlantic shows that it is not difficult to produce the kind of elegant teaser that is peculiarly handy for classroom analysis. The most immediate danger to poetry, in short, is that it will disappear as a living art and survive only as a more or less useful museum piece. (I ought to add that I am very far from thinking that poetry should not be treated as a discipline, provided it is a living discipline. But there is a tendency, mostly in the United States, where English seems now wholly to have replaced the classics, and there mostly among the most doctrinaire disciples of the New Critics, to formalize the art entirely and treat it in exclusively technical terms; to make of it, in fact, a kind of humanistic technology.)

It is, I suppose, slightly absurd to take up this elegiac note. The twentieth century has produced finer and more diverse creative work than any time at least since the death of Keats, and probably since the publication of *Paradise Lost*. Perhaps the vast, stony indifference of the semi-literate public has even irritated the poets into this effort. But in the last couple of decades or more the impetus has been lost. The sheer achievement of the early days of modern poetry may have had something to do with this; it set depressingly high standards for those who followed. Then the war and the present uneasy peace have left little time for creative optimism.

Yet both these reasons are, in a sense, rather abstract. Any writer who is properly caught up in what he is doing is arrogant enough to scale down established work to a manageable size. As for the wars, past and possible, their scale is so huge that they have almost ceased to have any bearing on the material of poetry. It is written, after all, about human beings, not about Humanity. Instead, that permanent sense of depression and the vague fear of ever chancing their arms which plague contemporary poets seem to have less to do with atomic bombs than with the recession. It is as though the poets felt they were about to lose their jobs.

I suggested earlier that all that remains of the poetry-reading public is largely an audience of specialists, thanks to the 'Keep Out' policy of the founders of the modern movement. This means that even though the standards of judgement are often far from high, at least there is some tolerance of novelty and a willingness to tackle difficult work. Yet it is this tiny but highly trained audience that is losing patience with contemporary verse, not the long-indifferent addicts of the mass media. The reason, I suggest, is not that poetry has become too difficult but that it has become too easy. And this is a matter less of technique than of substance. It is the poets, not the audience, who have become infected by mass communications. They have begun to ape the two popular images of themselves.

The first is that of the irremediably alien Genius, forever misunderstood and rejected by society (see Colin Wilson's *The Outsider*).

Originally, this was a Romantic concept, justified by a genuinely believed transcendentalism, or Platonism, as John Crowe Ransom called it. If the Imagination could pierce to a Reality behind appearances, then the poet was essentially dealing in mysteries; the reader at best could only pick up hints and approximations of his *real* meaning. Hence the continual use of that word 'magic' to describe the final effects of his work. The transcendental element of this has long since disappeared, but a superstitious belief in the incomprehensible mysteries of poetry has lingered on. Hence the contemporary Romantics have felt obliged to disguise their no doubt genuine but perfectly conventional human feelings in an elaborately obscured transcendental rhetoric, as though their reputations depended on the degree to which their work refused to yield up its meaning.

The second image was created as a reaction to this: to reassure the public that the poet is fundamentally as normal and down-trodden as every other man in the street. Despite the efforts of the literary journalists, this movement has very little to do with the plays and novels of protest of the 'Angry Young Men'. It is essentially a poetry of the *status quo*. Its unspoken theme is that even protest is impossible for those suffering from the motiveless benignity of the welfare state. The one dominant feeling is an uneasy nostalgia for the feelings the poets do not have. This wry, wistful decency, combined with great skill in handling traditional techniques, makes the best of these poets, Philip Larkin, seem to me like a contemporary, socialized descendant of Walter de la Mare. He has the same accomplishment and honesty, which depend on a nice sense of his own limitations. And like de la Mare's, his poetry is in its way almost perfect simply because he never oversteps these limitations. But its way is, by definition, limited. Mr Larkin's intelligence, skill and lack of pretension have established a poetry of reassurance and shown that there are still a few writers interested in recognizable processes of the intelligence. But the reassurance has been so much a matter of reasserting the value of conventions – of both poetry and the feelings – that it hardly seems a start in any new and unexpected direction.

The trouble with both fashions is that they ignore the fact that twentieth-century poetry is essentially different from what had gone before. When the founders set out to 'make it new', their experiments, those of a few publicists apart, had behind them more than mere technical curiosity or even impatience with worn-out conventions. Experimentation was, in a way, forced upon the poets by the discoveries of the psychoanalysts. They had offered insights into the nature of the emotions and the workings of the mind which showed the tired poeticisms of the previous era to be not only hopelessly inadequate but fundamentally false. I suggest, then, that the real impulse behind the modern movement was the desire to attain some degree of psychological realism. It was for this, rather than for his 'unified sensibility', that Mr Eliot praised Donne in an early essay in *The New Statesman.* Yet this element in both Donne and Eliot has been obscured because of their extraordinary technical achievements; so the 'unified sensibility' was translated as peculiar knack with complex images, while whatever it implied of psychological insight was ignored. In the same way, the whole story of Yeats's maturity, his change from a Rhymer to a major modern poet, is in the way he painfully brought himself to recognize the difference between his real emotions and his earlier romantic attitudes. Similarly, all D. H. Lawrence's poetry centres on his attempt to create a medium supple enough to follow precisely the complex ebb and flow of his feelings.

In picking on this concept of psychological realism as the main figure in modern poetry I am trying to suggest what it was that made the work of the great twentieth-century poets seem fresher and more serious than anything that had, for a long time, gone before. It is the same quality that made the nineteenth-century novel an infinitely more serious affair than most poetry of that time. By 'serious' I do not mean 'high-minded'; few poets have been more high-minded than Tennyson and Matthew Arnold. I mean simply that the reader finds himself continually caught up at the deepest level, continually faced with his most obscurely felt motives. It is this that makes for the power of Tolstoy's central realism and of Dostoevsky's tortured, peripheral realism of excess.

This is the kind of seriousness that seems to me to be lacking in the poetry of the 1950s. The work can too easily be dismissed; either the reader is baffled to know what all the fuss is about or he is impatient that the poet should be content to settle for so little. Either way, he is not called upon to re-examine his own motives, nor is he presented with any insights which, however grudgingly, he has to acknowledge as fresh and true. Hence the present disregard of poetry. For no one will go to the trouble of reading it only to be presented with the same clichés as the mass media purvey more easily and entertainingly. If, in the face of all the threats, poetry is to continue to be read, the least it can do is to keep a little ahead of contemporary fads and pieties. This means, I think, continuing in the line of exploratory realism on which it has tentatively started. It is, after all, far better for an art with almost no public left to risk being really unpopular than to content itself with being merely footling.

The Times Literary Supplement, 1958

2

VERSE CHRONICLE

Edith Sitwell*

Whenever a critic hesitates to sing Dame Edith Sitwell's hosannas there is sure to be trouble; the correspondence columns are full for weeks. Why, I wonder? If it is because there is a large public who passionately believe in the inviolability of poetry – all poetry – then that is indeed something. Or if there are enthusiasts who, without caring so much about poetry, are passionately concerned with the sanctity of the poet as a cultural symbol – well, that too is something, though rather less. But I doubt whether either of these reasons is true. Sitwellism seems something apart from a wider devotion to literature, something rather special, like a taste for the baroque.

I had better confess straight away that it is a taste I do not have. Consequently, I have always found it difficult to know what the fuss was about. And even now Dame Edith's work can be read complete in the *Collected Poems* I am still not much the wiser. When the earlier poems first appeared they were, no doubt, shocking. Because of them the poetess must have been subjected to a good deal of chivvying from an old guard who attacked the modern idiom in whatever shape, from Eliot downwards. At this distance, however, the poems do not seem so very outrageous. For all the belligerent mixing of sense impressions and the odd rhythms, Dame Edith's 'Façade', for example, seems no more 'abstract' (her word for it) than any other rather literary nursery rhyme:

* Edith Sitwell, *Collected Poems* (London: Macmillan, 1957).

Daisy and Lily,
Lazy and silly,
Walk by the shore of the wan grassy sea,
Talking once more 'neath a swan-bosomed tree . . .

This reminds me less of Mallarmé or Rimbaud than of

Minnie and Mattie
And fat little May,
Out in the country,
Spending a day.

Such a bright day,
With the sun glowing,
And the trees half in leaf,
And the grass growing . . .

That is by Christina Rossetti. If Dame Edith's verse is more striking, that has nothing to do with the feel of the thing; it is a matter of the sophisticated ornament.

Yet though the poetry may often have that charming, sophisticated, dream-like air of a Christmas panto for adults, does it really *matter*? Do the tricks of rhythm and rhyme, the exotic, improbable, nursery-tale objects make the early poems into anything more than delicious games? Was, in fact, Dame Edith, for all her inventions, ever 'modern' in any significant sense? I would suggest, instead, that she used the new taste for difficulty as an excuse to free herself not from outworn conventions of feeling and expression (she has her fair share of phrases like 'the glamour of eve'), but from the perennial convention that a poem should mean something.

Not that she doesn't give her works a meaning; the introduction to this volume is taken up with doing precisely that. But her interpretations prove only that her words, like Humpty Dumpty's, can mean anything she wants. This, for instance:

This melon
Sir Mammon,
Comes out of Babylon:
Buy for a patacoon –
Sir, you must buy!

It is, unquestionably, exuberant froth: Sir Mammon is put in his place by being rhymed with 'melon'; 'Babylon' comes from the nursery rhyme ('How many miles to . . .'); so does 'patacoon' (by 'pat-a-cake' out of 'doubloon'); the whole ebullient air depends on the speed of the movement. Dame Edith, however, seems unwilling to admit that any of her verse is, despite appearances, less serious than *Paradise Lost*. And so she comments:

> The change from the word 'melon' to 'Mammon' (the latter word is like thick dust that has gathered itself into some embodiment), the change from the dreaminess of 'Babylon' which is in part a matter of association, to the sharp sound, like that of a hard coin falling on dry ground, of 'patacoon' – that is deliberate.

Deliberate, perhaps; but hardly to be guessed by any except Dame Edith's most intimate associates. Of course, Dame Edith cannot be expected to translate all her poems; but without that, how is the uninitiated reader to manage, since her poems apparently mean neither what the syntax says nor what the rhythm and so on imply?

The answer, I suppose, is that he has to make up the poems for himself. But perhaps that is the secret of the admiration Dame Edith's work inspires. Instead of using poetry to express precisely the fullness of her experience, she has contrived with great care and invention a series of moulds into which the reader can pour just as much feeling as he wants. What she writes is not so much poems 'containing in themselves the reason why they are so and not otherwise' as challenges to his powers of free-association – a kind of 'do-it-yourself' verse.

Perhaps, too, this is why Dame Edith's later, more direct verse seems, compared with 'Façade' or 'Bucolic Comedies' or 'The Sleeping Princess', noisy and uncertain. She is so used to backing gracefully out of any definite commitment that she hasn't the means to handle full statements. For all the apocalyptic rumbling ('. . . In which the Megatherium Mylodon/Lies buried under Mastodon-trumpetings of leprous Suns . . .'), her anguish, however sincere it in fact may be, sounds more rhetorical than personal. In none of the later exclaiming is there anything that rings as true as that line in 'Colonel Fantock':

I always was a little outside life.

The Observer, 1957

Robert Lowell*

Few established poets ever change much once they have arrived. On the contrary, having struck a convincing posture, most of them have to struggle grimly merely to maintain it; they seem to be peering warily out at us from the shadows cast by themselves when young. But the ability to do something perfectly and then go on to do something quite different is a sure mark of creative power. T. S. Eliot's inaccessible and overarching achievement depends a great deal upon it: he has covered a huge poetical distance in extraordinarily few poems.

Robert Lowell, the most talented writer of all the enormously talented Bostonian Lowells, is one of the few poets to come into prominence in the forties who has this power of significant change. One's first impression of *Life Studies*, his first book for nearly ten years, is that here at last in all the dreary welter of 'new' verse, is something really new. Mr Lowell has dropped much of the rhetoric and all the contortion of his earlier work and is feeling his way to another kind of poetry. It is by no means less personal, but it is considerably less mannered.

The first poem in the book – on a train journey across the Alps to France – is one of the very few that might have sat comfortably among his earlier work. This is how it ends:

> *There are no tickets for that altitude*
> *once held by Hellas, when the Goddess stood,*
> *prince, pope, philosopher and golden bough,*
> *pure mind and murder at the scything prow –*
> *Minerva, the miscarriage of the brain.*

* Robert Lowell, *Life Studies* (London: Faber and Faber, 1959).

Now Paris, our black classic, breaking up
like killer kings on an Etruscan cup.

It is, by any standards, excellent rhetoric – a kind of invective of learning which, obviously, is more meaningful in its context. Even so, the words seem to pile up without ever quite defining their source. In the end, the only thing one is sure of is the murderous ominousness of the final couplet.

Compare that with the poem that follows and one sees how much Mr Lowell has gained in clarity (Marie de Medici is addressing her assassinated husband, Henri IV):

Your great nerve gone, Sire, sleep without a care.
No Hapsburg galleon coasts off Finisterre
with bars of bullion now to subsidize
the pilfering, pillaging democracies,
the pin-head priest, the nihilist grandee.
Sleep, sleep, my Husband. There at Saint Denis,
the chiselled bolster and Carrara hound
show no emotion when we kiss the ground. . . .
I rock my nightmare son, and hear him cry
for ball and sceptre; he asks the queen to die. . . .

The movement is larger, freer, yet, at the same time, more precise. The details add up and create both scene and emotion. So death is no longer an unmentionable threat in the background; it is a fact, recognized and awaited.

Mr Lowell's poetic advance boils down to this: the pressure is not off his work; but the torture, the sense of the inexpressibleness of conflict, has gone. In much of his earlier poetry the strain was almost unbearable. Only a prodigious effort of poetic will seemed to prevent it from splintering into incoherence. He imposed form on this passionate chaos by his superb ear for effects and by a rigorous use of Catholic symbolism. Even so, he maintained only a knife-edge and dangerous balance. There is neither symbolism nor debate, neither Catholicism nor oratory in *Life Studies*. In their place is a wry detachment, at times almost as painful as the great theological bust-ups of Mr Lowell's earlier poems, but now always lucid:

Azure day
makes my agonized blue window bleaker.

Crows maunder on the petrified fairway.
Absence! My heart grows tense
as though a harpoon were sparring for the kill.
(*This is the house for the 'mentally ill'.*)

The versification may look more casual than it did before, but it is still quite as canny; here, for example, the ironic meaning is forced home by suddenly inserting into the loose flow of the verse a perfectly regular ten-syllabled rhyming last line.

The change in Mr Lowell's work, then, is less a change of style than of heart. Instead of contorting his conflicts into a kind of savage and baroque theology, he seems now to be trying to trace them back to their source. The result is a series of controlled autobiographical reminiscences about the figures who loomed through his childhood: grandparents, father, mother, uncles and aunts. Granted they are caught, all of them, in their remorseless progress towards the family cemetery, but they are handled with a good deal of incidental tenderness and wit: for example, 'Aunt Sarah, risen like the phoenix/from her bed of troublesome snacks and Tauchnitz classics': or his uncle's student posters where 'The pre-war music hall belles/had goose necks, glorious signatures, beauty-moles,/and coils of hair like rooster tails.'

It is as though in these family portraits Mr Lowell were setting his house in order so as to assure himself of some firm, known base from which his work can start afresh. Perhaps this faint suggestion of poetic therapy explains a certain overlooseness in some of the pieces – 'Commander Lowell' and 'To Delmore Schwartz' in particular – that brings them dangerously near chattiness. But every minor fault is justified by a handful of poems at the end of the book. In these Mr Lowell faces his old passions – violence, hatred, exacerbation and love – but with a new and dispassionate control, a rhetoric that has been purified and made stronger by the flexibility acquired in the other poems:

Tamed by Miltown, *we lie on Mother's bed;*
the rising sun in war paint dyes us red;
in broad daylight her gilded bed-posts shine,
abandoned, almost Dionysian.
At last the trees are green on Marlborough Street,
blossoms on our magnolia ignite
the morning with their murderous five days' white. . . .

It may not quite match the massive achievement of Mr Lowell's 'Quaker Graveyard in Nantucket', 'Falling Asleep over the Aeneid', or 'Mother Marie Therese', but it is a magnificent start to a new phase in his work. In all events, poetry of this order needs neither to be justified nor explained; one should simply be thankful that there is still someone able to write it.

The Observer, 1959

Richard Eberhart*

Richard Eberhart's *Collected Poems* should set him up, once and for all, as an important writer. They also show the immense advantage it was for a poet, of a certain generation and a certain background, to be born American.

Eberhart is an exact contemporary of Auden and Company. He was born in 1904, came from the same comfortable bourgeois setting and went through much the same conventional education mill: an Ivy League college, Cambridge under I. A. Richards, graduate work at Harvard. For a time he kicked around in odd jobs, then taught in the American equivalent of one of the glossiest public schools. During the war, he was in the Navy. After it, he went into the family business until his reputation as a poet was firmly established. He then moved on to the Universities Circuit as Poet in Residence and teacher of Creative Writing. He has had all the best poetry prizes and serves on all the best poetry committees. In England he would have become a pillar of the Establishment and finished, no doubt, as a candidate for the Poet Laureateship.

Mercifully, they order these things differently in the States. As Auden once remarked, every poet is supposed to justify himself by producing a style that is utterly his own. And even when the inertia of established success overcomes him, he can't lapse back into an inoffensive traditional style because, for the serious poet, there is no traditional American style to lapse into. There, the only serious tradition is modernism. (America's first modern reactionary group is

* Richard Eberhart, *Collected Poems 1930–1960* (London: Chatto and Windus, 1960).

the Beatniks: they imitate Whitman.) So Eberhart has stuck to the basic premises of modern poetry: he has tried to make it new and make it intelligent.

His earliest work sounded, in style and intention, like a modern William Blake: it was a poetry which deliberately wooed the violence of immediate sensation, which tried to register experience with the directness of innocence. That sounds like a dubious virtue: we think of innocence in poetry as just another stylistic and emotional trick employed by any old literary crook who can't be bothered to use his intelligence. Not so in Eberhart's work. He is innocent only in being continually and vigorously open to experience. If this is the child's vision, it has gone through a peculiarly adult filter.

The theme that increasingly dominates his earlier poetry is that of death; not death as an abstraction but as a physical fact to be felt in the bones and the nerves and the flesh with a shocked, yet curiously detached absorption. But gradually the theme of death expands in his work until it includes not only the body but also that innocence he had so vigorously courted. The child dies and the mature man is born; physical pain is transformed into the pain of moral responsibility:

The full of joy do not know; they need not
Know. Nothing is reconciled.
They flash the light of Heaven indeed.
Let them have it, let them have it, it is mild.

Those who suffer see the truth; it has
Murderous edges. They never avert
The gaze of calculation one degree,
But they are hurt, they are hurt, they are hurt.

Eberhart's greatest maturity as a poet coincided with the Second World War. The sense of violence and bafflement in his thickened, muscular language, his apparent determination to resolve complexities without settling for any simplification, combined with a wonderfully unsentimental pity. 'Dam Neck, Virginia', 'The Fury of Aerial Bombardment' and 'A Ceremony by the Sea' are some of the best poems the war produced. Where weaker poets turned apocalyptic, he stuck indignantly to the human facts.

This central, purposeful note culminated after the war in an extraordinary poem called 'Fragment of New York, 1929'. It is simply a piece of reminiscence about working in a slaughterhouse – a job, I suppose, Eberhart took during the Depression. There are no melodramatics, no over-large gestures, no self-pity. There is only a steady strengthening and deepening of the poet's experience – from fact to meditation to fact – until the poem has built up an intense, Dantesque vision of evil. It seems to me a minor masterpiece.

Since then, Eberhart's verse has tended more and more to abstraction. I find this less impressive. There is always a certain deliberate awkwardness about his writing which, at its best, mirrors the kind of physical effort he puts into his thinking. But when used in directly metaphysical argument, it seems lumbering. Eberhart, however, is a prolific writer, so the metaphysical pieces may merely be poetic calisthenics to keep him fit until his next burst of creative energy. Anyway, he has written enough excellent poems to justify any number of mistakes.

The Observer, 1960

The Faber Book of Modern Verse*

There are three kinds of anthology. First, there are the representative, those large, overstuffed volumes which include everybody. Their standard is simply historical. Poets are in because they exist. They write, therefore they are; that is, are part of literary history or, if the anthology is contemporary, part of the Old Boy circuit. Hence the collections of Quiller-Couch and Oscar Williams, the Oxford Books of this and that, and the countless paperback guides to the monuments of literature, past and present. They are eminently useful but rarely significant.

Second, there are the idiosyncratic, which are as interesting, or as uninteresting, as the anthologist himself. He may have a special gospel to preach, as George Moore had in his *Pure Poetry*; or he may use literature to create an image of his own or his era's sensibility, as Aldous Huxley did in *Texts and Pretexts*. To judge by the use it has been put to, 'The Waste Land' itself might have been an anthology of this kind.

Finally, there are the critical anthologies, which make no claim to completeness, yet try to avoid the merely personal fad. Work gets in because it is good, because it has added something to literature and changed the standards a little bit. And these are the important anthologies, for they can create the taste of a period. Robert Graves once called one of his wilder lambastings of modern poetry, 'These be your gods, O Israel'. The title would apply without any irony at all to Michael Roberts's *Faber Book of Modern Verse*. It is still, twenty-five years later, the best anthology of modern poetry.

* *The Faber Book of Modern Verse*, edited by Michael Roberts, revised by Anne Ridler (London: Faber and Faber, 1951).

What makes *The Faber Book* as good as it is? Roberts, who included none of his own poems, claimed the freedom of a certain impersonality. Yet when the book appeared in 1936 it must have seemed 'modern' to the point of eccentricity. The reigning Establishment poets, whom Roberts called 'The House of Lords', were left out. So were poets who drew their strength from a style which had nothing to do with the new verse: Walter de la Mare, Edmund Blunden, Edwin Muir, Roy Campbell. In their place were young English and American writers, some of whom were scarcely known. It was modern then, and, to an extraordinary degree, it is modern now. Until the early fifties, it was the only English collection with a reasonable number of poems by William Empson and Wallace Stevens. It is still almost the only place for Hart Crane and Laura Riding.

Yet Roberts was right when he said he 'included only poems which . . . please me for reasons neither personal nor idiosyncratic'. He brought the verse together in the same way as he wrote his introduction: out of concern for and understanding of a whole new movement in poetry. In a sense, *The Faber Book* is a companion volume to Dr Leavis's *New Bearings in English Poetry*. Both analysed the new sensibility in verse and reordered tradition in the light of it. Both chose Hopkins as the first important 'modern' poet, for all that he had been dead for nearly half a century. Both concentrated on the achievement of Eliot and Pound.

Roberts went on to include a crowd of thirties poets, which was inevitable in 1936, but not in 1931, when *New Bearings* appeared. Roberts lost points by not including Hardy or Edward Thomas (the House of Lords again?), but made up with a host of American poets Leavis did not even mention. On quirks, they broke about even: Leavis has Ronald Bottrall, Roberts has eight Spender to one Eberhart. In short, where Leavis's criticism tried to set the house of poetry in order, Roberts's anthology showed how large and impressive the place was.

It has diminished surprisingly little. The anthology is still modernist and experimental in a way no contemporary equivalent would be. Or rather, if a contemporary anthology were experimental, it would probably be so in ways laid down by poets in *The Faber Book*. And this accounts for the queer excitement the collection still transmits. For the twenty-odd years before it was printed, poetry had changed into something not only richer and stranger but tougher, subtler, more concentrated and more European than had been seen for a long time.

Roberts set out to show what had happened and why. Perhaps the word which best describes his tone is not so much 'excitement' as 'optimism'. 'More often than prose or mathematics', his introduction begins, 'poetry is received in a hostile spirit'; and a little later he throws off the phrase, 'a bad poem, a psychologically disordered poem'. His optimism is in the way he speaks of poetry in the same breath as the sciences. Sensitivity and intelligence no longer seem mutually exclusive. It is the tone of the great Cambridge epoch when all the intellectual disciplines were being reordered.

It was the epoch of Principles: The Principles of Mathematics, of Ethics, of Literary Criticism. Its tone was analytical, quizzical, tough-minded and buoyantly determined – determined, that is, to explain things rationally and have done with nonsense, hostility and incomprehension. In its way, Roberts's thirty-five-page introduction is a Principles of Modern Poetry in miniature.

Alas, the new *Faber Book* is not quite what it was. Michael Roberts died before he was able to revise it. Anne Ridler took over, and partly transformed it into just another representative anthology. Where Roberts gave three dozen poets 350 pages, she added two dozen more in seventy-five pages. But she was attempting the impossible. When her revision appeared in 1951, modern poetry and its principles had changed: Symbolism and its poor sister, Imagism, were deceased, and the Anglo-American movement, with its eclectic, 'European' tradition, had sunk into a decline. English poetry had settled once more around the comfortable and comforting parish pump. So the anthology could never properly be brought up to date; it could only be done again.

It is a pity, then, that Faber does not reissue the book in its original form, instead of settling for the present compromise. For *The Faber Book of Modern Verse* is more than an excellent anthology; it is an important and original document in the development of modern literature.

The Observer, 1960

Hugh MacDiarmid*

Hugh MacDiarmid's reputation south of the border is uncertain, and he probably likes it that way. Until this edition of *Collected Poems* his work has been almost impossible to obtain; his last book of verse was published in London in the mid-thirties. Much of the present volume is in a particularly *recherché* form of Scots: he seems literally to have reinvented the language from a mixture of Dunbar's poems, Ibrox Park chat and Jamieson's *Etymological Dictionary of the Scottish Language*. Without him Lallans would never have existed. Scarcely any critics have written on him; although the new *Festschrift* has useful essays by members of the Scots Home Guard – David Craig, Edwin Morgan, David Daiches and Walter Keir – no comment by outsiders is included.

With his virulent Anglophobia, MacDiarmid clearly wouldn't give tuppence for what is thought of him here, anyway. Yet to celebrate his seventieth birthday the adulation, no doubt, will flow in. He is, after all, the most important Scottish poet since Burns, and the first English-speaking writer to make real poetry out of Communism.

MacDiarmid's *Collected Poems* represent a massive achievement. Massive in both senses: although a good many pieces have been dropped by the author, the volume still runs to almost 500 pages; and among them is poetry of the first importance.

But it is also an extraordinarily patchy achievement. Like

* Hugh MacDiarmid, *Collected Poems* (Edinburgh: Oliver and Boyd, 1962); *Hugh MacDiarmid, A Festschrift*, edited by K. D. Duval and Sydney Goodsir Smith (Edinburgh: Duval, 1962).

Shelley, who was the last important English radical poet, or like Ezra Pound with whom, despite their politics, MacDiarmid has a good deal in common, he has written far too much. Even the first slight lyrics run on and on. He finds it hard to let a subject be, or to distinguish between what he once called 'The Kind of Poetry I Want' and the kind of poetry he can write.

There are four stages in MacDiarmid's artistic evolution. In the first, he was a sharp but fairly conventional lyricist with hankerings after God. Then, in the mid-twenties, he started writing in Scots. The language he used put him in touch, at least theoretically, with the audience he was after. Though he was not yet in the C.P., he was a fierce Scottish Nationalist and far on the left. The vernacular poems were written for his ideal readers (whom he probably, like most influential poets, created): proletarian, intelligent, hard, witty, a bit battered and wholly un-English.

By the time his major Scots work appeared in 1926 – 'A Drunk Man Looks at the Thistle' – his confidence was complete; he was able to extend this 'common' style into a full-scale 'modern' idiom, competing with Eliot's, Joyce's, Pound's and Rilke's. Although his humour remained wry and pubby, his references were polyglot, and the argument was often complexly metaphysical.

When MacDiarmid joined the Communist Party during the Depression he began more and more to use English, but an English strengthened by his practice in Scots. The language was sparer, suppler, more concentrated than before, and was sustained by a subtly running, colloquial rhythm. At the same time the work had evolved a new centre: a Marxist-Leninism which had much less to do with general social theory than with a wholly unabstract human ideal. The kind of poetry he wanted reflected the kind of man he wanted. He once called it 'Unremittin', relentless,/Organised to the last degree'. In practice, it was something less cold-blooded than that. Disinterestedness did not preclude warmth nor manliness feeling. His ideal is of a man disencumbered by 'bourgeois' ambitions, morally straight and generously involved in the rhythm and give-and-take of life, in birth, love and death – which, in the context, is rather different from Eliot's sour 'Birth, copulation and death':

. . . the future fumbles,
A bad birth, not like the child in that gracious home
Heard in the quietness turning in its mother's womb,

A strategic mind already, seeking the best way
To present himself to life, and at last, resolved,
Springing into history quivering like a fish,
Dropping into the world like a ripe fruit due in time –
But where is the Past to which Time, smiling through her tears
At her new-born son, can turn crying: 'I love you'?

It is extraordinary that such a fusion of instinctive nature, human tenderness and a sense of history and of purpose could have emerged as a comment on the social mess of the thirties.

John Spiers once grumbled, and David Craig joins him in the *Festschrift*, that MacDiarmid's work has gone off badly since his moral and artistic honeymoon with Communism. Yet he was by no means perfect even then:

This Bolshevik bog! Suits me doon to the grun'!
For by fyke and finnick the world's no' run. . . .

To my unaccustomed ear at least, that sounds less like forthright complaint than mannered bullying. On the other hand, a recent poem like 'The Glass of Pure Water' combines meditation with physical subtlety as finely as most of his earlier work. Yet certainly he no longer often commands what he has called 'The genuine simplicity of immediate awareness'. Like Pound, all his reading has now become fair poetic game. He stuffs his verse with great dry wads of comparative philology, political wrangling, or even souped-up, heroical journalism. In the end, the poetry itself is crowded out.

But his best work more than makes up for the boredom, clumsiness and didacticism of the bad. He has managed a curious creative amalgam of old and new, uniting great feeling for his country, its traditions and language, with the strengths of the ideal modern industrial man: virile, unaffected, passionate and, like the poet himself, taking both poverty and learning for granted.

The Observer, 1962

Philip Larkin*

This is Philip Larkin's first book for nearly ten years. It contains only thirty-two poems – three more than *The Less Deceived*, which represented the previous decade's worth of his work. Clearly, no one is going to accuse him of writing too much or of publishing verse he is unsure of. Indeed, I imagine no one is going to accuse him of anything. His last book was received none too brilliantly; it is only since then that his reputation has slowly, almost silently, gathered momentum. Any moment now someone is bound to pin on him that heaviest of gold medals: the one inscribed 'Great Poet'.

If this happens, it will be a pity. For Larkin is an excellent poet, part of whose excellence is that he knows his limitations as precisely as his strengths, and he overestimates neither. So he has never thrown his hat into the heavyweight ring. If he is contending for any crown, it is Betjeman's or De La Mare's, and he is better than either. He has none of Betjeman's coyness or condescension – though, judging by a poem like 'Naturally the Foundation will Bear your Expenses', he also doesn't have Betjeman's touch with light verse. His serious poems are more squarely of one time, one place than De La Mare's, though less generous.

Perhaps his main achievement is to have created a special voice for that special, localized moment: post-war provincial England in all its dreariness, with the boredom of shortages no longer justified, the cheap, plastic surface of things which nobody wants and everybody

* Philip Larkin, *The Whitsun Weddings* (London: Faber and Faber, 1964).

buys. He did in poetry much the same as Kingsley Amis did in *Lucky Jim*: created a tone of voice for the witty, sharply literary provincial outsider who was a good deal cleverer and more perceptive than those on the metropolitan inside.

To do this Larkin brought about no spectacular transformation of the technique of poetry. He merely made another series of those minute adjustments to the tradition by which most English poetry in this century has managed to keep abreast of the times without risking a jump into the uncharted future. It is a question not of forms but of accent. This, for example, on Father Time:

> *So he patted my head, booming* Boy
> There's no green in your eye:
> Sit here, and watch the hail
> Of occurrence clobber life out
> To a shape no one sees –
> Dare you look at that straight?
> Oh thank you. *I said,* Oh yes please,
> *And sat down to wait.*
>
> *Half life is over now,*
> *And I meet full face on dark mornings*
> *The bestial visor, bent in*
> *By the blows of what happened to happen.*
> *What does it prove? Sod all.*
> *In this way I spent youth.*
> *Tracing the trite untransferable*
> *Truss-advertisement, truth.*

There are two main elements in this kind of success: first, the control which allows pub slang (all that 'clobbering' and stuff) to thicken naturally into serious metaphor (such as the 'bestial visor'); second, the thrown-away half-rhymes ('sod all' with 'untransferable') which are a formal equivalent of the disrespect in his voice. Technically, it is original, skilful and, as his imitators have sadly shown, unrepeatable. Without posturing or pretence, he has done something in poetry which is quite his own and quite undeniable.

Yet it is also extremely limited. In the last two books – that is, the last twenty years – Larkin's themes may have changed superficially but his style has developed not at all. And yet his style *is* his theme; it is a means of deprecation, of playing-down, a beautiful avoidance of coming out for anything. In *The Less Deceived* it was love and all that he was glancing off – all those modest proposals he had never made and risks he had never taken. In the new book the constant theme he edges around is death.

Two other poets recently have been much possessed by death, Sylvia Plath and Louis MacNeice. In Plath's poems death appeared as a positive act, an intense confirmation of identity, a fulfilment which created poetry. MacNeice treated death as a fact which, when accepted wryly, gave strength and depth to his work. Larkin is very different; for him death seems to be nothing more than a dank tailing-off which leaves behind only the sour taste of a wasted life:

Life is first boredom, then fear.
Whether or not we use it, it goes,
And leaves what something hidden from us chose,
And age, and then the only end of age.

'Death comes to nothing for one man,' wrote Norman Mailer, 'because he swallowed his death in his life, and . . . for another death is alive with dimension.' Larkin belongs very much to that first group. He writes of death as though it were merely the logical end to the denials he habitually practises in his work; if it scares or worries him, it does not do so for itself but because it lies outside routine and amiable comfort.

But no poetry can be made wholly of denials. What keeps Larkin's verse alive is his feeling for the life he never quite had, the life of chance and risk, marriage and movement. It is this that sustains the two best pieces in the book: the title poem – wedding parties seen from his comfortable seat in a train – and 'MCMXIV', an unusually convinced elegy for an England and an innocence he had never known, since both belonged to his father's generation. Given a safe, spectator's distance he is able to tap reserves not only of skill but of a depressed tenderness which rarely appear in his other work. (Elsewhere he can be, at times, sentimental, but that is another matter.)

It is, in the end, a question of choice. In order to write well Larkin has deliberately turned his back on what he calls 'unfenced existence; Facing the sun, untalkative, out of reach'. He has chosen instead a kind of suburban hermitage, with plenty of books and records, bottled beer in the cupboard and all mod. con. On the wall is a poker-work motto which reads: 'You'll never have it any better.'

The Observer, 1964

John Berryman*

John Berryman is one of those poets whom you either love or loathe. Yet even the loathers have grudgingly to admit that the man is extraordinary – too extraordinary, they would add – with a queer, distinct voice of his own. Personally, I find that voice powerful and undeniable, and one which, despite its vacillations and variations, already has to its credit a remarkably solid achievement, culminating in his intricate, anguished, unprecedented poem, 'Homage to Mistress Bradstreet'.

'Homage' is an intimidatingly difficult piece of work, but compared to 77 *Dream Songs* it is as clear as Mother Goose. The Dream Songs have been appearing here and there for some time – there were a couple in *The Observer* not too long ago – tantalizing fragments of a vast, sprawling work in progress. But this first bringing of them together doesn't make them any less baffling or seemingly more principled than, say, Pound's *Cantos*. There is, however, a difference: unlike Pound, Berryman is touting no theories, promoting no programme for Kulchur or society. The Dream Songs are, instead, the fragmentary inner biography, the perceptions by which he lives, of a character called Henry.

Henry is at once the poet – in that he is literary, learned, jagged and nervy to a degree – and yet not quite Berryman – in that he is held mockingly, quizzically at a distance, itching, lusting, worrying and fuming away in a not at all flattering light. There is also a second character who butts in with awkward questions at awkward moments, questions posed and answered in a joky mixture of blues and coon language. His name is Mr Bones; I presume he is Death.

* John Berryman, 77 *Dream Songs* (London: Faber and Faber, 1964).

So *77 Dream Songs* is a kind of poetic diary of the fantasies and probings of this half-loved, half-mocked joker in the pack, Henry, as he gets ill and drunk, makes passes, has a child, travels, quarrels with God and politicians, reads theology and talks of other poets (there are beautiful elegies on Roethke and Frost). Each Song is written in three six-line stanzas, though some rhyme, some don't, and the rhythm varies all through. So does the language. Berryman has been accused of borrowing like a magpie, and his sources have already been tallied: Pound, Stevens, Cummings, Joyce; there is also Hopkins and even, in the spelling, Bridges; plus baby talk, coon dialect and continual wrenchings of syntax, or, as he would say, 'grammaticisms, un—'.

It seems at first confusing, impenetrable, distracting. Yet finally it doesn't matter; as you get into the book you realize that these irritations are like nervous tics, simply part of the man. For Berryman is deliberately a mannerist who, out of his fraught nerviness, has made an original and remarkably flexible style. In his earlier work his wit was often swamped by his intensity. The Dream Songs, being more relaxed and personal, are at times very funny:

Black hair, complexion Latin, jewelled eyes
downcast. . . . The slob beside her feasts. . . . What wonders is
she sitting on, over there?
The restaurant buzzes. She might as well be on Mars.
Where did it all go wrong? There ought to be a law against
Henry.
– Mr Bones: there is.

But the jokes are not there for their own sakes – with the exception of a rousing attack on Ike. Instead, they are largely at his own expense. So they qualify and distance that anguish to which his style and preoccupations seem naturally to run. For Berryman is a poet of sleepless small hours' remorse. One of Thornton Wilder's characters, hungover after a terrible jag, flings up the window and shouts to the traffic far below: 'I apologize! I apologize to everyone!' Berryman has made major poetry out of that morning-after despair:

There sat down, once, a thing on Henry's heart
só heavy, if he had a hundred years
& more, & weeping, sleepless, in all them time
Henry could not make good.

Starts again always in Henry's ears
the little cough somewhere, an odour, a chime.

And there is another thing he has in mind
like a grave Sienese face a thousand years
would fail to blur the still profiled reproach of. Ghastly,
with open eyes, he attends, blind.
All the bells say: too late. This is not for tears;
thinking.

But never did Henry, as he thought he did,
end anyone and hacks her body up
and hide the pieces, where they may be found.
He knows: he went over everyone, & nobody's missing.
Often he reckons, in the dawn, them up.
Nobody is ever missing.

The precarious balance is kept by a just-detached attention to the details of feeling, a wryness, as it were, gone sensitive, an insistence, when tears might come, on thinking.

Not all the Songs are that straight. So it is best to start with the less resistant ones: Nos. 4, 14, 15, 18, 21–23, 27, 29, 52–54, 61–63, 69, 75–77. Even these can be uneven and maddening. But they are worth the trouble, for 77 *Dream Songs* is an utterly original work by a strange, talkative, learned, wrought poet who is continually writing his way around a central, unnerving perception:

We are using our skins for wallpaper and we cannot win.

The Observer, 1964

W. H. Auden*

Someone has said that once you have had a youthful love-affair with poems it's difficult later to be friends. This doesn't seem to be true for me of Auden's early work. When I was at school I knew great stretches of it by heart – particularly the section of his first *Collected Shorter Poems* called 'Songs and other Musical Pieces'. These still strike me as wholly compelling, original, inevitable. It is the later poems that stump me; they did then and, as volume has succeeded volume, they have ever since. I recognize that they are clever and witty and probably saner than the earlier stuff. I know, too, that Auden, with his subtle, aged, Wallace Beery face, has become an admirable figure on the literary landscape – a man of great generosity and charm. Yet his later poems strike me as shallow and prolix in a way that is utterly foreign to his early work.

The new edition of his *Collected Shorter Poems* and a reissue of *The Orators* show this, I think, all too clearly. Where the first *Collected* went from 1930 to 1944, the new volume spans thirty years, 1927–1957. It includes, that is, poems from *The Shield of Achilles*, *Nones* and half of *Homage to Clio*. To make room for them Auden has wielded a severe new broom. Poems, he says, have been 'thrown out because they were dishonest, or bad mannered, or boring'. These three categories account, alas, for some of his best work.

'I once,' he writes, 'expressed a desire for "New styles of architecture"; but I have never liked modern architecture. I prefer *old* styles.' So 'Sir, no man's enemy', a minor masterpiece, has gone

* W. H. Auden, *The Orators* (London: Faber and Faber, 1966); *Collected Shorter Poems, 1927–1957* (London: Faber and Faber, 1966).

because it was 'dishonest'. So, too, has 'Spain 1937', because, he says, the last line 'equates goodness with success'. I wonder. Mightn't the reason be that it is also, embarrassingly, a young revolutionary poem? How about the brilliant 'Gold in the North':

Some think they're strong, some think they're smart,
Like butterflies they're pulled apart,
America can break your heart.

Bad mannered, perhaps, to the country of his adoption, like that other famous casualty of his purge, '1st September 1939'? For the same reason, I suppose, his poem on Oxford has been carefully but fiercely castrated; it's bad form for a Professor of Poetry to talk about 'these quadrangles where Wisdom honours herself' and the stones echo 'The founder's equivocal blessing/On all who worship Success'. As compensation 'A. E. Housman', who 'Kept tears like dirty post-cards in a drawer', has been restored to the canon; after all, Housman was a Cambridge man. But on what conceivable grounds have lively, beautiful poems like 'Prothalamion' and 'Now through night's caressing grip' been removed? Or the whole of 'Paid on Both Sides', which is, for my money, the finest extended work Auden has ever done. Presumably, he is bored by lines like

Though he believe it, no man is strong.
He thinks to be called the fortunate,
To bring home a wife, to live long.
But he is defeated. . . .

and not by lines like

By all means sing of love but, if you do,
Please make a rare old proper hullabaloo:
When ladies ask How much do you love me?
The Christian answer is cosí-cosí. . . .

It's sad, it's almost tragic, but in the end it doesn't really matter. Some of the axed poems are so good that they have already become part of the language and literature, whether Auden accepts them or not. The only puzzle is why he should now dislike them so much. There is a clue in his foreword to the new edition of *The Orators*: 'My name on the title-page seems a pseudonym for someone else, someone talented but near the border of sanity who might well, in a year or two, become a Nazi.'

This border-line quality may well account for the knotted, wilful impenetrability of *The Orators*' prose, and for some of its tiresomeness. But it is also at one with whatever it was that made his poems tick: an unnamed, probably unnameable, but utterly pervasive sense of guilt and fear of retribution, which made him cast around unceasingly for solutions. So he went to politics, psychoanalysis and sociology, and refracted them all through a tense, thickened language, the poet's mind leaping like a salmon with energy and despair. It was all localized in those northern limestone uplands, a cold, bitten grazing country, sporadically patrolled by predators – foxes, hawks, men. In this chill and resistant landscape – 'North', he wrote, 'means to all *Reject*' – the guilt found some grim but objective relief – despite the schoolboy superstructure of code-words, mysterious orders and secret games. It also gave a sharp sense of the ominousness of the time, with Nazism rising and the old prep-school culture of England about to shatter.

Auden left these anxieties mostly behind him when he moved to America in 1939. Occasionally they appear later, but only as a fondly indulged habit, like some once recurrent but now vanished nightmare, a matter almost for nostalgia. In their place came complete assurance. The young poet who had prayed for 'New styles of architecture, a change of heart', got both in New York. He became *the* acknowledged craftsman and wit, writing comfortable, sociable, unexceptionable long poems, mostly to friends, full of learned jokes and personified abstractions, a kind of chatty, latter-day Roman.

Once in a while he produced something rather marvellous, like *The Sea and the Mirror*, but mostly his achievement was a matter of complete professionalism. He emerged, for example, as our foremost librettist. He forgot his earlier obscurities, his edginess, his unease and became, in a word, adjusted. He has gone on record as accepting all the Church's XXXIX Articles – more than even Matthew Arnold could manage. It reminds me of that folk-song of American psychoanalysis: 'I can't get adjusted to the you who got adjusted to me.'

But as I said, it doesn't matter. The poems are there, even if Auden now looks on some of the best of them with distinct distaste. The pity is that his hosts of admirers will now have to scrape around among out-of-print volumes to find their favourites.

The Observer, 1966

Louis MacNeice*

When Louis MacNeice died suddenly in 1963 he was writing as well as he had ever written. He was fifty-six, which is young to die but late for a poetic renaissance. Yet that sudden burst of creativity in his last couple of years was typical of his fitful, backwards-and-forwards progress as a poet. The best pieces in his *Collected Poems* are bunched together here and there like so many flourishing oases; around them are long, drab wastes of verse, often stylish but somehow as sprawling and unsustaining as sand. It runs in all to 560-odd pages, a sporadic, tantalizing, diffuse and utterly personal achievement.

Though his first volume was published in 1929, when he was twenty-two, it was nothing like as precocious as Auden's *Poems 1930*. MacNeice's earliest work was slacker, more casual, less attacking and complete. Apparently he recognized this, for he left out most of his juvenilia when he collected his work in 1948. It wasn't until about 1933 that he found his own ironic voice. Then, in a short space, he wrote a clutch of poems all of which have been in one or other of the selections and anthologies: 'Spring Voices', 'Sunday Morning', 'Perseus', 'Snow'.

In a way they were all lyrics – poems about a single, sharp perception – but urban lyrics. Their theme is: 'World is crazier and more of it than we think,/Incorrigibly plural.' The poems depend on the sudden, jolting realization that objects have a gaiety and solid presence of their own, quite independent of the moody vagaries of the poet. Unexpectedly, out of 'the city's haze . . . tilting by the

* Louis MacNeice, *Collected Poems* (London: Faber and Faber, 1967).

noble curve bus after tall bus comes/With an osculation of yellow light with a glory like chrysanthemums'.

To insist in this way on the shoddy-beautiful objects in the industrial landscape was one of the achievements of the thirties pylon poets. But when MacNeice wrote in this way it wasn't simply a question of chic or mannerism; things seemed vivid because they cut through the meditative gloom that prevailed elsewhere in his verse. For he was also beginning to evolve a style for long poems: relaxed, chatty, knowing, depressed. The voice was that of a man not so much disillusioned as without any illusions at all; it conveyed, above all, a sense of vague unease, of trouble just out of focus but wearily imminent. It was profoundly pessimistic. But it was also only intermittently successful. Most of MacNeice's long poems seem too long by half. Because he was witty, well read and technically adept he seemed effortlessly able to go on and on. His first two long poems – 'An Eclogue for Christmas' and 'Eclogue of a Five-Barred Gate' – are his best; there are brilliant period passages in the 'Autumn Journal'; the rest become progressively more prosy and thin-spread.

The reason, I suspect, is that behind the clever charm and off-hand intimacy was a core of indifference. That jumping intensity of invention which the young Auden brought to even his most intellectual performances was never MacNeice's style. He remained withdrawn – 'always under water or glass' – watching himself react with fascination and slight distaste. It implies, perhaps, a certain dubious talent for boredom; but this boredom, I think, gets right into the fabric of his long poems, deadening them.

It also implies a glum talent for expecting the worst, and this quality helped MacNeice come powerfully into his own as the Second World War approached. Around 1937 he began to experiment with light verse; perhaps the intricate techniques it demanded allowed him the same cooling objectivity he had found earlier in the 'incorrigibly plural' world. Certainly, between 1937 and 1941 he perfected a form of sardonic, deadly serious light verse which not only expressed, without fuss, all his anger and contempt but also seemed wholly appropriate for the time. 'Bagpipe Music', 'Bar-Room Matins', 'The Streets of Laredo' and the 'Novelettes' are some of the best poems written about 'the gathering storm' and the Blitz. MacNeice's dislike of heroics suddenly made sense of that nervous, battered period. The worst had happened and it turned out to be more or less tolerable; the relief gets into his poetry as a kind of jaunty indignation. The poems are perfect in their way, and part of the history of the time.

But the war ended, MacNeice stayed on at the B.B.C. and turned yet again to his fatal Cleopatra, the long poem. It was his worst period creatively. He seemed to write as though by conditioned reflex, with nothing particular to say and only a technique, a fascination with language and an unfortunate taste for puns and jingles to sustain him. The culmination of all this was 'Autumn Sequel', prattling and anti-climactic, his worst poem and his longest. Perhaps he managed to catch in it something of the bored London tone – sour, knocked-about, gossipy, soiled – but in doing so he was also caught and victimized by it.

In a late poem 'Goodbye to London', he wrote of the aftermath of war: 'reborn into anticlimax/We endured much litter and apathy hoping/The phoenix would rise.' Miraculously enough, it rose for him. When he was already in his fifties he turned back to the short, loaded forms he had always done best, and suddenly the poetry flowed again. Two themes seemed to possess him: his childhood and death, as though he were trying to forgive the past and, in a grim, joky way, accept whatever was about to happen. There were no histrionics; the texture was often tricksy, the style cool, the metaphors odd. But under it all ran the plangent refrain, 'Too late'.

These poems are a triumph of the nonchalant tone he had always worked for. He peered quizzically at the prospect of death and made of it poetry as wry, serious and, paradoxically, as lively as anything he had done in his prime.

The Observer, 1967

3

CLASSICS

Donne's *Holy Sonnets**

I suspect that Donne did not much like the sonnet as a literary form. There are, after all, none at all in the *Songs and Sonets*, despite the title. Elsewhere in his collected poems there are half a dozen verse letters to young friends-about-town, all sonnets, all early, and all – with one possible exception – worthless. To produce his best work Donne needed a form much freer than that of the sonnet, a form with subtler rhythms and a less defined rhyme-scheme, which could move with the movement of his sensibility, contain and echo the twists of his logic. Even when he used rhymed couplets, in the 'Elegies' and 'Satyres', he handled the meter with such freedom and treated the rhymes so off-handedly that his natural speaking voice was enriched by the ghost of that strictest of moulds; it became a kind of echo chamber enhancing his natural resonance and individuality.

This genius for using every metrical form as though it had never been used by anyone before, as though he had just invented it, casually and specially for the occasion, deserted Donne when he first turned seriously to sonnets in about 1607. That self-contained and intertwined series, 'La Corona', is, for him, startlingly unstartling and staid. It reads as though he had adopted the mode as a deliberate act of self-discipline, a means of chastening his Muse as he was gradually chastening his life and ambitions in his long decision to enter the church. The *Holy Sonnets* are later – though the bulk came only a couple of years after 'La Corona', if Dame Helen

* In *Master Poems of the English Language*, edited by O. Williams (New York: Trident Press, 1966).

Gardner is right in her dating, and in these scholarly matters she usually is. Certainly, they are an altogether more individual achievement than 'La Corona', but an achievement almost in the teeth of the sonnet form. They have none of the usual neatness or charm or grace that the Elizabethans had made seem obligatory. He merely used the inherent tightness of the sonnet to reflect both personal tensions and the highly organized, compressed thinking that, with Donne, always went with emotional disturbance. This taut complexity of tone defines the kind of poems the *Holy Sonnets* are. They have nothing to do with the certainties of faith. On the contrary, they are about the lack of faith, about guilt, hesitation, uncertainty and spiritual failure; about, in short, the obstructions to revelation rather than about revelation itself. I have written elsewhere* that, unlike George Herbert, Donne was continually arguing out his position with God in such a way as to make you believe that there was a good deal to be said on both sides. So the sonnets are inner debates, the outcome of which is never wholly certain. And they are carried out with a good deal of intricate theological argument.

The result is a distinct and unresolved clash between the private, the spiritual and the worldly. The best of them have that unforced and utterly individual note that was part of Donne's unique contribution to English poetry. They also have that other part of his contribution: the wholly unacademic effortlessness of intellectual reference. Donne's intellectualism, I mean, was very much that of a man of the world; his wide and intense learning was counterbalanced by an equally wide and intense sophistication. The clash, then, is in the way Donne used this worldly, sophisticated tone to cope with those moments at which personal anxiety and theology intersect. His gift is to make worldliness seem spiritual, and faith a matter of sense and sensibility.

> *And thou like Adamant draw mine iron heart. . . .*
>
> *Nor ever chast, except you ravish mee. . . .*

The writing is so convinced, the rhythm moves so subtly and individually, that you scarcely notice that, as figures of speech, these lines are two of the most extreme and 'conceited' in the series. The point – if it needs making again – is that in Donne's maturest work the conceit was in no way self-conscious, eye-catching or knock-you-down. It was, instead, an indication of the intellectual command and

* *The School of Donne* (London: Chatto and Windus, 1961), p. 78.

range of experience he brought to bear on his poems. It was a sign that he was not restricting his responses for the sake of propriety or of any false concept of purity of poetical tone. His triumph is that he makes it seem utterly natural to talk of the love of God and of religious conflict in terms of science and sex.

So his assurance is the product of great sophistication – intellectual and emotional as well as poetic. Consider, for example:

At the round earths imagin'd corners

Even at the beginning of one of the most powerful and, in every sense, rousing of all his sonnets, he does not relax his intellectual precision for rhetorical effect. Note, I mean, that 'imagin'd'. According to the notes, Donne had in mind a passage from Revelations: 'I saw four angels standing at the four corners of the earth.' But Donne the seventeenth-century intellectual, with his 'hydroptique, immoderate desire of humane learning and languages' cannot accept St John's inaccuracy: the earth is round, it has no corners. Precision above all things.

With this precision goes an intricate, personal theological questioning. In a way, the great dramatic outbursts – 'At the round earths imagin'd corners', 'Death be not proud', 'Batter my heart' – are not typical of the over-all tone of the *Holy Sonnets*. The note is generally more pausing, inturned and probing: 'Thou hast made me, And shall thy work decay', 'As due by many titles I resigne', 'I am a little world made cunningly', 'If faithfull soules', 'If poysonous mineralls', 'Why are wee by all creatures waited on?', 'Oh, to vex me, contraryes meet in one'; and so on. The questions, premises, suppositions and imagined situations are teased out in detail, with great exactness and shows of logic.

This is not, I think, always an advantage. Within the confines of the sonnet Donne's habitual logical compression sometimes jams up, so that, for example, when he plagiarizes himself, the religious verse sounds less convinced and convincing than the secular.

You which beyond that heaven which was most high
Have found new sphears, and of new lands can write,
Powre new seas in mine eyes, that so I might
Drowne my world with my weeping earnestly,
Or wash it, if it must be drownd no more:
But oh it must be burnt!

That is one of his favourite images, which he had worked out often and better before in 'The Good-Morrow', 'A Valediction: Of Weeping' and 'A Nocturnall Upon S. Lucies Day'. Compared with those three poems, the holy sonnet seems thinner, less urgent, more stilted and shriller.

The occasions of the *Holy Sonnets* are, of course, rather more formal and circumscribed than those of the *Songs and Sonets*. Indeed, the latest academic theory – which I don't believe – is that the poems are formal to the extent of being deliberate exercises in Ignatian meditation. Be that as it may, Donne certainly seems to have used them as a showcase for himself in the role of learned and devout theologian. In other words, they often read like a dry run for the sermons. And in some ways, the sonnets and the sermons are alike. We remember both for those marvellous outbursts when Donne, that tense, supremely intelligent and sensitive, and curiously modern intellectual, pulls out every trick of passionate rhetoric he can muster in order, finally, to convince himself of the truth of what he is saying. Yet in the sermons these are only isolated passages in long, scrupulous theological analyses. Even 'Death's Duell', that last and most extraordinary performance, which inspired one listener to comment that Donne had 'preach't his own Funeral Sermon', is meticulously argued and detailed, despite its intensity, eloquence and infinitely dramatic situation.

The *Holy Sonnets* record some of the private, internal conflicts which lay behind the grander public occasions of his preaching. Yet the poems, too, are most successful when most dramatic. Their drama, however, is less of situation than of language. It was a question of endowing a staid form with a certain intensity of action. Donne did so by using a technique he had discovered most triumphantly in an early poem, 'Elegie XVI':

> *. . . I saw him I,*
> *Assail'd, fight, taken, stabb'd, bleed, fall, and die.*

The best of the *Holy Sonnets* are informed by the same battering speed and attack:

> *All whom the flood did, and fire shall o'erthrow,*
> *All whom warre, dearth, age, agues, tyrannies,*
> *Despaire, law, chance, hath slaine . . .*

*

Thou art slave to Fate, Chance, kings, and desperate men,
And dost with poyson, warre, and sicknesse dwell,
And poppie, or charmes can make us sleepe as well,
And better then thy stroake . . .

*

Batter my heart, three person'd God; for, you
As yet but knocke, breathe, shine, and seeke to mend;
That I may rise, and stand, o'erthrow mee, and bend
Your force, to breake, blowe, burn and make me new . . .

It is a technical solution to a kind of behavioural problem. Part of Donne's perennial power came from his awareness of himself and of the figure he was cutting at the instant of writing. But this awareness depended, naturally, on the presence of an audience, whether it was one girl or a whole fashionable churchful. In contrast, the *Holy Sonnets* were debates with himself and with God, whose presence and reactions, even if they could possibly be presumed, certainly couldn't be predicted. So Donne created the drama and the audience by assault. He reversed the situation of his love poems, writing as though he himself were the recipient of the aggressive masculinity and seductive quickness of response which was always, whatever the circumstances, his peculiar *forte*. In his 'Elegie', Thomas Carew wrote of Donne:

. . . the flame
Of thy brave Soule, that shot such heat and light,
As burnt our earth, and made our darknesse bright,
Committed holy Rapes upon our Will. . . .

By some curious technical sleight of style Donne, in his *Holy Sonnets*, seems to be both the lover and the loved.

The problem, then, was how a highly sophisticated worldly man whose poetic force relied to a large extent on his awareness of himself acting *in* the world, wrote poetry of inner, spiritual debate without abandoning his natural strength and vitality. The answer was only partly in the usual Metaphysical solution – relentlessly worldly figures of speech – and only partly in Donne's adoption of his later scholastic role of the intricate theologian and preacher. The main solution was in creating drama out of the form and language themselves. It was the drama of language in continual, fruitful conflict with the stubborn and restrictive shape of the conventional sonnet.

1965

John Dryden*

Ever since Eliot's essay in 1921, Dryden has, nominally, been in. Yet although this is one of the few major judgements Eliot has amplified instead of going back on, an enthusiasm for Dryden is still rare enough. Every undergraduate can quote Donne as though he were one of the great modern poets, and a good many can competently denigrate Milton; but Dryden is still respected more than read. His poems which are in currency are those that always have been: *Absalom and Achitophel*, *Mac Flecknoe*, and a handful of lyrics, odes, elegies, prologues and epilogues. The reasons for liking them may have changed, but the poems that are liked have not. After all, since Mark Van Doren's book and Eliot's subsequent essays, there has been virtually no important criticism of the poet. And it has taken until now for a definitive, properly annotated text to appear; between Professor James Kinsley's magnificent new Oxford edition and the huge, eighteen-volume *Complete Works* of the last century, there are only a couple of student texts.

If, despite Eliot, Dryden is still not a cause of much enthusiasm that is because he is pre-eminently a public poet, and public poetry disappeared with Byron; even in his work it was already disastrously involved with the public version of the private life. Since then, however, poetry has been concerned almost exclusively with private lives. Even that new classicism that Eliot was pushing when he praised Dryden was a change in method, not in subject. Admittedly, Eliot's formidable intelligence, objectivity and feeling for the poten-

* *The Poems of John Dryden*, edited by James Kinsley, 4 vols. (London: Oxford University Press, 1958).

tiality of the language were all serving realism of a kind; but it was a psychological realism, the truth of the depths, whereas Dryden was concerned with the public surface, the truth and standards of the polite world. He transposed the political jostling and scheming, the literary feuds and personal jealousies, into poetry of great purity and control. Much of his achievement depends on what he managed to do with depressingly intractable material. He made major poetry out of occasional topics.

Today there is practically no occasional or political poetry; there is only private worry or semi-public rant which excuses itself by espousing more or less worthy causes. But traditionally, there are two ways of coping with politics in verse: there is political poetry and party poetry. In the great political poems – *Coriolanus*, *Antony and Cleopatra*, and Marvell's *Horatian Ode* – the politics are undogmatic and largely unexplicit. They are there as a dimension of the speaker's sensibility, the area in which public responsibility and private action merge. Political sense, in this kind of poetry, merely makes the individual judgement more serious, inclusive and fair. Whereas in party poetry there is declamation or satire, but no appeal. Instead of testing public occasions and personalities by his private judgement, the party poet merely sets into motion public, dogmatic principles. Since the judgements, in fact, are foregone, party poetry, like party politics, depends largely on the art of manipulation. It took an immense amount of brainwork, learning and social dexterity to produce *Absalom and Achitophel*'s endlessly elaborate correspondences between Biblical Israel and seventeenth-century England, by which, as Professor Kinsley's notes show, the jokes get better the more you know of the allusions.

It is all very clever and energetic and funny. But it is also faintly depressing. For party poetry has a shadier side, that of intrigue, personal rancour and money-grubbing. Dryden, who lorded it over Will's Coffee House and literary London, whose influence on poetry lasted well over a century, who virtually created the critical idiom of this country, was also the first master and victim of Grub Street. Ben Jonson had wielded much the same power fifty years before. But he had a fine, learned arrogance which put him a little beyond the range of the mud-slingers. His learning itself commanded respect enough to protect him. But after the Civil War, learning and wit became a little suspect; the Royal Society boasted that their experiments made all wits equal. So in Dryden there is a kind of naked, unrelieved literary professionalism. Inevitably, it is a bit sordid. There are, for example, his vicious personal feuds; he was beaten up for one of his satires. There are his endless dedications, with their almost abject eulogies of the great, wealthy and possibly useful. There is a steady stream of complaints about his penury and, as a result, the grinding contracts he let himself in for:

> Received then of Mr Jacob Tonson the sum of two hundred sixty-eight pounds fifteen shillings, in pursuance of an agreement for ten thousand verses to be delivered by me to the said Jacob Tonson. . . .

His collected poems are stocked with commendations, epilogues and prologues in verse, which were the seventeenth-century equivalent of the modern hack review, turned out to order. Apparently, even his funeral was the occasion of a vindictive brawl. As Dr Johnson remarked of one of Dryden's critical wrangles: 'This is not very decent.'

Perhaps it is the sordidness of the Augustans' literary warfare that makes their work, relatively, unpopular. It is not that they are too remote from us; on the contrary, they are too close. The principles of calm reason and order on which the Peace of the Augustans was founded were so grand that they seem hardly to touch the details of the poets' lives and work; or rather, when they do, they are undercut by the swarming professional malice. And unalleviated professionalism is hard to bear. Part of Donne's initial fascination for the writers of the 1920s was the ease with which they could read into him their own brand of metaphysical anguish. It can't be done with Dryden, Pope or Swift. For despite their occasional excursions into theology – *The Hind and the Panther*, *Religio Laici*, or the *Essay on Man* – Augustan poetry seems, to an extraordinary degree, secular, like our own. Their literary brawls, apparently free of any metaphysical or aesthetic ulterior motives, are uncompromising, bare and unpleasant. It is like reading our own miserable squabbles, but transformed out of reviewers' prose into poetry of wit and genius. It seems a waste of such formidable creative effort.

Yet professionalism was the essence of Dryden's poetry and his influence depends, in a way, on the amount he wrote. For in the continual grind of turning out translations and occasional verse as his patrons or his publisher required, Dryden created a new standard for the purity of the English poetic language. He did for English what the Academy was trying to do for French. Before him, Shakespeare had taken the language which was there to hand, still fluid and unshaped, and had forced it to its imaginative limits, so that all subsequent experiment has seemed almost footling. Compared with Shakespeare, Hopkins is mannered and Joyce merely accommodates the problem of poetic language to the sensibility of a Jesuit theologian. But where Shakespeare mapped the outer limits of poetic diction, Dryden gave it its norm. He created the great common language of poetry, the language of poetic common sense.

He had started as a pale, and not very promising, imitator of Cowley, 'the darling of (his) youth', writing in the decadent, polysyllabic, painfully conceited style that was the University affectation. By lurching ponderously from one wild image to another, the poet intended, in fact, to give the impression of great intellectual speed and dexterity. On these terms, Dryden was not a witty man. His imagination worked most forcibly when most forcibly controlled. And he learned this control, like Yeats, by writing for the stage. It was a question of deliberately slowing down the machinery:

To see this Fleet upon the Ocean move
Angels drew wide the curtains of the skies:
And Heav'n, as if there wanted Lights above,
For Tapers made two glareing Comets rise.

The condensed, twisted conceits were expanded until they became stately; and to be stately, they had also to be clear. Dryden transformed seventeenth-century poetry by replacing the corrupted standard of cleverness – the standard of Cowley, Cleveland and Benlowes – with the common-sense standard of clarity. Instead of dialectics, he wrote a poetry of exposition.

Not that that was enough; Waller had almost done as much before. But Dryden, having established his tough standards of the controlled purity of common sense, once more speeded up the grandiose for more personal ends. Compared with the Metaphysical poets or with Pope, Dryden, I suggested, was not a particularly witty man. Even as a person he was, apparently, a heavy, rather county figure and a reluctant conversationalist. But he is the greatest comic poet in the language:

Round as a Globe, and Liquor'd in ev'ry chink,
Goodly and Great he Sayls behind his Link. . . .

During his Office, Treason was no crime.
The sons of Belial had a glorious time. . . .

> *Can dry Bones Live? or* Skeletons *produce*
> *The Vital Warmth of Cuckoldizing Juice?* . . .

Dryden's comic satires are the final stage of his poetic self-criticism. He did not write mock heroics; his scale is larger than that. He simply viewed the great stately progress of his heroics in the wider air of common sense. But it was a common sense that had taken to itself all the imaginative speed and concentration his early verse had lacked. In Dryden's satires common sense itself achieves a creative strength more heroic than his heroics.

It had, however, its limitations. For common sense was also, for the Augustans, a criterion that was public and general. It demanded a clear sensibleness which the feelings very rarely have. So when Dryden attempted the positive emotions – love, respect, loss – he was so resolutely public and sensible about them that they ended, as often as not, by being merely general, grandiose. Only his negative emotions, his literary and political rancours, scorn and jealousies, could be expressed in all their strength and detail, for with them the poet could assume a kind of public indignation at his opponents' violation of the reasonable decencies.

This determinedly public appeal also affected his poetic language. Dryden, as Eliot suggested, is a great master of the natural style. And so, of course, is Donne. But Donne wrote merely for a few friends; he did not publish. And so his poetry has the colloquial vibrancy of intimate talk. Dryden, on the other hand, transformed into poetry the more formal strength of public conversation. It comes out in their versification: Donne's peculiar fluency was a matter of making the pattern of his verse follow the changing flow of his thinking; whilst Dryden's steadiness and power within the bounds of the couplet is a continual reminder of his central control of feelings, learning and standards, of his firm core of common sense.

He is the most competent poet in the language. He is also the most unflinchingly sensible. Both qualities brought their own deprivations. His professionalism led him to expend enormous creative energy in the services of dubious political feuds, personal animosities and what at least began as bread-and-butter versifying. And the confidence with which he limited his art to a public reasonableness makes him appear superficial compared to Pope, to whom the dominion of common sense seemed more precarious, difficult and threatened. But Dryden set, once and for all, the standard of tough clarity, unassuming purity of language, and ironic common sense by which all poetry, sooner or later, is judged. He created, in short, the public voice of poetry, and if to be popular now demands something less stringent, sane and clear, that is our loss.

The New Statesman, 1959

John Keats*

> A Man's life of any worth is a continual allegory – and very few eyes can see the Mystery of his life – a life like the scriptures, figurative . . . Lord Byron cuts a figure – but he is not figurative – Shakespeare led a life of Allegory: his works are the comments on it.
>
> JOHN KEATS: *Letters*

Compared with Keats himself, Shakespeare was lucky. Since we know so little of his life, we are forced to stick to his work. And that, mercifully, is enough to make all the diaries and laundry bills in the world irrelevant. Not so with Keats; his biography is insistent, inescapable. After all, he himself contributed so much towards it in his voluminous letters. And what he left out was filled in by the memoirs of his friends, their bickering and gossip, which raise a dust which begins almost to choke the poems.

For his life was, in pure form, an allegory of the Romantic poet. Cover his face: mine eyes dazzle: he died young. Had consumption not got him, the reviewers been kinder, and he and Fanny settled improbably into domesticity, the lure of his work would, I think, be much less – even if he had fulfilled his own most stringent ambitions. As it is, his life, or rather his death, somehow completes his poetry. For in terms of mere bulk, there is not all that much there.

> His *Endymion* [wrote Matthew Arnold], as he himself well saw, is a failure, and his *Hyperion*, fine things as it contains, is not a success. But in shorter things, where the matured power of moral interpretation, and the high architectonics which go with complete poetic development, are not required, he is perfect.

However much we would qualify Matthew Arnold's judgement, it

* Walter Jackson Bate, *John Keats* (Cambridge, Mass.: Harvard University Press, 1963); Aileen Ward, *John Keats* (New York: Viking Press, 1963).

remains more or less true. Yet that in itself makes Keats very much to the modern taste. Nobody writes long poems any more, and scarcely anyone reads them, unless forced. Indeed, in nearly every way Keats is the most modern of the Romantics: as Eliot once urged, he assimilated the lesson of Shakespeare's use of language in a wholly original way; he commands a thickness of metaphor and even occasional tricks of synaesthesia which pre-date the Symbolists; he has a steady ambivalence to death and the senses which goes well beyond the pleasure principle. Above all, he is one of us socially: not quite a gentleman, not quite properly educated, and continually willing to risk his social poise for his convictions: 'I always', he wrote, 'made an awkward bow.' Add to all that his sharp critical insights into his fellow Romantics, his belief in the impersonality of great art, his unromantic vigour and toughness with himself, and he seems a long way from the oversensitive darling of the senses, 'snuffed out by an article' and then immortalized in Victorian myth and Severn's posthumous sketches. 'There is', said his friend Woodhouse, 'a great deal of reality about all that Keats writes.'

The factual reality and the myth of Keats's life are investigated again by his two new biographers, Walter Jackson Bate and Aileen Ward. Professor Bate's massive record will, I imagine, be final until the scholars dig up substantially new material – if any remains to be dug. He meticulously goes through every provable detail of Keats's life: his day-to-day activities, journeys, meetings, dinner parties; the people he knew, the books he read; his dealings with his publishers, and with the literary tradition; the development of his metres, his ideas and his finances (Abbey, his guardian, turns out to be the villain of the book, embezzling the legacies of the Keats children). Every source is judged for its reliability, every rumour weighed, and few not found wanting. The result is not only a monumental scrupulousness, at times more monumental than readable, but also a fine scholarly detachment. For all the amassed detail, Professor Bate never pries; he has no theory to pin on his subject; as best as he can, he lets the man speak for himself.

Professor Ward is not quite like that. Like Bate, she gives a fairly detailed chronology (since they differ in places we will have to wait until the trade papers pronounce judgement). But she is far less insistent on facts. She uses even the chancier rumours, such as W. M. Rossetti's theory of his syphilis, and weaves from hints elaborate, and sometimes novelettish, arabesques:

As for Fanny, the nightmare of the summer was over. She was now simply and truly herself to him again, his young love, his beauty, his own, no longer a figure of bale.

The gush sorts oddly with the careful research which Professor Ward has obviously put into the book. Still, exactitude is not primarily her business. Her real interest is in the psychology of genius. With Keats, this means his relationship to his lively, seductive mother who, like Hamlet's, remarried too soon after his father's death, abandoned her children and returned only to die; the question then is how this conflict worked itself out in the psycho-symbolic patterns of his verse and in his behaviour. Professor Ward follows this line more or less convincingly, though without going very deep. Oddly enough, she is more incisive about Keats's first poem, the vapid 'Imitation of Spenser', than about those later gifts to the amateur psychoanalyst, like 'La Belle Dame Sans Merci' and the 'Ode to Melancholy'.

Yet despite their differences, both biographers are concerned with what is, fundamentally, the sheer improbability of Keats's poetic career. He was not, like Rimbaud, a prodigy from the start. He was almost nineteen before he wrote his first poem, and for some time after that his development was slow, his talent uncertain. He was, as Professor Bate insists, 'surprisingly, refreshingly remote from precocity'. Yet the whole progress, from the stiff, slow beginning, through the literary intoxication and Leigh Hunt-inspired affectations of the first volume, the strain of *Endymion* (in which he was, said Byron, 'viciously soliciting his own imagination'), to the more assured romances, and then to the final burst of great poetry, all this occupies a span of only three years. Keats is the supreme example of creative vitality and concentration. 'The Creature has a purpose and his eyes are bright with it.'

Each step in his development is logical; what is illogical is the speed with which the steps succeed each other. Under the pressure of his particular kind of talent, time seemed to collapse like a concertina. Yet the pressure was exerted not so much by some mysterious, specialized Genius as by a certain factual energy in his life. His letters foreshadow his poetry and define his creative strengths: his impatience with his poetic inadequacies and his critical gift for smelling them out; his courage in chancing his arm ('I was never afraid of failure'); his curiously impersonal literary ambition (he didn't want to get on in the literary world, he wanted to get on with literature). But beyond all that is the phenomenal *use* he put every experience to. The letters bear constant witness to the immediate and developing sureness of his responses to the society he moved in, to his reading, to ideas, to the flow of his own inner life. 'The Creature has a purpose and his eyes are bright with it.'

Yet this energy is only a necessary preliminary to the great work. His mature verse may depend upon this fullness of life, but it doesn't really start until the vitality was brought up short by the fact of death, and had the strength to acknowledge it. The cycle of his poetic apprenticeship begins and ends with a death: that of his mother turned him to literature – his almost obsessional reading at school dates from then; that of his brother made him a major poet – he began *Hyperion* while Tom was dying, and in the twelve months which followed produced all his most important poems. Why Tom's death should have triggered off such an incredible burst of creativity is, of course, impossible to say. No doubt the shock, the sense of loss and the memories which were stirred up of his mother's and father's deaths are all part of the process. But what seems to have mattered most was the contrast to his own vital energy; that is, the impersonality of death, the need to acknowledge that this thing happens despite all the care and love and passionate denial in the world. Critically, Keats had come to understand this when he first outlined his theory of negative capability. For that involves something more than a literary insight into the impersonality of great art. It also implies an essential step in psychological maturity: the acknowledgement of the independence of life outside oneself, of the fact that Iago and Cordelia exist in their own right, despite oneself. The stage beyond that is the more difficult acknowledgement of the fact that they can equally cease to exist, despite oneself.

William Empson once remarked that the line 'No, no; go not to Lethe; neither twist' 'tells you that somebody, or some force in the poet's mind, must have wanted to go to Lethe very much, if it took four negatives in the first line to stop them'. Yet that passive, feminine swoon into 'easeful death' is only one element in Keats's more complex effort to assimilate death into creative power, to make it, that is, part of his most intensely felt life. But that is precisely what he seems to have been doing when he rewrote *Hyperion*. The epic proper can only begin after the poet has undergone a kind of death:

Slow, heavy, deadly was my pace: the cold
Grew stifling, suffocating at the heart;
And when I clasp'd my hands I felt them not.
One minute before death my iced foot touch'd
The lowest stair; and, as it touch'd, life seem'd
To pour in at the toes . . .
. . . 'Holy Power,'
Cried I, approaching near the horned shrine,
'What am I that should so be saved from death?' . . .
Then said the veiled shadow: 'Thou hast felt
What 'tis to die and live again before
Thy fated hour. That thou hadst power to do so
Is thy own safety; thou hast dated on
Thy doom.' 'High Prophetess,' said I, 'purge off,
Benign, if so it please thee, my mind's film.'
'None can usurp this height,' return'd that shade,
'But those to whom the miseries of the world
Are misery, and will not let them rest.
All else who find a haven in the world,
Where they may thoughtless sleep away their days,
If by a chance into this fane they come,
Rot on the pavement where thou rotted'st half.'

What is in question here is neither suffering nor being miserable; it is, rather, the ability to understand what death means, to die, as it were, creatively, to transform the negative into a capability.

One of the nastier paradoxes of art is that, despite all the effort involved, it is not essentially therapeutic. Instead of summing up and so disposing of past experience, it more often seems to provide a rough sketch for what is to come. The poet in writing brings to the surface the conflicts which are nagging him and then finds himself acting them out. So though Keats's letters may have foreshadowed his poetry, his poetry, in turn, foreshadowed his life. Having got to the rare stage of being able to use his understanding of death for creative ends, he then found himself dying. Revisiting the house in Well Walk, where he had lived with his brothers, Keats told Hunt that he was 'dying of a broken heart'. I think he was lamenting more than the deprivation and ruin of his own life – his whole family either dead or inaccessible, and marriage with Fanny Brawne no longer possible – he was also lamenting his own death as a poet.

For he wrote nothing more. There followed only what he called his 'posthumous life' in Rome, and his own horrified attendance at his second death. Yet 'that which is creative must create itself'. Keats understood his death all too clearly, and he understood the terrible wastage it involved. What he could not have foreseen is that from these last pointless months the whole legend of Romantic genius should have been born – cold comfort, perhaps, but in the end sustaining.

The New York Review of Books, 1963

Arthur Hugh Clough*

When Arthur Hugh Clough died just over a hundred years ago the loftiest of the eminent Victorians combined to lament what might, or should, have been. Frederick Temple, headmaster of Rugby and later Archbishop of Canterbury, called him 'the ablest and greatest man I have ever come across'; Jowett granted that he 'certainly had great genius'; Carlyle, according to Froude, thought more highly of him than 'of anyone of our generation'; Matthew Arnold's *Thyrsis* was written in his memory. Everyone paid tribute and all were unanimous and eloquent on the theme that he had the makings of the most eminent Victorian of them all.

Their difficulty was to prove it to a sceptical public. Clough's immense promise had, by Victorian lights, drifted away into nothing. The hero of Dr Arnold's new Rugby, great footballer and effortless Balliol scholar, only got a second in Greats. He resigned from his Oriel Fellowship because of scruples about the XXXIX Articles, then from the principalship of University Hall, London, because of other religious hesitations. He drifted over to America, shiningly did the social rounds in Boston, and achieved nothing. He drifted back to England and lapsed heavily, though still uncertainly, into marriage with the conventional daughter of interfering parents. He finished as an Examiner in the Education Office, running errands in his spare time for Florence Nightingale. He died at the age of forty-two in 1861.

He published almost nothing and gained no reputation. *The Bothie*

* Katharine Chorley, *Arthur Hugh Clough* (London: Oxford University Press, 1962).

of Tober-na-Vuolich, 'a long-vacation pastoral', appeared in 1848 but was too much an Oxford in-group affair to have any success. The following year came *Ambarvalia*, over half of which was by the deservedly forgotten Thomas Burbridge. The book died unlamented and almost unreviewed. His masterpiece, *Amours de Voyage*, was published nine years after it was written, and then only in the States, serialized in the *Atlantic Monthly*. His friends disapproved of it. A few short poems appeared in magazines, but the rest – and he wrote more verse than Matthew Arnold – survived only in notebooks.

When his poems were collected together a year after his death, with a memoir by Palgrave, there was still a certain reluctance to see what all the fuss was about. The *Cornhill* suspected some kind of Establishment plot:

> The source of interest we feel in this volume [is] . . . in the intense conviction produced in friends, of some supreme excellence which Clough *might* have achieved, ought to have achieved, but somehow *did not*. In a word he was one of the prospectuses who never become works.

In the end, Clough did win a muted popularity: the more or less complete 1869 edition of his poems was reprinted fourteen times before the turn of the century; Walter Bagehot wrote splendidly on him; ten years ago he was immortalized by a definitive Oxford edition. But he has never quite taken on. The only poems of Clough's which everyone knows are 'Say not the struggle' and 'How pleasant it is to have money'. Michael Roberts may have praised *Amours de Voyage* to the skies, comparing it to Pound, Eliot and Laforgue; but even that didn't do the trick. And now Katharine Chorley, in her patient, thorough biography, has set out to vindicate him. But she does so apologetically, as though she too felt that Clough had somehow missed all the boats.

Perhaps the most brilliant man of his generation did fail as a public figure. But what would success have meant? Certainly, given Clough's fastidious, sceptical temperament, *not* a career in Parliament. What remained? The headship of an Oxford college, a Scottish University, or a public school? Had he wanted that, he would, like most of his contemporaries, have fought with his theological conscience and won. A bishopric? He hadn't the calling. Some sheikdom in the civil service? He was bored by the job he finally took there. At least, I suppose, success might have helped him to commit himself more strongly to his writing; he might have worked over his poems more and produced the usual volumes of essays, mainly theological, complete with the usual fighting footnotes.

Lady Chorley would no doubt reply that he might also, with success, have been less hesitant and unresolved in himself, less of a failure in his own eyes. His attitude of eternally hesitating withdrawal saddens her and so she produces good reasons why he had to think so poorly of himself: as an English child in the States, he was sedulously isolated from the local roughnecks and sucked dry by his attractive, lonely mother. Then, at the age of nine, he had been cut off from the demanding but safe and cosseting family circle and gone to school in England, shuttling from relative to chilly relative in the holidays. At Rugby, as Arnold's star pupil, he had had to stagger under an intolerable weight of moral virtue. At Oxford, at the height of the Tractarian–Liberal warfare, his Rugby-instilled pieties had been demolished by W. G. Ward, whose motives may have been more questionably emotional than high-minded. As a result, Clough carefully held back from all entanglements, theological as well as personal, and the long slide down to becoming Third Examiner in the Education Office began. Apart from his humdrum marriage, and a burst of Carlylean social invective whilst at Oriel, the only commitment he seems to have allowed himself was his weary dogsbodying for Florence Nightingale, the Dr Arnold of his last years. '*Il doutait de tout*', reads the motto of *Amours de Voyage*, '*même de l'amour*.'

Lady Chorley blames this instinctive reluctance to act on Clough's suppressed Oedipal fantasies and the consequent fear of primitive punishment – all of which she proves quite convincingly by some mild Jungian analysis of his poetic imagery. As the working principle of his life, she says, this means that 'there was a good deal of *anima* in his make-up, the feminine longing to be possessed by, in contrast to the *animus*, the aggressive masculine drive to possess'. In so many words, Clough's friends seem to have agreed with her: 'Pray, why not sign the XXXIX Articles,' J. P. Gell wrote to him. 'You must sign something unless you mean to have nothing to do with anybody.' And Clough himself was touchingly aware of his inadequacies: 'Yes, my dearest child,' he wrote to his dull little fiancée, 'you shall, please Heaven, bring me back into the real warm life.'

But whether or not Clough suffered the usual psychic wounds as a child is beside the critical point. After all, which interesting man didn't? The real question is always whether the wounds utterly debilitate or produce a compensating strength. And for Clough, the second. His public career may have been stifled by his inability to act, but in *Amours de Voyage* he raised this hesitancy to the level of genius. It is by the standard of such poetry that one can see precisely what was wrong with the conventional Victorian love lyric – of which, of course, Clough wrote his fair share. As Graham Greene says in *The Quiet American*: 'He was an adult poet in the nineteenth century. There weren't so many of them.' If one dislikes the Victorians still, it is not so much for their smugness, that complacent prosperity squatting on social mean-mindedness, nor because their uneasiness ran so to undefined sadness, as though the whole of their inner landscape, when the buoyant mood wasn't upon them, were some grey Doré illustration of ruined chivalry and broken hearts. One dislikes them because their moral righteousness produced such throttling simplifications. Clough's failure as a Victorian figure and his strength as a poet lay in his inability, in the face of his own complexities, to accept the stock answers. As Bagehot said:

> He had by nature an exceedingly *real* mind. . . . The actual visible world as it was and as he saw it exercised over him a compulsory influence. . . .

Clough's genius was to see that, whatever pressure to conform his age and friends exerted on him, his unique brand of touchy, choosy sophistication couldn't be expressed in the language of mid-nineteenth-century romanticism. Like Henry James's intimations of morality, his own needle-fine responses required a subtly polished language of manners. Through that casual formality alone he could catch what he called, in one of his best similes,

> *. . . in a stream when the wave of the tide is*
> *Coming and not yet come – a sort of poise and retention.*

This critical poise and retention of sensibility is given perfect form only in *Amours*. The *Bothie* has its moments, but they are overborne by that Landseer-like doggedness which overtook the Victorians whenever they went north of the border. As for *Dipsychus*, by which Lady Chorley sets great store: it strikes me, in both verse and argument, as crude – for all the insights it may provide into Clough's troubles. Just as the jingling couplets make it sound, at times, like nothing so much as 'Savonarola Brown', so the staring contrast between earnest young Dipsychus – one of Dr Arnold's little prefects on the loose – and his cynically tempting Spirit is obvious to the point of self-parody. Despite flashes of urbane insight, *Dipsychus* is on the way to the platitudinous seas of *Mari Magno*, while *Dipsychus Continued* is already drowned in them.

Clough's claim to fame rests squarely and solely on *Amours de Voyage*. But in that, I think, he wrote better than any Victorian poet apart from Hopkins:

There are two different kinds, I believe, of human attraction:
One which simply disturbs, unsettles, and makes you uneasy,
And another that poises, retains, and fixes and holds you.
I have no doubt, for myself, in giving my voice to the latter.
I do not wish to be moved, but growing where I was growing,
There more truly to grow, to live where as yet I had languished.
I do not like being moved: for the will is excited; and action
Is a most dangerous thing; I tremble for something factitious,
Some malpractice of heart and illegitimate process;
We are so prone to these things with our terrible notions of duty.

This kind of insight into that most terrible of the Victorian notions of duty – married love – seems to me not only as fine as anything in Hopkins but, in a sense, more difficult to come by. In one way, Hopkins's isolation in the Society of Jesus was an advantage: the pieties demanded of him were spiritual not social. Clough, on the other hand, when he wrote like this from his position in the centre of the intellectual establishment, was swimming against the whole flood-tide of mid-nineteenth-century convention. And yet he still managed to maintain that 'sort of poise and retention' of individual judgement.

No doubt something approaching this detached, knowing, but utterly unflinching analysis sustained the best efforts of his colleagues. But it is missing from their poetry. Only Clough, who published almost nothing and would have no truck with literary talk or with what he called 'common, wine-bibbing, punning, hand-to-mouth-living' scribblers, managed in *Amours de Voyage* to convert this sophisticated strength into poetry. It makes all the defences, inadequacies and suffering on which Lady Chorley's book centres more than worthwhile.

The New Statesman, 1962

4

CONTINENTALS

Albert Camus*

If the English have little taste for ideas disguised as literature – and not much for ideas at all – the French have even less for creative work without theories to support it. There is almost no public role for the literary intellectual in England unless he is also a novelist, poet or playwright, whereas in France a man's imaginative writing often seems to be not much more than a handy way of drawing attention to his ideas. The hero of *The Fall* remarks, a little sourly: 'It always seemed to me that our fellow-citizens had two passions: ideas and fornication'; and in Paris even fornication has something a little abstract about it, as though it were a brand of physical chess.

Camus seems to fit effortlessly into the French system. His first novel, *The Outsider*, was bolstered by *The Myth of Sisyphus*, his formal defence of the Absurd. *The Plague* was followed by a new definition of his position in *The Rebel*; although they were published four years apart, the second volume of his *Notebooks* shows that they grew together in counterpoise. The third novel, *The Fall*, moves on from *The Rebel* and leads, according to the *Notebooks*, to yet another vast summa, *Création corrigée ou Le Système*, which was to have been a 'big novel + big meditation + unactable play'. Or rather, it would have led there had not the Absurd caught up with Camus again in January 1960, when the car he was being driven in wrapped itself round a tree.

Despite this, the coherence of his work is not really logical. It is

* Albert Camus, *Carnets. Janvier 1942–Mars 1951* (Paris: Gallimard, 1965).

the individual coherence of something organic in which interconnecting veins of life run between every part. The cult of the Absurd gave way to his later rejection of nihilism, not by any clear intellectual choice, but by a process of natural growth. He did not adopt a new theory, he gave instead reasons for his maturity; he argued it out in a way which was at once historically profound and very personal. Throughout his career he remained an artist who was also an intellectual, rather than an intellectual, like Sartre, who used the arts for polemical and theoretical ends. Although he did his university work in philosophy – his thesis was on Plotinus – he was never a professional, or even a particularly natural philosopher; he was a moralist who managed to make a persuasive system out of his novelist's preoccupation with conduct. *The Rebel* may be a remarkably probing and sustained intellectual performance for a man of letters, but it is also, for such a difficult, abstruse work, curiously beautiful. The man of letters triumphed over the philosopher, not only in the lucid rhetoric of the close, but in the texture itself of the book. What gives it that sombre, unexpected beauty is something beyond mere style as artifice; it is the quality that forms and controls style: an unwavering sense of justice, a tense humility.

Late in 1950, when his success was complete, his reputation enormous, Camus wrote in the *Notebooks*: '*Oui, j'ai une patrie: la langue française*.' This was no exaggeration; the French language seems the only place where he ever felt himself easily at home. In Metropolitan France he was an outsider from colonial Algeria, his working-class background detached him from Parisian chic, he belonged to no church, was a member of the Communist Party for not much more than a year, his first marriage lasted even less than that time. To all that was added a further double load of alienation: he was tubercular and, in effect, an orphan – his father died on the Marne within a year of his birth and his mother farmed him out to a forbidding, harsh grandmother.

There was, in short, a shell around him, a continual loneliness which neither fame nor a second marriage could shift. The detached purity and sustained impersonality of his style was part of that shell. (It was startlingly consistent: the new *Notebooks*, for example, cover his time in the Resistance without ever mentioning it, even obliquely; in 1946 he ironically excused the intrusion of personal matters into working notes by saying that his memory is going.) Yet it was through his style itself that he created and tested his life and values. It is a question, above all, of the use to which he put his uncanny gift for sensuous impressions. All the indifference and remoteness and displaced anxiety, the discouragement, bitterness, absurdity and nihilism return finally to an assured core of sensuous calm. It is not sensual, since the women in his work are felt more powerfully as absences than as presences. It has, instead, something to do with Mediterranean North Africa: with the heat, the salt and the swimming, with the cool winds and settling noises of evening, with the way the light intensifies and fades in a sky so clear, so luminous that there might never have been a cloud.

For most European writers, all this would be the setting for one of those Durrell-like Never-Never lands where all the girls are beautiful, eager and inventive, and hangovers never happen. Camus, who was born there, was always aware of the dirt and poverty and discomfort of North Africa, the unspeakable suburbs, the dust and cold of the uplands. But underneath that he knew what else it could give: an assured ease and sense of well-being, which is the one unchanging moral positive in his work.

'The secret of Europe', he wrote in *The Rebel*, 'is that it no longer loves life.' Camus was certain of himself at least on that score. But of not much else. The rest of his work was an attempt to show what remains when you love only life, how you must conduct yourself without the support of any of the other comforting abstractions: God, politics, nihilism, family, history, even love. He was involved with morals without organized morality, with the politics of loneliness.

In his famous quarrel with Sartre, Camus seems to have been made the scapegoat for the whole of the bourgeois left wing's resentment of utopian liberal humanism. This was less than just. One of his greatest strengths as a thinker was that he demonstrated from the inside just how hopeless the liberal humanist position has become. It is not simply that modern industrial states are too vast and highly organized for the creed to be effective, or even meaningful. It is rather that they are organized in such a way that they exert on all beliefs an intolerable pressure which forces them into totalitarianism. Both the nineteenth century's nihilism and its revolutionary utopianism produced their separate brands of totalitarianism – of the right and of the left, Hitler's and Stalin's. Against them, liberal humanism was too vaguely loving, hopelessly enlightened and full of optimistic intentions to be a viable alternative.

What Camus set in its place was not a philosophy but a personal stance that assumed nothing, expected nothing and was critical of everything. His early concept of the Absurd was, I suppose, a secularized sense of tragedy, an analysis of the way a meaningless death gratuitously calls in question a life without meaning, or a life amounting, at best, to no more than that death. 'Nothing, nothing had the least importance, and I know quite well why. . . . From the dark horizon of my future', says Meursault the Outsider, 'a sort of slow, persistent breeze had been blowing towards me, all my life long, from the years that were to come.'

Camus's experience in the Resistance changed his attitude but not his assumptions. Accepted nihilism becomes nihilism criticized, absolved by the possibilities of action. *The Rebel* is a critique of romantic absolutism in all its forms and also of whatever seems malicious, willed and slightly paranoid in the cult of the Absurd. All that remains is the individual freedom to say no, and some kind of self-knowing courage which can be expressed in action and the senses. There is also a mild nostalgia for what he calls 'the delicate equilibrium between humanity and nature, man's consent to the world, which gives ancient thought its distinction and its refulgence'. If this is humanism, it is humanism in total isolation, assuming no community with anyone else.

Freedom, moreover, was not natural or instinctive; it was something to be acquired the hard way and learned, as it were, end on. 'There is only one liberty,' he wrote in the *Notebooks*, 'to come to terms with death. After which, everything is possible.' This idea that you should work from the end of your life back to the present, that you must consent to your death before you can properly, knowingly, live now, is perhaps inevitable in a man who, like Camus, had been tubercular. But it is also typical of his work. His heroes are men with no childhood; they have only, at best, an adult past they can reach back to, a handful of sharp yet casual sense impressions. This means that each begins with a life that is more or less in control, more or less formed, understood and accounted for. It makes them impervious to romanticism.

Yet by cutting the roots to his childhood, a writer not only cuts off much confusion and mess and darkness, he also runs the risk of cutting himself off from the sources of real feeling. Camus avoided this by giving himself with extraordinary generosity to the present. He did so without drama or self-pity, without preconceptions, regrets or illusions, with great intelligence and modesty, and by creating a style which was lucid, unfailingly objective, yet humane, tentative and lonely. He was courageous without making claims; he had, above all, no conceit. Simply by recognizing the present impossibility of systematized morality he emerged as the one genuine imaginative moralist of our time. In the *Notebooks* for February 1951, he wrote a final footnote on *The Rebel* which seems to apply to all his work: 'I have wanted to speak the truth without ceasing to be generous. That is my justification.'

The Spectator, 1965

Jean-Paul Sartre*

In his time, Sartre has gone into the ring with nearly every literary form, except poetry: novels, plays, stories, philosophy, aesthetics, politics and criticism. With immense industry, spouting ideas like some huge, hard-working Moby Dick of the intellectual life, he has effortlessly dominated the Paris scene since the war. Yet he is a curious phenomenon: a great influence, a great figure in the landscape, yet never quite a great writer. His philosophy, apparently, is not startlingly original and is, certainly, expressed far too obscurely to have had anything but a most sidelong influence. How many of the professed Existentialists have really read *L'Être et le Néant*? And how many of them have really understood it? It strikes me as being written as though deliberately to defy analysis. Even more certainly, he is not a great creative writer, for all the compulsive readability of his novels – like a highbrow Ian Fleming – or the tensely dramatic situations of his plays. All that brilliance gets in the way of the human thing which is, after all, what literature is about. The books are too full of good ideas to be true. Tease them out as problems and they seem all very profound and subtle; but they *feel* shallow.

Yet this combination of talents – both exceptional, neither quite overwhelming – blends into something wholly pervasive. Sartre is influential because he is a philosopher who gave his ideas flesh and set them intriguingly in action. He is also a novelist and playwright whose work gains dignity by echoing an elaborately structured

* Jean-Paul Sartre, *Baudelaire* (London: Hamish Hamilton, 1964); *Words* (London: Hamish Hamilton, 1964).

world of ideas. As such, he belongs to a special sub-division of literature, the School of Brilliance: its alumni include Voltaire and George Bernard Shaw, Anatole France and Aldous Huxley. It is a school that relies, to use old-fashioned terms, more on invention than imagination. That is, the writers' fecundity with plots, situations, aphorisms and striking, unexpected ornaments is endless, but their people are two-dimensional props for ideas, voices in a crackling but bleak world of abstractions. The opposite of the inventors is someone like Shakespeare, who was more or less incapable of thinking up his own plots, but who could imaginatively fill out any given situation with a self-generating depth and insight.

Occasionally Sartre has faced the problem of turning his rather baffled and baffling brilliance on to the realm of insights. He has had only mixed success. His now reissued study of Baudelaire, for instance, is less criticism than a series of free variations on the existential themes implicit in the poet's life: on what he chose to make of his talent, his past, his personal relationships, his laziness, his ennui and, almost by the way, his poetry. It is a blinding *tour de force*, yet in some curious manner, it makes you feel that Baudelaire never properly *existed* for Sartre, Existentialism or no Existentialism. He is merely an excuse for the ontological flourishes, like a saint's bones in a Baroque church.

Baudelaire was first published in 1947, when Existentialism was very much a fighting creed. So by pillorying an idol of French culture Sartre was showing where he stood in a particularly strong way. Now the creed is less urgent and the situation more complex, Sartre has created fresh drama by turning on himself. In the first volume of his autobiography, *Words*, he does a job on his own childhood, at times in much the same terms as he attacked Baudelaire's. But there is a crucial difference: in *Baudelaire* Sartre was diagnosing something wrong in the French cultural tradition, or cultural attitudes; in *Words*, in a far less detached way, he is getting his own back on his life.

So the brilliance is more attacking, more detailed, and considerably more stimulating. The book is written in a positive fury of wit, aphorisms flashing from every page:

> He was a nineteenth-century man who, like so many others, including Victor Hugo himself, thought he was Victor Hugo.
>
> I lived beyond my age as people live beyond their means: enthusiastically, exhaustedly, expensively, and all for show.

> I was to have the sex of angels, indeterminate but feminine round the edges.

The whole book is like this: crisp, elegant, bracing, arrogant, sadistic. 'I loathe my childhood', he explains, 'and all that remains of it.' I suppose we all do. The question is why Sartre, at the age of fifty, feels he must attack his with such concentrated virulence. His problem, I think, was not that his childhood was unhappy, but that it was not unhappy enough; not that he was insufficiently loved, but that he was insufficiently hated. He felt himself guilty without a cause.

His father died when he was a few months old and his mother went back to live with her parents: 'chilled by gratitude, [she] sensed the blame beneath their decency: families naturally prefer widows to unmarried mothers, but only just.' Still, they all duly adored little, fatherless Jean-Paul and his supremacy, from infancy on, was unchallenged. He shared a bedroom with his mother, each in his own chaste, narrow bed, and she loved him vaguely but hopelessly. His grandfather Charles Schweitzer, uncle of Albert, bearded like God the Father, vain, pompous and contemptuous of all the world, doted on the child. So did his cynical, bed-ridden wife. Abetted by the women, Jean-Paul's every lisping was preserved and repeated to admiring adults. By guile, exaggeratedly good behaviour and a deliberately cultivated hypocrisy, he ran the whole show.

Yet somehow it wasn't enough, somewhere his real loves and hatreds were frustrated and unexpressed. His own explanation is an odd one:

> My father's hasty retreat had conferred on me a very incomplete Oedipus complex; no Super-Ego, I agree, but no aggression, either.

Considering that this is the most aggressive book that I, for one, have ever read, Sartre is presumably pushing back something rather powerful. My guess is that his Oedipus complex was complete, all right, but it seemed motiveless. His omnipotence was unchallenged, but it wasn't taken seriously. The adoration was a bit remote and all his canny outlets for aggression – his cleverness, his charming-outrageous sayings, his precocious literariness, even his long curls – were in some way made to reflect glory on the family. He had all these things, yet he didn't properly exist. He was merely, in his own words, 'a cultural possession'. If he was spoilt, it was only because he was *used*; he became a flattering trick mirror for his grandfather's overwhelming narcissism. He hated it, but felt guilty for his apparent ingratitude – as he no doubt also felt guilty for his father's death and his complete possession of his mother. So he made amends by changing the focus, so that it was he, the child, who was using the adults:

> We would remain a few seconds, face to face, a pretty group in porcelain, then I would dash forward, laden with fruit and flowers and, to my grandfather's joy, rush to his knees, pretending to be out of breath; he would lift me off the ground, raise me at arms' length to the skies, then clutch me to his heart murmuring: 'My darling child!' This was the second position, closely watched by the passers-by.

His contempt is not wholly destructive; rather, it is the driving force behind his cleverness. But if both are the reactions of a grown man to a farce he was made to play out when he knew no better, they are also a new model of his old childhood defences. The young Jean-Paul was obscurely aware that the feelings in scenes like these were all wrong, but he presumably must have given himself over to them; whereas the adult writer is determined to detach himself from his partially duped innocence. So Sartre has invented a technique which I would call 'schizophrenia by brilliance'. The cleverer he is, the better he is protected from hurtful reality; his brains save him from his feelings. Which brings us back to the difference between invention and imagination.

Isolated from other children, bored, spoilt and loved only in as much as he presented a flattering image to his elders, he saved himself from the failure of all drive and passion and feeling by turning author. Ludicrously young, he began to churn out novels, lurid adventure stories in which he was hero, saviour, essential – in short, someone. 'I was born from writing: before that, there was only a reflection in a mirror.' So he scribbled endlessly, airing his omnipotence fantasies in a world in which he really was omnipotent, since he created it. His family, of course, adored him all the more, gloating over his talents. But they also left him alone, they let him work, they allowed him the beginnings of his own independent identity. Only his Jehovah grandfather seemed unimpressed – jealous perhaps, since he, too, had a book to his credit – but he never missed a chance of showing the clever little fellow off.

At ten, when the book ends, there are hints that the tensions began to tell on him; Sartre seems to have had the symptoms of genuine schizophrenia: voices in the head, total identification with other people and objects. But they went, exorcised by that brilliance which, by then, was bluntly, rigidly set on using everyone and everything as he himself had been used. Now, he says, a day never passes without his writing something. With endless industry and perseverance, he has manipulated puppets in plays and novels to his greater glory as he himself was once manipulated to someone else's glory. But instead of discovering his identity, he has created it, deliberately, from the outside, almost in the abstract; and he has created also a theory to justify the process. If his brilliance still seems to demand the lurking presence of an adoring, slightly dumbfounded public, waiting with bated breath for his next outrageous remark, that is only the vaguely magnified and now faceless ghost of his doting but unsatisfactory family, peering over his shoulder – not lost but gone behind.

The Spectator, 1964

Miroslav Holub*

Miroslav Holub is a curious mixture, perhaps a unique one: he is one of Czechoslovakia's most prolific and original poets and also a distinguished scientist, a clinical pathologist who has travelled widely on both sides of the Iron Curtain, researching and attending scientific congresses. So far his publications include eight books of poetry, two travel books and twenty-five learned papers on pathology; he also edits a Czech popular science magazine.

The combination of poetry and science is not altogether unprecedented; Lucretius made experiments of a kind, so did Goethe; and then there was Erasmus Darwin who versified *The Lives of the Plants.* What makes Holub so unusual is his distinction in both fields. When scientists turn to verse the results usually resemble the poems of that eminent Cambridge physicist, the late Professor Andrade: elegant in their old-fashioned way, but over-mellow, coy, soft at the centre, a sentimental Mr Hyde to his formidable Dr Jekyll. The gloomy general rule seems to be that, even with the best will in the world, the split between the two cultures is radical, if only because the scientists won't take the discipline of the arts seriously. So they go to poetry simply as a *relief* from the intellectual stringency and sophistication of their professions.

Nothing could be less true of Holub's work. I do not know – and if I did, could not judge – the intellectual qualities that distinguish him as a scientist. But I imagine they have much in common with the subtlety and precision of his poetry, and with the openness to

* Introduction to *Miroslav Holub: Selected Poems* (Harmondsworth: Penguin, 1967).

experience which so continually informs and controls it. If Holub remains a scientist in his verse, it is not because he is dry or schematic, dogmatic or aggressively intellectual; it is, instead, because he is always experimental. According to Karl Popper, the basis of every scientific law is the principle of falsifiability: a law, that is, is valid only if it can be, but has not been, disproved. Holub seems to write his poems as though with that in mind; his attitude, as he moves between the two cultures, is tentative, empirical, alert:

We gave a helping hand to grass –
and it turned into corn.
We gave a helping hand to fire –
and it turned into a rocket.
Hesitatingly,
cautiously,
we give a helping hand
to people,
to some people. . . . [*A Helping Hand*]

Born in 1923, the son of a railway worker and a language teacher, Holub did not begin to write poems until he started his clinical research at the age of about thirty. So experimental science and experimental verse have flowered together throughout his career. When I met him last in Prague, I asked him if he had any poetic theories I should know about. He came back the next day with a couple of pages of typescript with a characteristic heading: 'Some very individual points/valid on 8 June 1965, 17.00 hrs.' The fourth of these eleven points was this:

> There is no deep difference between the scientific mind and the artistic mind: both include the maximal creativity with the maximal freedom. Science is both theoretic and experimental. Art is only experimental.

The heart of the matter is the word 'experimental': he was, I believe, referring more to the content than to shape and technique of verse; or rather, since these elements cannot be separated, the stress is on what the poem is saying rather than how it says it. Granted, the form of Holub's work is strenuously anti-traditional; he invariably uses the freest of free verse, and has employed in his time some elaborate tricks to break down the purely literary limitations of poetry (I will come back to these). But that, in a way, is only a part of a traditional battle perennially fought in Czech verse between the lyrical romantics and the analytic poets. So as the foremost 'analyst' Holub belongs to a tradition of anti-traditional writers. The real experimentation in his verse is not a question of new literary devices, but of the use of *anti-literary* devices to evolve a form that is flexible enough to take any kind of experience or pressure as it comes. And for Holub, 'experience' includes, or is defined by, the scientist's energy, cunning and sharpness.

Seen in one light, the whole of the modern movement, from the turn of the century up to the present, has been concerned with the problem of extending the possible range of the arts, with breaking down conventional responses and expectations, and working out forms to express whatever the present urgencies are felt to be. But in general, the movement the arts have taken has been inward: poets and painters have become more and more concerned with exploring the extreme edge of the viable, with harnessing in their work the insights and energy released by breakdown, neurosis, paranoia, despair and drugs. In its way, Holub's poetry is no less exploratory than that of the Extremist poets of the West, but it takes the opposite direction. His business is with the way in which private responses, private anxieties, connect up with the public world of science, technology and machines, with the way, as he said in an interview on Prague Radio, we put out 'tips into this world of scooters, skyscrapers and streptomycin'.

Perhaps this is inevitable, since he is a Marxist. But his Marxism is in no sense dogmatic or party biased. His overtly political poems are sharply against the Establishment, with its attendant bureaucrats and manoeuverers. His politics, no less than the rest of his work, are continually exposed to that tension between theory and experienced reality which he calls 'experiment'. The whole point of his longest and most ambitious poem, 'The Root of the Matter', is to set life as it is lived in the feelings and senses against the slogans and clichés through which you must continually thread your way:

Some mistakes are now mistakes
others are still virtues

That could stand as the ironic motto for the whole of post-Stalinist Czechoslovakia.

Perhaps the key to what he is after as a political scientist-poet is to be found in poems like 'Pathology', or 'In the Microscope':

Here too are dreaming landscapes,
lunar, derelict.
Here too are the masses
tillers of the soil.
And cells, fighters
who lay down their lives
for a song.

Here too are cemeteries,
fame and snow.
And I hear murmuring,
the revolt of immense estates.

It is a kind of embattled Communist Party vision of the world reduced to microscopic dimensions; and thereby judged ironically; and thereby also dignified. For this scaling down of politics by means of science is not done for the sake of satire but for the sake of proportion. The final standard is a sense of common humanity, and in the final analysis science is just one among many of the human gifts, like the gift of curiosity or inventiveness or creativity or patience or love:

We have
a map of the universe
for microbes,
we have a map of a microbe
for the universe.

We have
a Grand Master of chess
made of electronic circuits.

But above all
we have
the ability to sort peas,
to cup water in our hands,
to seek
the right screw
under the sofa
for hours

This
gives us
wings. [*Wings*]

In the light of this kind of writing it is as meaningless to call Holub a humanist as it is to call him a Marxist; both imply some programme and dogma, even if, for the humanist, they are only the vague programmes and vaguer dogmas of optimistic liberalism. Holub's poems are rooted in something harder and more empirical than that: in a resistant, decent, unbelieving sense of the realities of people and their troubles. If he seems optimistic, it is only with the practical, untheoretical optimism of the scientist who is kept going through all the dragging boredom of an experiment by the hope somewhere of a genuinely new result:

Here in the Lord's bosom rest
the tongues of beggars,
the lungs of generals,
the eyes of informers,
the skins of martyrs,

in the absolute
of the microscope's lenses.

I leaf through Old Testament slices of liver,
in the white monuments of brain I read
the hieroglyphs
of decay.

Behold, Christians,
Heaven, Hell, and Paradise
in bottles.
And no wailing,
not even a sigh.
Only the dust moans.
Dumb is history
strained
through capillaries.

Equality dumb. Fraternity dumb.

And out of the tricolours of mortal suffering
we day after day
pull
threads of wisdom. [*Pathology*]

This is where the experimental poet joins with the experimental scientist: common to both is a sense of discovery. But where the pathologist makes his discoveries in his specialized field, the poet makes them about feelings, about situations, about a shared, troubled humanity. At the core of both is a wary, critical, open attitude to experience. Thus science and poetry become two ways of looking at the same reality, differing only in technique:

> There are [runs the third of Holub's 'very individual points'] no different realities. What can be created by art is not a new reality, but a deeper approach to the intrinsic and extrinsic facts of human life. These facts are the kingdom of the arts and philosophy only to that moment when they become accessible to scientific methods.

All Holub's technique is concentrated on the exposure and analysis of reality. He speaks fluent English, reads widely in it and claims to have derived his free verse forms from William Carlos Williams. But the results are very different. Williams used his simple, stripped-down forms for two purposes: first, to achieve an American accent and rhythm, which had nothing to do with the traditional British iambic pentameter; second, in order to make the rather simple perceptions and objects of his poems come out clear and strong. Complexity was not his *forte*, and when he attempted it the result, as often as not, was muddle. Holub, in comparison, is intellectual, sophisticated. Consider, for example, 'Love':

Two thousand cigarettes.
A hundred miles
from wall to wall.
An eternity and a half of vigils
blanker than snow.

Tons of words
old as the tracks
of a platypus in the sand.

A hundred books we didn't write.
A hundred pyramids we didn't build.

Sweepings.
Dust.

Bitter
as a beginning of the world.

Believe me when I say
it was beautiful.

The technique is that of the early abstract painters: he reduces the confused uneasy situation to its bare elements, and then reassembles it so that the complexity is somehow clarified, validated by an ironic compassion. He uses free forms so that they won't get in the way of what he has to say. They allow him complexity without padding. And this is as it should be for an intellectual who has no taste for abstractions. In his poetry, as presumably in his science, he continually insists on probing below the surface of received, everyday experience to reveal new levels of meaning, to lay bare new emotional facts. It is as though his poems and his researcher's microscope worked in the same way, and towards the same end.

It is in this realm of at once confirming and extending reality that he has made some of his most fruitful experiments. He is much concerned with widening the potential audience of poetry. As he said in a Prague Radio interview:

> Most of all I like writing for people untouched by poetry; for instance, for those who do not even know that it should at all be for them. I would like them to read poems as naturally as they read the papers, or go to a football game. Not to consider it as anything more difficult, or effeminate, or praiseworthy.

If this is in part the good Marxist speaking, the results have nothing at all to do with the inert, pedantic code of 'socialist realism'. Holub has experimented with what he calls 'synthetic art. Poetry plus music plus pictures plus I know not what.' This is in line with the work of another brilliant Czech artist, the stage designer Josef Svoboda, who in his *Magic Lantern* and in many of his productions at the National Theatre has triumphantly and cunningly fused live theatre with the cinema. Holub's attempts at synthesis have been made in collaboration with a young photographer, Jan Pařík, whose chief subject is life in hospital wards and operating theatres. Holub's poems begin where the photographs leave off; they are meditations which go, in his own words, 'beyond them and behind them'. This, for example, accompanies a photograph of an empty operating theatre:

The small worms of pain still wriggled
in the limpid air,
The trembling died away and
Something in us bowed low before
the fact of the operating-table

the fact of the window
the fact of space
the fact of steel
with seven blades.

The silence was inviolable
like the surface of a mirror.

Though we wanted to ask
Where the blood was flowing
And
Whether you were still dead,
darling. [*Reality*]

The impulse behind these free variations on Pařík's photographs is an attempt to make people think about what they experience from day to day, to make them connect up what they see with what they read and feel.

This refusal to separate modern life into neat, isolated compartments is fundamental to all Holub's work, and to his importance. In the second of his 'points' he remarks:

> Art has to be the product of a complete personality aware of all information and assumptions valid for the citizen of the modern world. Superstitious exclusion of science from arts and humanities does not preserve creativity; it preserves only old approaches and old reactions, which become more and more confused in the modern world.

This, I think, cuts through a good deal of the muddle which plagues discussion of the modern arts, a muddle about traditional values and the contemporary situation. When, for example, the Leavisites assert that there is a total discrepancy between mass society and minority culture, or the American existentialists insist on the equally total 'alienation' of the artist from his technological consumer society, both are on to a partial truth; but for the sake of it they are denying whatever is positive and hopeful in the industrial, electronic world. Both are, in some degree, rejecting what we have in favour of a tense nostalgia for what we have lost. No doubt, what has been lost was very valuable; no doubt, the close-knit, mutually self-supporting, pre-industrial-revolution communities had a strength and assurance that our own lack. But they had also ceased to exist at least by 1918, probably long before. To lament their passing may be right and proper, but utterly to reject what has taken their place is mere conservative utopianism. It is, after all, difficult to feel deprived of what one never knew.

This is not a trap Holub has ever fallen into. On the contrary, the source of his strength is his subtle, critical acceptance of the realities as they are, his refusal either to shut things out or to praise them simply because, like Everest, they are there. His poetry is based finally on an unsentimental, probing, compassionate, witty sense of the modern world. As he says in 'The Root of the Matter':

> *There is poetry in everything. That*
> *is the biggest argument*
> *against poetry.*

1967

Zbigniew Herbert*

In Western Europe we take for granted that there is a fundamental split between poetry and politics. The problem is not that the twain can never meet but that they can do so only at a great cost. The complexity, tension and precision of modern poetry simply doesn't go with the language of politics, with its vague rhetoric and dependence on clichés. This is the argument against Yevtushenko, against much of Mayakovsky, against Auden's 'Spain', or the young Spender's nugatory Marxism. It amounts to the belief that political poetry, *as poetry*, must be relatively but debilitatingly simple-minded. This means that, although it may on occasions be effective, it can't finally be 'good', since our criteria of excellence are defined by qualities more inturned and subtly discriminating than politics leaves room for.

To all this Zbigniew Herbert is an exception. He is an *avant-garde* poet whose experiments and precise, restrained rhythms have sent Polish prosody off in a new direction. Trained in law, he is a man with a passion for classical literature and for history, and with all the intellectual tautness associated with a poet like T. S. Eliot. Yet his verse is unremittingly political. In the circumstances, it could never have been otherwise. Born in Lvov in 1924, he wrote his first poems during the appalling Nazi occupation of Poland and served a peculiarly savage apprenticeship in the underground resistance. When the war ended he went to university at Cracow and Thorn, where he

* Introduction to *Zbigniew Herbert: Selected Poems* (Harmondsworth: Penguin, 1968); also appeared in *The Review*, 1967.

took a degree in Civil Law. During the grim years of Stalinism the magazines he wrote for tended to get themselves banned and he pushed his pen uncreatively in an office. His first book of poems, *A Story of Light*, was not published until the thaw was well under way, in 1955.

Clearly, he is not political in the conventional sense: he does not purvey, in suitably touched-up forms, the predigested truths supplied by any party. He is political by virtue of being permanently and warily in opposition. Yet that, too, is a misleading, over-dramatic way of putting it. His opposition is not dogmatic: during the Nazi occupation he was not, to my knowledge, a Communist, nor during the Stalinist repression was he ever noticeably even Catholic or nationalist. Herbert's opposition is a party of one; he refuses to relinquish his own truth and his own standards in the face of any dogma.

The best Western poets, arguably, do much the same. By implication at least, they too are deeply committed to the politics – or anti-politics – of protest. But where they create worlds which are autonomous, internalized, complete inside their own heads, Herbert's is continually exposed to the impersonal, external pressures of politics and history. This makes for a curious reversal of values. Poets in Western Europe and America react to the cosy, domesticated, senselessly sensible way of life in a mass democracy by asserting the precariousness of things and deliberately exploring the realm of breakdown and madness. For Herbert, on the other hand, madness and disintegration are all on the outside, the products of war and totalitarianism. In a poem called 'Our Fear' old-fashioned horrors of death and the supernatural have been replaced by political terror. In a totalitarian situation only 'the dead are gentle to us', and the only sanity lies in the brief, ironic tenderness of one person for another.

This has been his theme from the start. In one of his first poems, 'Two Drops', written when he was about fifteen, a man and woman make love as the bombs fall. This ultimate existential gesture – as though a kiss could annihilate annihilation – is the clue to all his subsequent work: it is a question of quarrying for himself a little area of light and sense in the engulfing darkness of total war and repression. The pressures he is fighting against are defined at the end of a poem called 'Parable of the Russian *Émigrés*', when all the touching, elegant survivors of the old order have been swept away:

after a couple of years
only three of them were spoken about
the one who went mad
the one who hanged himself
she to whom men used to come

the rest lived out of the way
slowly turning to dust

This parable is told by Nicholas
who understands historical necessities
in order to terrify me, i.e. to convince me

Most of Herbert's poetry is concerned with reasons for being neither terrified nor convinced, and with his strategies for survival.

Most important of these strategies is irony. Yet Herbert's irony has nothing to do with the dandified, touch-me-not distaste – by Eliot out of Laforgue – which was fashionable among the post-Symbolist poets of the twenties and the American academics of the forties. For that irony was, in essence, a slightly less than noble art of self-defence; it protected those who wielded it from emotions they felt they would be better without – feelings for other people, the temptations of commitment. In contrast, Herbert's irony is neither elegant nor embattled:

First there was a god of night and tempest, a black idol without eyes, before whom they leaped, naked and smeared with blood. Later on, in the times of the republic, there were many gods with wives, children, creaking beds, and harmlessly exploding thunderbolts. At the end only superstitious neurotics carried in their pockets little statues of salt, representing the god of irony. There was no greater god at that time.

Then came the barbarians. They too valued highly the little god of irony. They would crush it under their heels and add it to their dishes.

('*From Mythology*')

Irony of this kind is a two-edged weapon, which turns on the poet as readily as on the world outside. It is based on a sense of his own ineffectual fragility when faced with the steam-roller of political force. It is, in short, the irony of a vulnerable man. In his love poems, like 'Silk of a Soul' or 'Tongue', it inhibits nothing; it simply helps him gently to preserve a sense of proportion, the watchful compassion of a man who, like his 'Pebble', has come to terms with his own limits:

The pebble
is a perfect creature

equal to itself
mindful of its limits

filled exactly
with a pebbly meaning

with a scent which does not remind one of anything
does not frighten anything away does not arouse desire

its ardour and coldness
are just and full of dignity

I feel a heavy remorse
when I hold it in my hand
and its noble body
is permeated by false warmth

– Pebbles cannot be tamed
to the end they will look at us
with a calm and very clear eye

Herbert's irony is in the service of an ideal of balance and repose. It is not a safety device which ensures that the outer world will impinge on the poetic only in discreet, carefully regulated doses; it is, instead, a way of focusing the whole mass of his experience so that 'to the end [his poems] will look at us with a calm and very clear eye'.

This sense in his verse of a strong and steady light, which, without denying the shadows, somehow makes them easier to tolerate, is the core of that 'classicism' always invoked to describe his work. There are also other related qualities: for example, his preoccupation with the Greek and Latin classics, cannily modified so that contemporary experience is constantly held in the long, cooling perspective of myth. Then there are his subdued, chaste rhythms and spare language, which leave no room for romantic excesses:

my imagination
is a piece of board
my sole instrument
is a wooden stick

I strike the board
it answers me
yes – yes
no – no

Herbert's poetry is also classical in the tautly intellectual control that edges it continually towards some Platonic point of rest, some poise of art and understanding. In poem after poem he strains cunningly towards the moment of final silence – 'the heart of things/ a dead star/a black drop of infinity' – only, at the last moment, for the postman to knock and nudge him back into the fallen world. For all his fine classical yearning, he never tries to betray or even to escape the unredeemed obduracy of things and people and situations.

This tension between the ideal and the real is the backbone on which all his work depends. It is what allows him to be at once classical and insistently political. For everything he writes is founded on the realization that poetry, by its nature, is idealistic, hopeful or, as William James put it, 'tender-minded', while the situation in which he must function as a poet is savagely 'tough-minded' – pragmatic, political, destructive, controlling. And he has come to this understanding not abstractly but from his own experience: first under the occupation of the Nazis, who massacred one in five of the Polish population; then under the long years of grinding Stalinist repression. So the facts of his whole life since early adolescence strain continuously against his education and philosophical inclinations. His gift is to be able to express this contradiction whole and without falsification.

To some degree, this tension places him firmly in the tradition of Polish literature, which has developed during the last two centuries despite constant domination by one foreign power or another. But where most Polish poets derive some support from their fierce nationalism, Herbert seems to work without any illusions at all. He is a poet of complete isolation. Soon after the thaw he wrote an ironic ode to his desk drawer; the theme was simply that now he was able to publish all the work he had kept locked away for so long, he no longer had anything to write about. According to the code of Herbert's politics of isolated opposition, even publication is a betrayal of standards, a loss of dissident freedom.

Yet his final strength lies in the fact that he refuses the consolations even of being exclusive and apart. In one of his finest poems it is Fortinbras, the soldier and politician, who writes an elegy for Hamlet, the idealist, dreamer, poet and tragic hero. It is, in its way, a kind of love poem, and its poignancy lies in Fortinbras's acceptance of his unromantic limitations. The more necessary his practical ruthlessness seems to be, the more urgently he yearns towards Hamlet's unworldliness, and the more utterly separate the two men become:

Adieu Prince I have tasks a sewer project
and a decree on prostitutes and beggars
I must also elaborate a better system of prisons
since as you justly said Denmark is a prison
I go to my affairs This night is born
a star named Hamlet We shall never meet
What I shall leave will not be worth a tragedy
It is not for us to greet each other or bid farewell
We live on archipelagos
and that water these words what can they do What can they do
Prince

In 'Elegy of Fortinbras' Herbert tenderly and regretfully acknowledges the ascendancy of worldly sanity over poetic idealism. It is the inevitable choice of a poet who, like all his compatriots, has lived through a violent historical nightmare. I have written elsewhere that 'Herbert's steadily detached, ironic and historically-minded style represents, I suppose, a form of classicism. But it is a one-sided classicism, based not on order matching order, a regulated style displaying the regularity of the world, but on a strict and wary attitude to a situation which is at best prone to romanticism and at worst a violation of all sanity. It is a way of coping coolly with facts which could easily slide out of control'.* Classicism of this order is political; in his poetry Herbert is creating a minority politics of sanity and survival.

1967

* *Under Pressure* (Harmondsworth: Penguin, 1965), p. 31.

Hungarians*

The first thing to remember about Hungarian literature is that, like that of most Eastern and Central European countries, it is relatively young. Until the middle of the nineteenth century there was little writing of much significance in Magyar. The official language of the aristocracy, of parliament and of law was Latin – it was sometimes even spoken in the private homes of the upper classes – while the language of the Hapsburg rulers was German. The native tongue was for peasants; it was devalued, non-literary, sub-cultural.

The first major Hungarian writers, using Magyar as a serious literary vehicle, came when they were needed, pat on time for the Kossuth Revolution in 1848. The poets Mihaly Vorosmarty, Sandor Petöfi and Janos Arany, and the novelist Mor Jokai, were all deep in revolutionary politics, and all used Hungarian as a kind of political gesture. It was a token of independence, an attempt to switch not merely interest but the whole focus of attention away from the imposed, foreign ruling élite towards the native, Magyar-speaking peasantry. Hence Petöfi's epic, *John the Hero*, had a double importance: it was one of the first major poems written in the native language and also, equally for the first time in Hungarian literature, a work in which the hero was a peasant, his ideals nationalistic.

If Petöfi, Arany and Jokai had a double importance, they also left a double inheritance. Their work meant that the first great classics of Magyar literature were firmly, passionately Romantic

* Introduction to *Hungarian Short Stories* (London: Oxford University Press, 1967).

in style. It also meant that literature became rooted in radical politics. Petöfi and Arany both fought in the War of Independence; Petöfi died in the battle of Segesvar. Both they and Jokai were involved with literary magazines which were vital for the dissemination of revolutionary political ideas. Their example has become a tradition. Contemporary poets like Sandor Weöres, and novelists like Magda Szábo, who keep aside from politics, are rare in Hungary. In the 1930s it was the writers of the Populist Movement – Zsigmond Móricz and Gyula Illyés among others – who helped draw attention to the appalling plight of the 'three million beggars', the incredibly poor and backward dispossessed peasants who swarmed over the vast feudal estates before the war. Hungary's greatest living novelist and its greatest critic – Tibor Déry and George Lukács – were both prominent, active Communists; in his time, Lukács has held government office. It was a gathering of writers and intellectuals – significantly named the Petöfi circle – which sparked off the revolution in 1956.

This political embroilment of the artists – expected, honoured, almost necessary – is a tradition in Central and Eastern Europe, where the intelligentsia is much smaller, more closely knit and less specialized than in the West. It is also inevitable in countries with long histories of invasion and rule by foreign powers. The Turks overran Hungary in the sixteenth century. When they were finally thrown out the Hapsburgs took over. Hungary has only been independent as a state since 1919, and since the last war it has been firmly within the Russian sphere of influence. In such circumstances, nationalism becomes a major preoccupation of the writers. They are important not just for their art but also as teachers, helping the nation to an awareness of itself, its aspirations, its troubles.

I have written elsewhere that this dual inheritance of romanticism and political involvement has resulted in a curious Hungarian trick of the sensibility, a simultaneous doubleness of response: the ability to feel romantic about politics and political about romance. Without any strain or falsification, lyricism and cynicism coexist in the same man at the same moment. It is a kind of national schizophrenia, and it permeates the whole of Hungarian culture. Their intensely-felt cults of love, bravery, patriotism and fine feeling exist side by side with equally intense cynicism, a national genius for arranging things, for seeing through shams, for knowing the right official, for comfort, for not being taken in. The two poles on which

Hungarian life turns are, in short, sense and sensibility; a passion for good living and a passion for culture.

All this makes it an amiable country to visit but a hard one to come to terms with. The same is true for these short stories: they are intriguing, amusing, extremely perceptive, sometimes moving, often sour, but there is, around most of them, a shell of cleverness that keeps the reader at a distance. It is always present in the stories with urban settings, even when they are little more than light-weight comedies of manners. No matter how trivial the theme, the writers seem at once in love with their own cynical clear-sightedness, which helps them see the shams and pretensions for what they are, and at the same time they are mildly shocked by this vision. So they write as though with a distaste for themselves, a worldly yearning for some lost innocence. Occasionally, cleverness turns into vigour but that kind of affirming energy is rare.

It is the same at the other end of the social spectrum. Many Hungarian writers, for example, are preoccupied with peasant life and things rural. Yet, despite this similarity of theme, they are a world apart from an English novelist like Thomas Hardy, who appears in his books as a rather slow-minded, private man, whose genius lay in his utter truth to his own elegiac insights into loss and deprivation. That kind of writer is almost unthinkable in Hungary. A Magyar, to qualify as an author at all, must continually parade a tense knowingness. To the outsider, it is stimulating enough; but it can become, in the not-too-long run, rather exhausting. As the quibble was to Shakespeare, according to Dr Johnson, so cleverness is to the Hungarian writers: a fatal Cleopatra.

Perhaps one reason for this continual and compulsive show of wit is the intensity with which the arts are cultivated in Hungary. There is a saying that nine of the ten million inhabitants of the country are writers. Certainly, Budapest seethes with cultural activity. Everyone has read everything and is producing something. To survive in that gossipy café world it is essential to be in the highest degree sophisticated, polyglot, cynical, chic. This concentration of talent and its fierce cultivation is not new to the mid-twentieth century. It derives from the time when the dispossessed gentry and rising, largely Jewish, middle classes drifted together in the capital and established their own embattled league of intelligentsia. It was an intelligentsia existing in the teeth both of incredible general poverty and ignorance and also of a tiny, ruling élite of corrupt, disproportionately rich aristocrats. Today the intelligentsia is far less exclusive than it was. The Communists have mounted a huge, and hugely successful, attack on illiteracy. Serious books are cheap, plentiful and avidly consumed; adult education and spare-time culture thrives. Yet it seems to me that there is still, under all the optimism and effort, a slight feeling of precariousness. The swarming world of metropolitan art is counterbalanced by a rural culture which has only slowly been wakened out of its feudal apathy. Before the last war the life of the peasants on the great estates was still as debased and controlled as that of the serfs in early medieval England, or of the peons of Peru. In some areas, there was even enforced abortion to prevent the birth of more than one child to each family. The change from these habits of centuries has been tentative and gradual, however successful. The Great Hungarian Plain is still there, beyond the cities and the playground round Lake Balaton, like some hole in the nation's head. It gives the nervous polish of metropolitan cultural life a certain insubstantiality.

Just as the Hungarian temperament balances between romanticism and cynicism, the social range of literature is suspended between sophistication and simplicity, between town and country. The best work is done when these opposites blend and fertilize each other. When the writers stick purely to the urban scene cynicism dominates everything else; there is an obsession with the corruption, arrogance and triviality of the complacent rich. This fascinated anger with the rottenness of everything and everyone controls the oddly disturbing stories by Sandor Hunyadi and Gyula Krudy. Both have about them a sense of underlying violence and exasperated humour which, in Krudy's story particularly, has the disjointed intensity of a nightmare, however debonair the literary manners may seem. The authors make their points and put their subjects in their places with a positive fury of cleverness. It is all very sharp and knowing, sometimes comic, often brilliant, but it is founded essentially on contempt – which is a piercing enough response, but a limiting one. In contrast, a deeper level is touched only in a curious interchange between urban and rural, between innocence and corruption.

Mor Jokai's 'The Frog' is the prototype for this kind of writing, and the stories of Jozsef Lengyel, Sándor Brody and Andor Endre Gélleri are all in the same school. But, for me, the two best pieces in this collection, are those by Zsigmond Móricz and Tibor Déry. Both are about children, both centre on this clash between innocence and guile, and both are controlled by, above all, anger. It is as though only the innocents – children and peasants – were able to rouse Hungarian writers from their knowing contempt for adult corruption. This might, I suppose, be a way in which Magyar romanticism works its way out; yet the writing is better than that, the children are in themselves not in the least romantic. Déry's war orphans are thieves who thoughtlessly commit and accept murder; Móricz's girl heroine is, by her own pitiful lights, devious and cunning. The authors' controlling anger is against the injustice of an adult world which forces children into such desperate necessities. Yet the compassion underlying all this, and purifying it, is an instinctive tenderness for the outcast, a sentient, watchful, ironic identification with the lost and delinquent.

Perhaps it is precisely these last qualities which define the essence of Hungary itself for its artists. The country survives isolated in the heart of Europe. Before the war its feudal ruling oligarchy kept it largely shut away from the processes of industrialization which might have transformed it into a modern democracy. Now it is finally emerging fully into the twentieth century and its massive substratum of illiteracy is being eroded, it remains, for the writers, land-locked by its impenetrable language, which is linked to no other European tongue except Finnish. The Hungarians are, of necessity, superlative linguists; in Budapest everyone you meet seems fluent in at least two or three foreign languages. But nobody, apart from the Hungarians, speaks Magyar. It is a lost language. The effect of this on a nation with a genius for lyric poetry and a general obsession with literature and communication must be a sense of intolerable loneliness. The country may swarm with talent, but the only Hungarians with a genuine hope of an international reputation are those whose genius lies in the international languages; the musicians, mathematicians and scientists; even the chess-players and footballers have more chance than the writers.

This may account for the almost incestuous intensity of Hungarian literary life, and also for the edge of frustration in all the continual cleverness. But it also accounts for that instinctive sympathy with the orphaned, the put-upon, the outcasts, with all those who are at once pathetic, lost and murderous. Whatever its political commitments, Hungarian writing has all the characteristics of a minority literature. Indeed, the isolation of the country and its language produces its own special strength: it is a strength which comes from a community of shared experience extending to every level of society, a sense of fundamental, lonely sympathy, despite all the local antagonisms and bitchiness. It is like some wrought, quarrelsome but passionate family; they know that, when all the rows and back-biting are done, there is no one else to love or understand them.

It seems to me that this mixture of compassion, anger, isolation and cunning in the best Hungarian writing is rare and valuable. It is also increasingly relevant to the contemporary situation of all artists, whatever their nationality. 'Isolation', 'failure of communication', 'alienation', 'extremism' – all these are fashionable labels pasted over the one trouble twentieth-century artists have in common: whatever their success and acceptance, the language they use seems, in its essence, to be foreign and incomprehensible to their audiences. In a sense, all original modern artists are spiritual Hungarians.

1967

Jan Kott*

The Poles have a tradition of double-talk. It is an inheritance from a long history of invasion, division and political rape by hordes, of greater or less barbarity, sweeping in from the east and the west. But specifically it is the inheritance from a time when straight talk was impossible: the century and a half or more of the Partition, when the country was carved up between Russia, Prussia and Austria. Then the nation's unity and identity were preserved only by the use of the Polish language. So to write in it became, willy-nilly, a political act, a gesture of independence. Authors stood in for politicians; instead of factions, there were poems and novels.

The result is a national genius for ambiguity, an obsession with allegory. Everything is written in what they call 'Aesopian language', which makes it impossible to publish even 'Ba, ba, black sheep' without someone interpreting the thing as a parable of the Polish economy, a veiled but barbed comment on production and distribution. In the Polish arts, every statement is loaded, every image is more than it seems.

Jan Kott is a master of this two-tone style. Poet, critic, one-time Resistance fighter and now Professor of Literature at Warsaw University, he is a man of immense intellectual influence. Like his colleague, the philosopher Leszek Kolakowski, he is concerned with working out a possible stance to fit the present situation, a way of coping and understanding. Like Kolakowski, his politics are revisionist, his attitudes existential; and both work from behind a

* Jan Kott, *Shakespeare our Contemporary*, translated by Boleslaw Taborski (London: Methuen, 1965).

smoke-screen of scholarship: Kolakowski is an expert on theology and seventeenth-century philosophy, Kott on Shakespeare.

So the difficulty for the western reader of *Shakespeare our Contemporary* is that, although Kott may mean what he says, he doesn't always say what he means:

> What world did Shakespeare write about, what times did he want to depict? Was it the world of feudal barons, slaughtering one another in the middle of the fifteenth century, or perhaps the world of the good, wise and devout Queen Elizabeth? That same Elizabeth, who cut off Mary Stuart's head when Shakespeare was twenty-three years old, and sent to the scaffold some fifteen hundred Englishmen, among them her own lovers, ministers of the realm, doctors of theology and doctors of law, generals, bishops, great judges. . . . What in fact did the Grand Mechanism mean for Shakespeare? A succession of kings climbing and pushing one another off the grand staircase of history, or a wave of hot blood rising up to one's head and blinding the eyes? . . . A dense and impenetrable night of history where dawn does not break, or a darkness that fills the human soul?

In passages like this Kott is updating Shakespeare even more rigorously than Shakespeare updated Holinshed. The Bard would scarcely have encouraged anyone who found similarities between Elizabeth and Richard III, but those 1,500 clever Elizabethans who went to the block look remarkably like the 3,500 Polish intellectuals murdered in the Nazis' 'Operation AB'. As for the dark night of history, Shakespeare may not have known one, but Kott has lived through two: the first under the Germans, when twenty per cent of the total population was killed; the second under the Stalinists, when the intellectual life of the country was bureaucratized, censored and policed to a standstill.

That, anyway, is the first part of the allegory. The tone is that of a teacher addressing a sympathetic undergraduate audience. All of them would rather be talking about what is going on outside the lecture hall; all tacitly understand that that is what they really are discussing; but the formal, scholarly pretence is kept up to mollify the authorities, as though the whole performance were a joke at the expense of officialdom – a joke which could be exploded by a single footnote: 'For "English" read "Polish" throughout.' It is the strategy of an occupied nation, almost the only form of political debate a one-party system will allow. The second half of the quotation is, however, rather different: the question is no longer what is happening, but how you cope with it. Does the ultimate responsibility for the situation rest with 'historical inevitability' or does it devolve finally on the individual? In the Polish context, that means, quite simply, a choice between Marxism and Existentialism. The professor, in short, is not teaching his students about Shakespeare, he's advising them on how to manage, how to behave in their own society and how to recognize the forces that shape it.

If this all sounds a little far-fetched and hectic, that is only because I have, in effect, been doing a Kott on Kott. It seems the only way of getting much out of the book. From the point of view of scholarship it is wild, more or less half-baked and wilfully contemptuous of everything we know of the traditions Shakespeare worked in. As a piece of straight literary criticism it is even worse. Kott is impervious to the richness of Shakespeare's poetry and the insights it gives – through its endless fertility, humour and energy – into a complex, variable, self-renewing world of values. You would never guess from his comments that Shakespeare is the greatest poet we have, nor even – if it weren't for the shape of the quotes – that he was a poet at all. He is interested only in such present comfort as he personally can get out of the Bard. Shakespeare, in short, is Kott's straight man.

He is perfectly frank about this:

> Shakespeare is like the world or life itself. Every historical period finds in him what it is looking for and what it wants to see. A reader or spectator in the mid-twentieth century interprets *Richard III* through his own experiences. He cannot do otherwise.

So Kott gives us Shakespeare the nihilist, first master of the Theatre of Cruelty, definer of 'the Auschwitz experience' and protagonist of the naked unaccommodated man. His moral world is stripped bare, the heavens are invariably 'cruel, empty, unalterable and silent', 'relentless and merciless' (all those epithets are used in the space of five lines). Down below, there is a choking metaphysical fog in which those two monster buses, Marx and Kierkegaard, loom and occasionally collide, and a handful of lonely, sour tramps, dressed in slightly beat Renaissance finery, tentatively pick their way.

It is a gloomy vision and a rhetorical one; yet for all the melodrama and souped-up prose, the results are curiously compelling. It is not that Kott is particularly original in his interpretations – Professor Kermode devoted an elaborate hatchet job in the *New York*

Review to disproving that theory – but he is utterly committed to the present relevance of the plays, and infatuated with the modern, political, Polish poet he has created. And his passion is contagious. As he describes them, Richard III really is Stalin, and Prospero a grand revisionist philosopher-prince in semi-retirement – a kind of George Lukács without the evasiveness. He justifies *Hamlet* in terms of the Twentieth Party Congress and the Cracow production, with no soliloquies, continual intrigue and spying, and a Prince who has 'read only newspapers' and looks like a student agitator; Kott's Hamlet, in fact, is no longer Hamlet, he is a failed Fortinbras.

Similarly, his *Midsummer Night's Dream* is a failed *Troilus and Cressida*. By altogether ignoring the tone of the poetry he makes the play into a vast, salacious orgy in which everyone's buried sexual fantasies are acted out: the young lovers, dead drunk, change partners a couple of times in one night, and 'the slender, tender and lyrical Titania' rapes herself a phallic donkey. (It is typical of Kott's 'originality' that in this essay he sounds as though he were just about to invent the theory of the unconscious.) More complicated still is his attitude to *Coriolanus*, which he admires in the teeth of the politics; perhaps the hero's arrogance chimes with something in Kott's Polish sensibility. So he resolves the moral paradox by reading the play as though it were the first western: the background is that of a classic class struggle, but the hero who 'falls victim to his own mythology' is transformed into a prototype of the fastest sword alive, lonely, contemptuous and unable to beat his fate, a Shane in Roman toga.

This is not quite as ridiculous as it sounds, for a great deal of Kott's flair and freshness comes from his ability to see Shakespeare through the eyes of a compulsive film-goer. His influence in the west has percolated through actual productions – Peter Brook's and, to a lesser extent, Peter Hall's – and the reason, I think, is not that his ideas are particularly revolutionary, but that he can, to an extraordinary degree, *visualize* the plays in contemporary terms. Wilson Knight first talked about the grotesque in *King Lear* in 1930; but he read the play primarily as a poem. Kott's contribution was to *see* it in terms of the metaphysical pantomime of Samuel Beckett. In a way, this is a simpler job; it demands less tact, less discipline, less rigorous care and less insight into what Shakespeare actually wrote. But what it does demand is an exacerbated insight into present troubles, present preoccupations, present styles.

All this Kott has with an uncanny, though sometimes faddish, intensity. He also has the headlong, argumentative enthusiasm of a man for whom literature is instinctively an expression of politics. The result is not a new Shakespeare, nor any transformation of Shakespearian criticism. Indeed, it is hardly Shakespearian criticism at all. Instead, it is a wonderfully sharp and suggestive analysis of the whole bracing, hypersophisticated, double-dealing and bloody-minded intellectual life that seethes in modern Poland.

The Spectator, 1965

August Strindberg*

The fiftieth anniversary of Strindberg's death misfired in 1962. Elizabeth Sprigge's lovingly prepared translation of twelve of his plays does not seem to have been ready in time. All we got here was *Inferno*, the record of his breakdown after he separated from his second wife, which is fascinating as a case-history but a non-starter as a work of art. The Royal Shakespeare Company's contribution was a burlesque of his quite good one-acter, *Playing With Fire*. And that was that.

Yet it was typical. Strindberg has nearly always had the wrong kind of success and the wrong kind of failure: both have been scandalous, noisy, racked. He seems only to have been able to stomach public acclaim provided it was accompanied by a proportionate public fury. He was, from the start, a tortured man who exploited his tortures, who chronicled his appalling autobiography as it happened, and wrote to hurt. He was as self-destructive as he was paranoid; conversely, he pitied himself as much as he persecuted himself. He had a flair for disastrous marriages and melodramatic affairs. He quarrelled with everyone – particularly his friends – and had his first collection of stories prosecuted for blasphemy. He fancied himself as an alchemist and dabbled in theosophy and occultism. At his worst, he seems hopelessly preoccupied by his own sinfulness, his 'passions' and the sweet smell of decadence.

But these last *fin de siècle* mannerisms are a mere irritation on the

* August Strindberg, *Twelve Plays*, translated by Elizabeth Sprigge (London: Constable, 1963); *Inferno*, translated by Mary Sandbach (London: Hutchinson, 1962).

surface of his work. Eliot once remarked that the odd thing about the British writers of the Nineties – Wilde, Dowson, Lionel Johnson – was that they suffered so much and yet wrote so superficially. They were protected, he thought, by their histrionics. Strindberg lacked that extra thickness of skin. Instead, his genius was directly related to the rawness of his nerves. The state of mind he so meticulously described in *Inferno* is, in the technical sense, psychotic; he shows, I am told, all the symptoms of a paranoid schizophrenic. More simply, he commanded neither the defences nor the sense of reality to keep him in the manageable realm of neurosis. Yet it was from precisely this failing that his power and his curiously contemporary air come. In painting, Expressionism may have gone a long way beyond Edvard Munch, whom Strindberg knew in Paris during his *Inferno* period. On the stage, however, it is still catching up with Strindberg.

He seems to have invented what now passes for the *avant-garde* theatre, and a great deal of what we take for granted in the cinema. As early as the foreword to *Miss Julie* he had set about the reform of the stage. He wanted to get rid of the footlights, the distractions of orchestra and intervals, the boxes 'with their tittering diners and supper-parties', and the heavy encumbrances of elaborate sets. In their place he wanted a fluid stage – of the kind, presumably, which Svoboda has perfected in Prague – and acting fluid enough to include improvisation, ballet and mime; also a fluidity of writing, to avoid

> the symmetrical, mathematical construction of French dialogue, and let people's minds work irregularly, as they do in real life where, during a conversation, no topic is drained to the dregs, and one mind finds in another a chance cog to engage in.

Above all, he was after 'a *small* stage and a *small* house' and 'total darkness in the auditorium'. It sounds like the usual attack on the conventionality, complacency and philistinism of the socialite theatre. But it has little to do with the naturalist programme of Ibsen. Strindberg's brand of realism was more like that of the cinema, where the darkness and the looming black and white images are closer not to life but to dreams.

This fits with Strindberg's preoccupation as an artist. He was continually trying to cut through the polished surface of ideas and manners to examine the springs of action. 'We want', he wrote, 'to see the wires themselves, to watch the machinery.' Perhaps Beckett works in the same way. But he is more limited, more negative;

the essence of his people is their isolation, and their most passionate relationship is with Nothingness. Strindberg, on the other hand, was too close to Ibsen to be able to abstract his obsessions so tidily. And the obsessions themselves were all concerned with the destructive complexity of his feelings for women.

He is the master of sexual ambivalence and uncertainty. Pathologically jealous, he was a sensualist who yearned always for 'masculine virginity'. He courted rejection and reacted savagely to any positive show of love. It is as though he were unable to get over the fact that women have their own sexual desires. That is the chief offence of Miss Julie, of Henriette in *Crime and Crime* and of Alice in *The Dance of Death*. It seemed to open to him menacing perspectives of feminism, lesbianism and a whole world in which embattled women usurped the rights of men. His perfect heroines were all virginal, suffering, bodiless: Swanwhite, Eleanor in *Easter*, Indra's Daughter in *A Dream Play*, and the Girl in his masterpiece, *The Ghost Sonata*. All his heroes, meanwhile, suffered maternal agonies of tenderness for their children, shared even their wives' labour pains and were passionately involved with their wives' former husbands or lovers. The result is an endless and unresolved sense of outrage. His couples destroy each other in acts of what, in *Creditors*, he calls 'pure cannibalism'. In his works there are no solutions, only at times a grudging acceptance of the horror of the other person's individuality. His talent lay in catching that note of human violence in constricted surroundings. In comparison with his chamber plays, the more ambitious open-scene poetic quests, like *To Damascus* and *The Great Highway*, are diffuse and unconvincing. His genius needed the domestic prison for the full expression of its ferocity. He was the inventor of marital Expressionism.

The core of Expressionism is in an impossible intensity of feeling which lies just behind the work of art but which is never quite expressed by it. You are constantly forced back from the work to its creator. In his famous essay on *Hamlet*, Eliot wrote:

> The only way of expressing emotion in the form of art is by finding an 'objective correlative'; in other words, a set of objects, a situation, a chain of events which shall be the formula of that *particular* emotion; such that when the external facts, which must terminate in sensory experience, are given, the emotion is immediately invoked. . . . Hamlet (the man) is dominated by an emotion which is inexpressible, because it is in *excess* of the facts as they appear.

By this reckoning, *Hamlet* is the first Expressionist play. But what is an exception with Shakespeare is the rule with Strindberg. *The Father*, for example, begins with the bullying, insistently masculine hero trapped in a houseful of women and in a heartless, mutually destructive marriage. The situation has all the makings of a piece of Ibsen-like claustrophobia. Then it explodes. His wife has only to drop two hints – that he is mad and that their daughter is not his, both legitimate manoeuvres in the style of battle they are fighting – and he promptly becomes insane. For despite appearances, the madness was already there, though neither in the situation nor in anything you are told of the Captain's character. Instead, it existed in Strindberg's own mind, as a permanent background of horrified anxiety. To understand the play you must understand Strindberg: his history of breakdowns, excesses and frenzies; his love-hatred for his first wife and the man he had taken her from, and for his icy father who had married the housekeeper directly his own first wife died, when Strindberg was at puberty. The play calls for a kind of Method reading, just as it calls for Method acting. The words, in order to make sense of the actions they go with, must imply intensities which they do not in fact define. This is the opposite of Shakespeare's way, where the feelings develop with and through the language, the images releasing layer after layer of meaning. In Strindberg's chamber plays the language and the feeling are always a little apart.

He seems to have been aware of the split. It was, I think, in the hope of mending it that he tried to break down the conventions of his contemporary stage and turned more and more to poetic drama. As he said in the note to *A Dream Play*:

> The Author has sought to reproduce the disconnected but apparently logical form of a dream. Anything can happen; everything is possible and probable. Time and space do not exist . . . And since on the whole, there is more pain than pleasure in the dream, a tone of melancholy, and of compassion for all living things, runs through the swaying narrative.

This is a stage further on from the theatre he postulated in the foreword to *Miss Julie*. In that play Strindberg himself is divided equally between Miss Julie and Jean; in *A Dream Play* he is deliberately fragmented through all the characters. He used the dream convention as a way through to the emotions. The feelings experienced in dreams are both more intense and more direct than any experienced in waking life. So by creating in his 'swaying narrative' the condition of dreams, he was able to tap the roots of his obsessions without feeling constricted by that reality which, in his sickness, he was never properly able to face.

Yet the pure dream plays lack the power of his earlier, more firmly localized works. He needed the 'objective correlative' of domesticity to fix that tension between love as he felt it should be and marriage as he knew it was. He was possessed by the idea of marriage. But only in *The Ghost Sonata* did he manage to reconcile its constrictions with the imaginative freedom of his dream narrative. The result was a kind of acted-out, personified poetry. 'Not reality,' as he says in *A Dream Play*, 'but more than reality. Not dreams but waking dreams.'

The New Statesman, 1963

5

NOVELS

Laurence Sterne's *A Sentimental Journey**

Le moral, c'est le travelling.
JEAN-LUC GODARD

Laurence Sterne is a distinctly 'modern' novelist. He has the freedom, the total originality, the sense of a man creating the form from scratch and for himself, that we now expect of any serious artist. He has, too, the modernist's apparent indifference to rules, as though aesthetic formalities were, in the final analysis, boring, and the only vindication of a work of art were the immediacy with which it expresses the personality of its creator. Casualness, in short, was his declared artistic principle:

> . . . of all the several ways of beginning a book which are now in practice throughout the known world, I am confident my own way of doing it is the best – I'm sure it is the most religious – for I begin with writing the first sentence – and trusting to Almighty God for the second.†

Obviously, he wasn't anything like as haphazard as he wished to appear. We know from his manuscripts that he wrote and meticulously rewrote, crowding the margins with changes and alternatives, in order to give his prose precisely that casual, dashed-off air, the surface flicker of a sensibility in motion.‡ Yet the effect he achieved with all this effort was of a fined-down disregard for art.

He was also the first modernist in the way in which he cut the novel clear from the constrictions of traditional narrative, setting it

* Introduction to *A Sentimental Journey* (Harmondsworth: Penguin, 1967).

† *Tristram Shandy*, VIII, ii.

‡ See Wilbur L. Cross, *The Life and Times of Laurence Sterne* (New Haven, 1929), 3rd edition, pp. 471–7.

free into the realm of personality, almost a kind of proto-expressionism. Granted, he took his method largely from the picaresque novel; his masters were Rabelais and Cervantes. Yet the picaresque is essentially the form for obsessional story-tellers: one tale leads compulsively to another, as though the fate of the narrator of the *Arabian Nights* hung over every picaresque author's head. In comparison, Sterne seems not much interested in stories. Occasionally he digresses into narrative, but mostly he simply digresses, as yet another fascinating and seemingly urgent side-issue crosses his mind. And these digressions, like his two novels themselves, are substantially without plots. The whole rickety substance is supported and validated simply by the flow of talk, talk, talk. It reads like a picaresque novel transformed into abstract art.

There is a belief, which Sterne himself encouraged, that he learned this method from John Locke and his theory of the association of ideas.* It seems to me equally possible that it was merely part of his Irish inheritance. Though his father, Ensign Roger Sterne, was English – an amiable Army failure descended from a long line of tough and successful Yorkshire churchmen – his mother had Irish connections (she, too, was an apparent disaster: a nagging wife and an indifferent, rapacious mother, she was the stepdaughter of a camp sutler to whom Roger Sterne owed money). Laurence himself was born in Dublin and spent the early part of his childhood billeted on occasional Irish relatives. Although most of his schooldays and the rest of his life were spent in Yorkshire – with intermittent forays on London and the Continent – his work is controlled by the same compulsive talkativeness as you find undiluted only in an Irish bar-room virtuoso. And he re-created the novel in that image, evolving a style of pure talk, of controlled inconsequentiality, irrelevance and continual interruption. This was a form both new and not immediately usable. So, although his influence was enormous in his day, it by-passed the nineteenth century, when the novel became more settled and staid in its ways. His lineal descendants are the heroes of Samuel Beckett's fiction, with their endless 'qua-qua'.

Given this lack of plot or even moral purpose, either improving or scurrilous, you are left for connections and artistic control simply with a personal tone of voice, the flow of casual, intimate, highly idiosyncratic conversation. Even *Tristram Shandy*'s extraordinary

* See John Traugott, *Tristram Shandy's World* (Berkeley: University of California Press, 1954).

gallery of eccentrics – Uncle Toby, My Father, My Mother, Trim, Dr Slop, Yorick, the Widow Wadman – have very little substance of their own; they rely on the author's amused, vague tenderness towards them to make sense of their lives. They are less characters in their own right than obsessions held together by his indulgence.

This is still more marked in *A Sentimental Journey*, where the people are described hardly at all. It is perhaps the most bodiless novel ever written. Though incident is piled on incident, none really amounts to much, and the book relies for its effect entirely on Sterne's ability to buttonhole his readers. For that he had an unprecedented genius. He was master of some curious sleight of tone which sucks you at once into the most intimate and private workings of his mind. He had, as another Irishman, W. B. Yeats, said of a third, George Moore, 'the terrible gift of intimacy'.

Maybe this gift was so unfalteringly his throughout his literary career because he began so late and was spared a hesitant apprenticeship. His first effort, a pamphlet called *A Political Romance* was not published until the beginning of 1759, when he was already in his mid-forties; *Tristram Shandy* began to appear at the end of the same year. By the time he came to *A Sentimental Journey*, nine years later, his intimacy with the audience was instinctive and assured. Indeed, the novel is elaborately that of a famous man. Sterne writes as though from a certain height of success; he is knowingly a public personality, a fashionable figure on the literary landscape, confident and rather delighted by the exposure. The incident with the Comte de B*** – who suddenly realizes that the shabby charmer who is begging his help in obtaining a passport is in fact a famous author – and the description of how he rode the circuit of smart Parisian parties are done with the evident relish of a man who enjoyed his fame.

Yet clearly something more is involved than naïve pleasure in his success and his distance from his Yorkshire parsonage and half-mad wife. By 1768, Sterne's fame, his novels and his personality were, to an unusual degree, all of a piece. He had wholly entered the Shandean world he himself had created. The first-person narrator is himself a character from the earlier novel: he is Yorick, parson and friend of the Shandys', whom Sterne had prematurely killed off in the first volume – mourning his decease with two pages of solid black – and then resurrected whenever convenient, thanks to a time-scheme which leaps years between lines and extends seconds through whole paragraphs. Granted, the personalities of Sterne and Yorick were inextricably entwined well before the final novel: Sterne called himself Yorick in his letters and even published his sermons under that name. But by the time he came to *A Sentimental Journey* the name was something more than a semi-private joke to draw the initiated reader into the author's élite circle. Instead, it seemed to sum up a whole nexus of Sterne's preoccupations: with wit and melancholy and death. Yorick the jester was also Yorick the death's head, and Sterne, who had spat blood with increasing seriousness since his undergraduate days at Cambridge, was knowingly a dying man when he began the *Journey*. So perhaps it gave him a soothing illusion of immortality to identify so completely with a character in his own work. More probably, it allowed enough free air to circulate between himself and his situation, so that his wit had space in which to manoeuvre.

There were also certain practical advantages. In part, Sterne wrote this last novel to clear, or at least to redefine, his name. As a writer, his reputation was, by then, vast and international, but as a parson it had suffered correspondingly. His difficulty was that, like most compulsive talkers, he could never resist the joky, bawdy possibilities of whatever turned up along the way in his monologues. His fellow-clerics objected accordingly: his work was altogether too smutty, too obsessed, too unseemly for a man of the church. So one purpose of *A Sentimental Journey* was to prove his innocence. His letters at the time ring with the theme. He wrote to his daughter that the design of the book was 'to teach us to love the world and our fellow creatures better than we do – so it runs most upon those gentle passions and affections, which add so much to it'. To another, slightly older, young woman it was the same story:

> . . . I have something else for you, which I am fabricating at a great rate, and that is my Journey, which shall make you cry as much as ever it made me laugh – or I'll give up the Business of sentimental writing – and write to the Body.

It was even the same to his diplomat friend, Sir George Macartney, though the tone was a little cooler: 'I shall', he said, 'have the honour of presenting to you a couple of as clean brats as ever chaste brain conceiv'd.'

Sterne had always written from his nerve-ends, with a quivering, edgy liveliness; the new novel was to show that this was genuinely the product of an intensity of emotion, not of mere nerviness. On the surface, there was something almost didactic in its purpose: it would teach people how to react, show them that the simplest incident – an innocent exchange with a mendicant monk, a peasant with his dead donkey – swarmed with high feeling. It would show them that the value of travelling was not in stunning adventures or strenuous sight-seeing or exquisite views exquisitely rendered back into prose; it was, instead, in the traveller's receptiveness to feelings, and the flair and subtlety with which he expressed them.

Admittedly, Sterne was cashing in on a fad. Almost twenty years before, a Lady Bradshage had written querulously to Richardson:

What, in your opinion, is the meaning of the word *sentimental*, so much in vogue among the polite. . . . Every thing clever and agreeable is comprehended in that word. . . . I am frequently astonished to hear such a one is a *sentimental* man; we were a *sentimental* party; I have been taking a *sentimental* walk. . . .

Sterne took this London fad and made it into an international obsession. The word was adopted into French and German because of his novel. There were circles of Sterne addicts in Germany who studied the master, cultivated exquisite feelings and, after the manner of Yorick and the friar, presented each other with little horn snuff-boxes, promising, according to Professor Cross, 'to cultivate Yorick's gentleness, content with fortune, and pity and pardon for all human errors'. No doubt it was excessive; certainly, all this stood Sterne in peculiarly bad stead with the Victorians: he was credited with all the morbid sensibility and snobbish high feeling which they loathed. In *The English Humourists* Thackeray attacked him as a supreme hypocrite, flailing him for his combination of sentimentality and prurience.

To be disliked by Thackeray, of course, is a fair recommendation. Even so, Sterne has never quite escaped the charge of playing up his sensitivity. Even his defenders imply that he overdid things and, in his concern not to appear bawdy, went too far the other way, ending as a dandified tear-jerker. This seems to me to disregard the whole strategy of the novel: every exquisite moment is promptly undercut either by irony or by deliberate absurdity. Consider, for example, the much-abused episode of the peasant lamenting his dead donkey. It was a kind of eighteenth-century death of Little

Nell, energetically wept over at the time and strenuously savaged later. Neither the admirers nor the detractors seem to have got the point. Sterne ends the passage by drawing the inevitable moral:

> Shame on the world! said I to myself – Did we love each other, as this poor soul but loved his ass – 'twould be something. –

The next chapter begins immediately:

> The concern which the poor fellow's story threw me into, required some attention; the postilion paid not the least to it, but set off upon the *pavé* in a full gallop.
>
> The thirstiest soul in the most sandy desert of Arabia could not have wished more for a cup of cold water, than mine did for grave and quiet movements; and I should have had a high opinion of the postilion, had he but stolen off with me in something like a pensive pace. – On the contrary, as the mourner finished his lamentation, the fellow gave an unfeeling lash to each of his beasts, and set off clattering like a thousand devils.

So instead of being able to lie back and soak in his feelings, Yorick is promptly embroiled in a shouting match with the postilion. Only when his nerves are so thoroughly jangled that he needs the release of a hard gallop does the coachman slow to a walking pace. The whole thing is a paradigm of frustration, and a joke at his own expense.

This, I think, is the rule for the novel, not the exception. The more elegantly sentimental the narrator's responses, the more absurd the after-effects. It is Sterne's particular strength as a comic writer that no matter how whole-heartedly he pursues high feeling, unredeemed reality keeps breaking in. So whatever the immediate propagandist issues for his contemporaries – for or against the sentimental education – it seems to me now to be genuinely impossible to read him as anything except a supreme, and supremely consistent, ironist.

Perhaps that is the least that can be expected of an eighteenth-century wit. Yet Sterne's irony, like most other elements of his writing, has a distinctly modern taste to it. The incident with the beautiful Grisset, for example. Yorick, strolling in Paris, is more or less lost; 'more or less' since he doesn't bother to ask the way until he can find someone attractive enough to be worth asking. Finally, he sees the beautiful Grisset working in her shop; together they go through an elaborate ritual of question and answer, she giving him directions, he repeating them to her, she repeating them back to him; he leaves, forgets the directions in a few paces, and returns; at length they settle down to an intimate *tête-à-tête* in her shop. It is like the mating dance of two tropical birds. Finally, by way of elegant compliment, he takes her wrist and feels her pulse:

> I had counted twenty pulsations, and was going on fast towards the fourtieth, when her husband coming unexpected from the back parlour into the shop, put me a little out in my reckoning. – 'Twas no body but her husband, she said – so I began a fresh score – Monsieur is so good, quoth she, as he pass'd by us, as to give himself the trouble of feeling my pulse – The Husband took off his hat, and making me a bow, said, I did him too much honour – and having said that, he put on his hat and walk'd out.

The beautifully poised and pausing rhythm of the prose, by which Sterne passes off an outrageous situation as though it were utterly normal, is the essence of his art. It is also the essence of the modern 'cool' style, the art of controlled and detached delinquency. Yet this is not a quality which has yet been expressed with any great subtlety in prose. And this is the crux of the matter when calling Sterne a modernist: the closest equivalent to his work is not to be found in any contemporary novelist; it is, instead, in the films of the French director, Jean-Luc Godard.

What they have in common is a style and an obsession, or rather, a style to cope with an obsession. By style I mean something beyond their elegance and wit and detachment. Instead, it is the ability to maintain all those qualities whilst not leaving anything out, whilst refusing a narrow, exclusive focus. The novelist's sensibility and the director's camera are so alive, so eclectic, that when they move down a street the whole casual scene is drawn into the action: 'I walked up gravely to the window in my dusty black coat, and looking through the glass, saw all the world in yellow, blue, and green, running at the ring of pleasure.' And the action itself is casual. The plot in Godard's movies may be marginally tighter than in Sterne's novels, but it is rarely more important. What matters are the incidents that proliferate along the route, and the way in which they are handled. In *Bande à part*, for example, even the chief actors in the farce are bored by the robbery they are so elaborately planning; what interests them, and the audience, are the side issues – a dance in a café, a lesson in a language school. Hence casualness and unprejudiced receptivity become an artistic procedure. And this, in a way, is a kind of delinquent aesthetic: the artist creates a work at the same time as he comments, implicitly but nihilistically, on the art-form and the whole choosy business of art. Neither Sterne nor Godard seems to believe in anything beyond what is there, present to the senses, at the moment. Questioned by a pompous interviewer on the morality of his films, Godard replied, '*Le moral, c'est le travelling*'. He was implying, to say the least, that morality is strictly empirical, since '*le travelling*' is a technical film-maker's term to describe a tracking camera. Morality, that is, is to be picked up, and discarded again, as you go along. Sterne has precisely the same unrehearsed attitude to what occurs. So both are delinquent to the extent of, first, being unconcerned with any preordained moral order and, second, in their seemingly delighted assumption that, beneath all the elegance, their protagonists are interested only in gratifying their momentary impulses – though without unnecessary viciousness; the wit of both is essentially gentle. In their worlds everyone, elegantly, sadly, in one way or another, is on the make.

This, I think, is the basic assumption behind all Sterne's ambiguities. For example, the intense, finger-tip flirtation between Yorick and Madame de R***'s 'fair *fille de chambre*' in the chapter called 'The Temptation'. The narrator returns to his hotel to find her waiting; in that curious, typical, slow-motion narrative, where every slight gesture can endure for whole lines, he takes her back up to his room and then, little by little, leads her from the desk, to the door, to the bed, where they sit exchanging quivering civilities:

> A strap had given way in her walk, and the buckle of her shoe was just falling off – See, said the *fille de chambre*, holding up her foot – I could not for my soul but fasten the buckle in return, and putting in the strap – and lifting up the other foot with it, when I had done, to see both were right – in doing it too suddenly – it unavoidably threw the fair *fille de chambre* off her centre – and then –
>
> THE CONQUEST
>
> YES – and then – Ye whose clay-cold heads and lukewarm hearts can argue down or mask your passions, tell me, what trespass is it that man should have them? or how his spirit stands answerable to the Father of spirits but for his conduct under them?
>
> If Nature has so wove her web of kindness, that some threads of love and desire are entangled with the piece – must the whole web be rent in drawing them out? – Whip me such stoics, great Governor of nature! said

I to myself – Wherever thy providence shall place me for the trials of my virtue – whatever is my danger – whatever is my situation – *let me feel the movements which rise out of it, and which belong to me as a man – and if I govern them as a good one, I will trust the issues to thy justice*; for thou has made us, and not we ourselves.

As I finish'd my address, I raised the fair *fille de chambre* up by the hand, and led her out of the room – she stood by me till I lock'd the door and put the key in my pocket – *and then* – the victory being quite decisive – and not till then, I press'd my lips to her cheek, and, taking her by the hand again, led her safe to the gate of the hotel.

This is *double entendre* raised to high art. The lines I have italicized could as easily describe the act of making love as the reasons for abstaining from it. So who is conquered in 'The Conquest': Yorick or 'the fair *fille de chambre*'? Sterne avers that it is the former, but the whole passage seems to point the other way.

It was presumably this kind of moral punning that Coleridge objected to in his *Literary Remains*:

With regard to Sterne, and the charge of licentiousness which presses so seriously upon his character as a writer, I would remark that there is a sort of knowingness, the wit of which depends, first, on the modesty it gives pain to; or, secondly, on the innocence and innocent ignorance over which it triumphs; or, thirdly, on a certain oscillation in the individual's own mind between the remaining good and the encroaching evil of his nature – a sort of dallying with the devil – a fluxionary art of combining courage and cowardice, as when a man snuffs a candle with his fingers for the first time, or better still, perhaps, like that trembling daring with which a child touches a hot tea-urn, because it has been forbidden; so that the mind has its own white and black angel. . . . We have only to suppose a society innocent, and then nine-tenths of this sort of wit would be like a stone that falls in snow, making no sound, because exciting no resistance; the remainder rests on its being an offence against the good manners of human nature itself.

To some extent this is justified, but only by virtue of misreading the tone of the man. Sterne seems to snigger only if read with the bias of nineteenth-century moral solidity and assurance. Judged by the more improvised standards he seems to have shared with the mid-twentieth century, the nastiness disappears entirely. The joke is there for those who can see it, but is not insistent enough to offend those who can't. Either way, it remains a joke; the criterion is enjoyment; the author demands simply that the reader relish as much as he does the full, ambiguous subtlety of the situation, with no moral *parti pris*.

Yet neither Sterne nor Godard are as cool as they would appear. Rather, their coolness is what William Empson once called 'a style from a despair'. Under it runs a continual, plangent note of obsession. With Godard the obsession is single: it is with a girl – embodied usually by the beautiful Anna Karina – baffling, ungettable, promiscuous yet frigid, narcissistic, rejecting, and yet, with her queer honesty, always a bit pathetic, almost innocent, certainly lost. The camera becomes an instrument of his obsession, as though he were trying to catch with it something of her elusiveness and fix it on film for keeps. Sterne, by his own confession, also thought of himself as a man obsessed by women, a perpetually pining lover. It seems to me to be nearer the truth to say that he was obsessed by feeling itself. Hence that extraordinarily consistent air of suspended eroticism which runs through most of *A Sentimental Journey*, a continual, quivering, aroused nervousness. Granted, he was constantly undercutting it, as I suggested earlier; so it became an irritant instead of a destroyer of wit. Yet there is a curious rawness about his sensibility: he is so quick and aware and brimming with responses that he writes as though he had one skin too few.

That is natural enough, considering the circumstances under which he wrote this last book. He was in the final months of his life, knowingly dying of consumption, racked by the after-effects of a savage cure for venereal disease, and desperate at the loss of a woman with whom he was – or imagined himself to be – violently in love. Mercifully, none of this gets into the *Journey*. Instead, it is chronicled at length in his *Journal to Eliza*, which was written literally in tandem with the novel. The *Journal* was never intended for publication; he kept it solely for the benefit of his latest passion, a Mrs Elizabeth Draper, who had unwillingly left him to return to her elderly husband in India. He planned to give it to her when they were reunited to show how painfully he had endured her absence. So to say that it is a terrible production – indulgent, self-pitying, hysterical – is beside the point. Yet by the tiresome excess itself, the *Journal* somehow validates the *Journey*. For it helps to define a quality in the wit which is otherwise hard to pin down. I mean the sense, which Sterne also shares with Godard, that the wit, for all its cool, is romantic; it is based on an illusion, even an idealism of feeling. But it is redeemed from common sentimentality because the artist is so quick and subtle and perceptive that he sees through the illusions long before the reader. Indeed, the illusions are a force impelling him into wit. So he undercuts them before anyone else has the chance.

This precarious poise is difficult to maintain at the best of times. And all the evidence seems to show that *A Sentimental Journey* was, in fact, written at the worst of times, with illness, heartbreak and death all crowding in one on another – not to mention the unexpected return of his nagging wife, which prematurely put a stop to the *Journal*. Yet it was through this private record that he managed to draw off the excess of feeling – that emotional rawness which consumptives are particularly prey to – leaving himself free to mock himself in his real art, leaving his urban, and supremely urbane, irony in complete mocking control. This is why *A Sentimental Journey* was finally not quite the spotless and improving novel he threatened in his sickness and depression. The witty, sharp-edged, casual monologue, perceptive almost to the point of over-breeding, and so cool that it begins with a casual remark and ends in the middle of a sentence in the middle of a bawdy story, was an infinitely more difficult work of art to achieve.

The Hudson Review, 1967

Thomas Hardy's *Jude the Obscure**

Jude the Obscure is Hardy's last and finest novel. Yet its publication in 1896 provoked an outcry as noisy as that which recently greeted *Lady Chatterley's Lover*. The press attacked in a pack, lady reviewers became hysterical, abusive letters poured in, and a bishop solemnly burnt the book. The fuss may seem to us, at this point in time, incredible and even faintly ridiculous, but its effect was serious enough: '. . . the experience', Hardy wrote later, 'completely cured me of further interest in novel-writing.' After *Jude* he devoted himself exclusively to his poetry, never returning to fiction.

What caused the uproar? It was not Hardy's fatalism; after *Tess* his public had learned to live with that and even love it. Nor was his attack on social and religious hypocrisy particularly virulent, though there was certainly a good deal of entrenched resentment of his criticism of those two almost equally venerable institutions: marriage and Oxford. Zola's name was invoked by one or two reviewers, but not seriously. The real blow to the eminently shockable Victorian public was the fact that Hardy treated the sexual undertheme of his book more or less frankly: less frankly, he complained, than he had wished, but more frankly than was normal or acceptable.

Despite the social criticism it involves, the tragedy of *Jude* is not one of missed chances but of missed fulfilment, of frustration. It is a kind of *Anna Karenina* from the male point of view, with the basic action turned upside down. Where Anna moves from Karenin to

* Afterword to *Jude the Obscure* (New York: New American Library, 1961); also appeared in the anthology *Thomas Hardy*, edited by A. Guerard (Englewood Cliffs and London: Prentice-Hall, 1963).

Vronsky, from desiccation to partial satisfaction, Jude, swinging from Arabella to Sue, does the opposite. For all his – and Hardy's – superficial disgust, Jude and Arabella are, physically, very much married: their night at Aldbrickham after years apart is made to seem the most natural thing in the world; Jude's subsequent shame is prompted less by the act itself than by his anger at missing Sue and fear that she will somehow find out. On the other hand, his great love for Sue remains at its high pitch of romance and fatality largely because she never really satisfies him. Hardy himself was quite explicit about this in a letter he wrote after the novel was published:

> One point . . . I could not dwell on: that, though she has children, her intimacies with Jude have never been more than occasional, even when they were living together (I mention that they occupy separate rooms, except towards the end, and one of her reasons for fearing the marriage ceremony is that she fears it would be breaking faith with Jude to withhold herself at pleasure, or altogether, after it; though while uncontracted she feels at liberty to yield herself as seldom as she chooses). This has tended to keep his passion as hot at the end as at the beginning, and helps to break his heart. He has never really possessed her as freely as he desired.*

So Jude's tragedy, like every true tragedy, comes from inner tensions which shape the action, not from any haphazard or indifferent force of circumstance. Jude is as frustrated by Sue, his ideal, intellectual woman, as he is by Oxford, his equally shining ideal of the intellectual life. Frustration is the permanent condition of his life.

I am not, of course, suggesting that the book has no theme beyond the sexual relations of Jude, Sue, Arabella, and Phillotson. That was D. H. Lawrence's interpretation in his wonderfully perceptive, startlingly uneven *Study of Thomas Hardy*. But then Lawrence was writing not as a critic but as an imaginative artist who owed a great personal debt to Hardy. His critical method was simply to retell Hardy's plots as though he himself had written them, isolating only what interested him. The result was considerable insight and an equally considerable shift of emphasis away from the novel Hardy actually wrote.

Obviously, *Jude the Obscure* does have its declared social purpose: to criticize a system which could, for mainly snobbish reasons, keep

* F. E. Hardy, *The Later Years of Thomas Hardy*, 1930, p. 42.

out of the universities 'one of the very men', as Sue says, 'Christminster was intended for when the Colleges were founded; a man with a passion for learning, but no money, or opportunities, or friends. . . . You were elbowed off the pavement by the millionaires' sons.' A figure who for Thomas Gray, a Cambridge don elegizing in his country churchyard, was an object of mildly nostalgic curiosity, became in Hardy's work a living, tragic hero. And by this shift of focus Hardy helped make the issue itself live. In his postscript of 1912 he wrote 'that some readers thought . . . that when Ruskin College was subsequently founded it should have been called the College of Jude the Obscure'. Hardy may not have had as direct an influence on social reforms as Dickens; but he helped.

Yet *Jude the Obscure* is clearly more than a criticism of the exclusiveness of the major English universities. Surprisingly early in the book Jude realizes that his Christminster ambitions are futile. After that, though the University remains an obsession with him, it plays very little part in the novel itself. Instead, it is a kind of sub-plot echoing the main theme in slightly different terms, just as Gloucester and his sons repeat on a smaller scale the tragedy of King Lear and his daughters. But with a crucial difference: Jude is the hero of both the main plot and the sub-plot. Christminster may drop out of the major action, but his continuing obsession with it repeats, in another tone of voice, his obsession with Sue. In the beginning, both Sue and the university seem objects of infinitely mysterious romance; both, in the end, land Jude in disillusion. Both seem to promise intellectual freedom and strength; both are shown to be at bottom utterly conventional. Both promise fulfilment; both frustrate him. All Jude's intellectual passion earns him nothing more than the title 'Tutor of St Slums', while all his patience and devotion to Sue loses him his job, his children and finally even his title of husband.

Hardy himself knew perfectly well that the Christminster, social-purpose side of the novel was relatively exterior to its main theme. Years later, when there was talk of turning *Jude* into a play, he wrote: 'Christminster is of course the tragic influence of Jude's drama in one sense, but innocently so, and merely as a crass obstruction.' There is, however, nothing exterior in the part Sue plays in Jude's tragedy. At times, in fact, she seems less a person in her own right than a projection of one side of Jude's character. Even Phillotson remarks on this: 'I have been struck', he said, 'with . . . the extraordinary sympathy, or similarity, between the pair. He is her cousin, which perhaps accounts for some of it. They seem to be one person split in two!' And, in harmony with the principle by which all the major intuitions in the novel are given to the men, Jude himself perceives the same thing: when he lends Sue his clothes after she has escaped from the training college and arrived, soaking wet, at his lodgings, 'he palpitated at the thought that she had fled to him in her trouble as he had fled to her in his. What counterparts they were! . . . Sitting in his only arm-chair he saw a slim and fragile being masquerading as himself on a Sunday, so pathetic in her defencelessness that his heart felt big with the sense of it.' The situation, in which the hero dresses in his own clothes his wet, lost, desperate double, is exactly the same as that of the masterpiece of double identity, Conrad's *The Secret Sharer*.

Considering the ultimate differences between Sue and Jude, Hardy perhaps thought that their similarities merely emphasized the contrasts of which, he wrote, the book was full: 'Sue and her heathen gods set against Jude's reading the Greek testament; Christminster academical, Christminster in the slums; Jude the saint, Jude the sinner; Sue the pagan, Sue the saint; marriage, no marriage; etc. etc.' But the geometrical neatness of Hardy's plan does not make his psychological insight any less profound or compelling. All through the book Sue is Jude 'masquerading as himself on a Sunday'. As even her name implies (Sue, Hardy says himself, is a lily, and Bridehead sounds very like maidenhead), she is the untouched part of him, all intellect, nerves and sensitivity, essentially bodiless. That is why her most dramatic and typical appearances have always something ghostly about them. When, for example, Jude suddenly and guiltily comes across her after his night with Arabella at Aldbrickham, 'Sue stood like a vision before him – her look bodeful and anxious as in a dream'. Or, when she unexpectedly returns to Phillotson in his illness, and does her odd, characteristic conjuring trick with the mirror: 'She was in light spring clothing, and her advent seemed ghostly – like the flitting in of a moth.' It is this combination of non-physical purity with exaggeratedly sharp intellect and sensitivity which preserves her for Jude as an object of ideal yearning, hopeless and debilitating. It is a yearning for his own lost innocence, before his Christminster ambitions were diverted by Arabella. Even when he finally rounds on her, after all their years and tragedies together, he can still only call her 'a sort of fey, or sprite – not a woman!' Despite everything he can do, she remains a bodiless idea, an idea of something in himself.

Sue and Arabella are, in fact, like the white and black horses, the noble and base instincts, which draw Plato's chariot of the soul. But because Hardy too had a passion for Sue's kind of frigid purity ('She is', he wrote, 'a type of woman which has always had an attraction for me'), he exaggerated the case against Arabella almost to the point of parody. Lawrence wrote:

He insists that she is a pig-killer's daughter; he insists that she drag Jude into pig-killing; he lays stress on her false tail of hair. That is not the point at all. This is only Hardy's bad art. He himself, as an artist, manages in the whole picture of Arabella almost to make insignificant in her these pig-sticking, false-hair crudities. But he must have his personal revenge on her for her coarseness, which offends him, because he is something of an Angel Clare.

Where Hardy thought Arabella 'the villain of the piece', Lawrence tried to make her out the heroine. Both views are wrong, not because Sue is any more or less of the heroine than Arabella, but because *Jude the Obscure* is fundamentally a work without any heroines at all. It has only a hero. I will return to this. Lawrence was, however, right when he said that Arabella survives Hardy's deliberate coarsening of her. The artist does her justice against the grain of his tastes. So it is she, not Sue, who shows flashes of real intelligence:

'I don't know what you mean,' said Sue stiffly. 'He is mine if you come to that!'

'He wasn't yesterday.'

Sue coloured roseate, and said 'How do you know?'

'From your manner when you talked to me at the door. Well, my dear, you've been quick about it, and I expect my visit last night helped it on. . . .'

And it is also she, not Sue, who really wants Jude:

In a few moments Arabella replied in a curiously low, hungry tone of latent sensuousness: 'I've got him to care for me: yes! But I want him to more than care for me; I want him to have me – to marry me! I must have him. I can't do without him. He's the sort of man I long for. I shall go mad if I can't give myself to him altogether! I felt I should when I first saw him!'

With fewer exclamation marks and without the moralizing

qualification of 'latent sensuousness' – as though that were so reprehensible! – Arabella's words would sound more frank and serious than any protestation Sue manages in the whole book. Similarly, despite everything, it is Arabella whom Jude really wants physically. There is no doubt about this from the moment when, without a flicker of distaste, he picks up the pig's pizzle she has thrown at him:

> . . . somehow or other, the eyes of the brown girl rested in his own when he had said the words, and there was a momentary flash of intelligence, a dumb announcement of affinity *in posse*, between herself and him, which, so far as Judy Fawley was concerned, had no sort of premeditation in it. She saw that he had singled her out from the three, as a woman is singled out in such cases. . . . The unvoiced call of woman to man, which was uttered very distinctly by Arabella's personality, held Jude to the spot against his intention – almost against his will, and in a way new to his experience.

This may have in it none of the refinement of Jude's passion for Sue, but it is considerably more human and spontaneous. Jude, after all, fell in love with Sue's photograph before he fell in love with Sue herself; and the first time she saw him 'she no more observed his presence than that of the dust-motes which his manipulations raised into the sunbeams'. So they are never really married because the connection between them is of the sensibility, not of the senses. The only real moment of ecstasy Jude shares with Sue is bodiless, precipitated by the scent and brilliance of the roses at the agricultural show. 'The real marriage of Jude and Sue was', as Lawrence said, 'in the roses.' So it is Arabella who gets the last word; however much Hardy may have disliked her in principle, artistically he acknowledged the sureness of her physical common sense, to the extent at least of allowing her to make the final, unqualified judgement of the tragedy:

> 'She may swear that on her knees to the holy cross upon her necklace till she's hoarse, but it won't be true!' said Arabella. 'She's never found peace since she left his arms, and never will again till she's as he is now!'

Yet although his final attitude to Sue may have been ambiguous, in creating her Hardy did something extraordinarily original: he created one of the few totally narcissistic women in literature; yet he did so at the same time as he made her something rather wonderful. Her complexity lies in the way in which Hardy managed to present the full, bitter sterility of her narcissism and yet tried to exonerate her.

Bit by bit, even Jude is made to build up the case against her: she is cold, 'incapable of real love', 'an epicure of the emotions', and a flirt; she wants to be loved more than she wants to love; she is vain, marrying Phillotson out of pique when she learns that Jude is married, and going to bed with Jude only when Arabella reappears on the scene; she is even cruel, in a refined way, her deliberate, 'epicene' frigidity having killed one man before the novel even starts. Yet despite all this, Jude loves her. Part of his love, of course, is rooted in frustration: he wants her endlessly because he can never properly have her. And he loves her, too, because he loves himself; he has in himself a narcissism which responds to hers, a vanity of the intellectual life, of his ideals and ambitions, of the refinement of intellect and sensibility which he had first projected on to Christminster.

But the truth and power of the novel lie in the way in which Jude, in the end, is able to understand his love for Sue *without lessening it.* Until the closing scenes, he manages to make her conform to his ideal by a kind of emotional sleight of mind: he dismisses his glimpses of the unchanging conventionality below the bright surface of her non-conformity by invoking both his own worthlessness and that vague marriage-curse which has been the lot of his family. The turning-point is the death of the children.

One thing troubled him more than any other; that Sue and himself had mentally travelled in opposite directions since the tragedy: events which had enlarged his own views of life, laws, customs, and dogmas, had not operated in the same manner on Sue's. She was no longer the same as in the independent days, when her intellect played like lambent lightning over conventions and formalities which he at the time respected, though he did not now.

Where Jude matures as a man, reconciling himself to the endless tragedies and disappointments until he can accept them more or less without self-pity, Sue remains fixed in her narcissism. She does not change, she simply shapes her outer actions to the commonplaces which at heart have always ruled her. Convention – which she calls High Church Sacramentalism – is simply a way of preserving her vanity intact. To break her self-enclosed mould would mean laying herself open to the real tragedy of her relationship with Jude

– of which she, not Fate, is the main instrument – and thus giving herself to him completely. Because she is unable to do this, she denies the true marriage between them and perverts it to fit a conventional idea of matrimony. Arabella may occasionally have turned whore for practical ends – that presumably, is how she raised the money to make Jude drunk before remarrying him – but it is Sue whom he accuses, when she returns to Phillotson, of 'a fanatic prostitution'. What began as intellectual freedom ends as prostitution to an idea. So when Jude finally turns on her with the cry 'Sue, Sue, you are not worth a man's love!', he is passing judgement not only on her but also, because he never once denies that he loves her, on something in himself. That cry and Arabella's closing words represent a standard of maturity which Jude only slowly and painfully attains.

There is something puzzling about *Jude the Obscure* as a work of art: in impact it is intensely moving; in much of its detail it is equally intensely false. The dialogue, for example, is, with very little exception, forced and awkward. Even granted the conventional formalities of the time, no character ever properly seems to connect with another in talk. Despite all the troubles they have seen together, Jude and Sue speak to each other as though they had just been introduced at a vicarage tea-party. As a result, their grand passion becomes, on their own lips, something generalized, like the weather or religion or politics. They are, in Sue's own words, 'too sermony'. Conversely, Arabella, apart from her few moments of truth and an occasional, ponderous slyness, is reduced to a kind of music-hall vulgarity of speech. Widow Edlin is archly folksy and Father Time is almost a caricature of Hardy at his most Hardyesque. The only people who seem able to talk more or less naturally to others are the solitaries, Phillotson and, in a slighter way, Vilbert.

It may be that Hardy had very little ear for dialogue; it is something he rarely does well. But his clumsiness in *Jude* is more than a fault, it is part of the nature of the work. For the essential subject of the novel is not Oxford, or marriage, or even frustration. It is loneliness. This is the one condition without which the book would show none of its power. When they are together the characters often seem amateurishly conceived, and sometimes downright false. But once they are left to themselves they begin to think, feel, act and even talk with that strange poignancy which is uniquely Hardy's. The brief, almost cursory paragraph in which Jude tries to drown himself after the failure of his first marriage is a far more effective and affecting scene than, for example, the elaborately constructed pig-killing – and largely, I think, because nothing is said. None of the emotional impact is lost in heavy moralizing or awkwardness. When Jude is on his own, as he is for a great deal of the novel, walking from one village to the next, one Christminster college to another, then he emerges as a creation of real genius.

The novel's power, in fact, resides in that sustained, deep plangency of note which is the moving bass behind every major incident. This note is produced not by any single action but by a general sense of tragedy and sympathetic hopelessness which the figure of Jude provokes in Hardy. And the essence of his tragedy is Jude's loneliness. He is isolated from society because his ambitions, abilities and sensibility separate him from his own class while winning him no place in any other. He is isolated in his marriage to Arabella because she has no idea of what he is about, and doesn't care. He is isolated in his marriage to Sue because she is frigid. Moreover, the sense of loneliness is intensified by the way in which both women are presented less as characters complete in themselves than as projections of Jude, sides of his character, existing only in relation to him. In the same way, the wonderfully sympathetic and moving treatment of Phillotson in the scene at Shaston – his surprising delicacy and generosity and desolating loneliness – is essentially the same as the treatment of Jude. The two men, indeed, are extraordinarily alike: they are both in love with the same woman, both fail in much the same way at Christminster, both inhabit the same countryside and suffer the same loneliness. Their difference is in age and ability and passion. Phillotson, in short, is as much a projection of Jude as are the two women. He is a kind of Jude Senior: older, milder, with less talent and urgency, and so without the potentiality for tragedy. In one sense, the entire novel is simply the image of Jude magnified and subtly lit from different angles until he and his shadows occupy the whole Wessex landscape. And Jude in turn is an embodiment of the loneliness, deprivation and regret which are both the strength and constant theme of Hardy's best poetry. Hardy may have been perfectly justified in denying that the book was at all autobiographical, but it is a supremely vivid dramatization of the state of mind out of which Hardy's poetry emerged.

This is why Father Time fails as a symbol. He is introduced in one of the most beautiful passages of the novel:

He was Age masquerading as Juvenility, and doing it so badly that his real self showed through crevices. A ground-swell from ancient years of night seemed now and then to lift the child in this his morning-life, when his face took a back view over some great Atlantic of Time, and appeared not to care about what it saw.

And he is finally left in a paragraph of equal force:

The boy's face expressed the whole tale of their situation. On that little shape had converged all the inauspiciousness and shadow which had darkened the first union of Jude and all the accidents, mistakes, fears, errors of the last. He was their nodal point, their focus, their expression in a single term. For the rashness of those parents he had groaned, for their ill-assortment he had quaked, and for the misfortunes of these he had died.

But in between these two points, his ominous remarks, desolation, and self-consciously incurable melancholy are so overdone as to seem almost as though Hardy had decided to parody himself. Even the death of the children, and Father Time's appalling note – 'Done because we are too menny' – is dangerously close to being laughable: a situation so extreme, insisted on so strongly, seems more appropriate to *grand guignol* than to tragedy. But Hardy, I think, was forced to overdraw Father Time because the child is redundant in the scheme of the novel. What he represents was already embodied in fully tragic form in the figure of Jude. There was no way of repeating it without melodrama.

The power of *Jude the Obscure* is, then, less fictional than poetic. It arises less from the action or the fidelity of the setting than from the wholeness of the author's feelings. It is a tragedy whose unity is not Aristotelian but emotional. And the feelings are those which were later given perfect form in Hardy's best poetry. The work is the finest of Hardy's novels because it is the one in which the complex of emotions is, despite Father Time, least weakened by melodrama, bad plotting, and that odd incidental amateurishness of detail by which, perhaps, Hardy, all through his novel-writing period, showed his dissatisfaction with the form. It is also the finest because it is the novel in which the true Hardy hero is most fully vindicated, and the apparently fascinating myth of immaculate frigidity is finally exploded. But I wonder if Hardy was not being slightly disingenuous when he claimed that the treatment of the book by the popular reviewers had turned him, for good, from the novel to poetry. After *Jude the Obscure* there was no other direction in which he could go.

1961

Henry James's Travel Essays*

Henry James's essays on travel are essential, masterly and relatively neglected. They serve as a kind of dark side of the moon to the rest of his work; the harmony and incandescence of it all depends upon them. For the novels, they represent what has to an extraordinary degree been left out, or at least left understood. For James himself they are part of that great internal debate in which he argued out the morality of his cosmopolitanism.

A good deal of the sharpness of his social analysis, his habit of probing his surroundings to a depth at which he could no longer remain comfortable with them, was prompted by a distaste for his own fate:

> It is hard to say exactly what is the profit of comparing one race with another, and weighing in opposed groups the manners and customs of neighbouring countries; but it is certain that as we move about the world we constantly indulge in this exercise. This is especially the case if we happen to be infected with the baleful spirit of the cosmopolite – that uncomfortable consequence of seeing many lands and feeling at home in none. To be a cosmopolite is not, I think, an ideal; the ideal should be to be a concentrated patriot. Being a cosmopolite is an accident, but one must make the best of it. If you have lived about, as the phrase is, you have lost that sense of the absoluteness and the sanctity of the habits of your fellow-patriots which once made you so happy in the midst of them. You have seen that there are a great many *patriae* in the world, and that each of these is filled with excellent people for whom the local idiosyncrasies

* Henry James, *The Art of Travel*, edited by Morton Dauwen Zabel (New York: Doubleday, 1959).

are the only thing that is not rather barbarous. There comes a time when one set of customs, wherever it may be found, grows to seem to you about as provincial as another; and then I suppose it may be said of you that you have become a cosmopolite. You have formed the habit of comparing, of looking for points of difference and of resemblance, for present and absent advantages, for the virtues that go with certain defects, and the defects that go with certain virtues.

There is a hint of weariness and dis-ease about the tone, as of a man who is lamenting his fate more than he is defending his choice. For, in a way, James was born to cosmopolitanism. Professor Morton Zabel, in his thorough, perceptive introduction, produces a statement by brother William to the effect that Henry's real nationality was 'a native of the James family'. He was brought up, that is, to standards of civilization and morality that had not merely lost their general effectiveness but were hardly even pertinent to the great new powers and influences at work in the country. During James's lifetime the standards of the old American culture began to seem those of a less and less significant minority group. To the new criteria of power, wealth and technological skill James was by instinct and training wholly alien. When he returned to the States late in his life, he analysed in a curious way the failings of the New Hampshire landscape:

The teams, the carts, the conveyances in their kinds, the sallow, saturnine natives in charge of them, the enclosures, the fences, the gates, the wayside 'bits', of whatever sort, so far as these were referable to human attention or human neglect, kept telling the tale of the difference made, in a land of long winters, by the suppression of the two great factors of the English landscape, the squire and the parson.

What the squire and the parson do, between them, for appearances (which is what I am talking of) in scenes, predominantly Anglo-Saxon, subject to their sway, is brought home, as in an ineffable glow, when the elements are reduced to 'composing', in the still larger Anglo-Saxon light, without them. Here was no church, to begin with. . . . One lives among English ancientries, for instance, as in a world toward the furnishing of which religion has done a large part. And here, immediately, was a room vast and vacant, with a vacancy especially reducible, for most of the senses, to the fact of that elimination. Perpetually, inevitably, moreover, as the restless analyst wandered, the eliminated thing *par excellence* was the thing most absent to sight – and for which, oh! a thousand times, the small substitutes, the mere multiplication of signs of theological enterprise, in the tradition and on the scale of commercial and industrial enterprise, had no attention worth mentioning. The case, in the New Hampshire hills at least, was quite the same for the pervasive Patron, whose absence made such a whole . . . we lost ourselves in the intensity of the truth that to compare a simplified social order with a social order in which feudalism had once struck deep was the right way to measure the penetration of feudalism. If there was no point at which they had perceptibly begun, there was on the other side of the world no point at which they had perceptibly ceased. One's philosophy, one's logic might perhaps be muddled, but one clung to them for the convenience of their explanation of so much ugliness. The ugliness – one pounced, indeed, on this as on a talisman for the future – was the so complete abolition of *forms*.

The point James seems to be circling around is not just a lack of instinctive order and social hierarchies, nor is it the curiously untouched quality of the American landscape itself. That vibration in the American air which both excited and chilled him was of a wholly new type of culture: a culture that is apart from Europe's not merely because it is untouched by feudalism, but because it is completely post-Industrial Revolution, based squarely on technological achievement. The moral tradition of New England and the James standard of personal culture were about to be replaced by 'the American Way of Life'; that is, physical luxury, ease and the consumption of produced goods were about to become the standards by which the civilized life was to be judged. What James called the 'abolition of forms' might also be called the secularization of culture. It implies, among other things, a separation of general standards and individual morality.

James travelled, then, because his upbringing had made him something of an alien in his own country. The peculiarly social dimension of his moral sense did not, as he often complained, have enough to work on in the States. Neither did his almost metaphysical sense of order and form. So he travelled, as perhaps no European writer was by that time able to travel, as the last of the aristocrats. Professor Zabel suggests that James's wanderings have something in common with the Grand Tours of earlier generations. This is a question of something more than the classic route and the classic leisure. It is also a question of attitude: his alien, impartial curiosity, and his aristocrat's air of expecting to be amused. To be sure, the amusement was always of a most serious kind, that of a connoisseur of moral distinctions and fine experiences, yet amusement of a sort it seems to have been. Perhaps this is what he meant when he called himself 'a mere taster of produced tastes'. There is about his work a continual air of detachment, as of a man deliberately sampling views and customs and manners and climates, always a little from the outside, always as one who partakes only as it pleases him, not from need or loyalty, but to satisfy the endless requirements of a critical morality. 'It is', he remarked, 'a singular fact that a society that does nothing is decidedly more pictorial, more interesting to the eye of contemplation, than a society which is hard at work.' Were it not for his intelligence, he would seem at times to be engaged merely in a vast and slightly trivial exercise of his sensibility.

If I hesitate to use that phrase of a writer of James's calibre, it is because it calls up all too patly the brand of inert sensitivity associated with nether Bloomsbury and the Sitwells. The enormous difference is, of course, precisely in James's intelligence:

> Your first impression is therefore of the – what shall I call it? – of the abundance of petticoats. Every woman you meet, young or old, is attired with a certain amount of richness, and with whatever good taste may be compatible with such a mode of life. You behold an interesting, indeed a quite momentous spectacle; the democratization of elegance. If I am to believe what I hear – in fact, I may say what I overhear – many of these sumptuous persons have enjoyed neither the advantages of a careful education nor the privileges of an introduction to society. She walks more or less of a queen, however, each uninitiated nobody. She often has, in dress, an admirable instinct of elegance and even of what the French call 'chic'. This instinct occasionally mounts to a sort of passion; the result then is wonderful. You look at the coarse brick walls, the rusty iron posts of the piazza, at the shuffling negro waiters, the great tawdry steamboat-cabin of a drawing-room – you see the tilted ill-dressed loungers on the steps – and you finally regret that a figure so exquisite should have so vulgar a setting. Your resentment, however, is speedily tempered by reflection. You feel the impertinence of your old reminiscences of English and French novels, and of the dreary social order in which privacy was the presiding genius and women arrayed themselves for the appreciation of the few. The crowd, the tavern-loungers, the surrounding ugliness and tumult and licence, constitute the social medium of the young lady you are so inconsistent as to admire; she is dressed for publicity.

This is from one of his earliest essays, on Saratoga, when James's irony was still faintly defensive; there are moments in it where I, for one, could wish that his sense of being cultured, and therefore slightly apart, did not make him so superior. Yet even if the irony occasionally and almost imperceptibly wavers, the passage has a distinction which the merely sensitive could never achieve: quite simply it shows at every turn an extraordinary ability to *think*. None of the detail is there simply for its own sake. Running beneath it all is a logic which makes the description take its place in a larger order of values and concepts.

James, in fact, seems to have cultivated his sense of the object in order to clarify his world of values. That hint of amusement I mentioned comes from what seems, at first glance, to be a curious impartiality, or an indifference, as to what the object is: a cathedral or a woman's dress, the Grand Canal or the unemployed; it all seems equally useful material for 'the patient, the inner vision' – in other words, for his own ends. This is, presumably, the cosmopolitan's critical impartiality, the privilege of, to use James's own phrase, 'the restless analyst'. But it presumes on a calm lack of commitment not merely impossible in our day, but faintly improper. Since the burden of social guilt has become more evenly spread, that pause and deliberation of James's discriminations has set him utterly apart from our present age and habits. For all his wit, intelligence and seriousness, for all the quickness and impartiality of his eye, James the traveller is, fundamentally, very remote. He can be admired but, despite the American *littérateurs* in Paris and Rome, despite the American undergraduates in Oxford, he cannot, with any conviction, be copied.

His genius for catching the essence of what he described was born of two qualities: first, his aristocratic knack of treating everything as though it were created for his own private satisfaction; second, the leisurely, spacious style of his investigations:

> I spent a long time looking at this monument. I revolved around it, like a moth around a candle; I went away and I came back; I chose twenty different standpoints; I observed it during the different hours of the day, and saw it in the moonlight as well as the sunshine. I gained, in a word, a certain sense of familiarity with it; and yet I despair of giving any coherent account of it.

(The *it* in question is Chartres Cathedral.) This is the style of the Grand Tour, where each accredited object of historic importance is treated as an essential cultural document, to be studied with as much relish and intensity as Shakespeare's plays. And James, with his wonderful ability of turning everything to his own uses, created from each 'required' scene images of his own sensitized intelligence. Hence there is something rather static about the world he creates in these sketches; the richness of his civilized sensibility seems composed of the richness of places and things frozen in their motion. The modern traveller, on the other hand, seems far less concerned with things than with the surrounding air. 'Comes over one an absolute necessity to move': that is Lawrence at the start of *Sea and Sardinia*; it is a motto for the age. The modern writer, in fact, is driven by restlessness, by irritation, by the sense of confinement. He is less interested in scenes and the accretions of culture than in a change of sky. Perhaps this is why the main stream now flows towards America, where the skies are larger, instead of towards Europe. For since its power has begun to decline, Europe has been left with a sense of history without a corresponding sense of potentiality. The landscape has begun to seem so cluttered with traditions gradually emptied of their significance – much as the English horizons are eternally cluttered with clouds boding bad weather – that there is no longer the elbow-room for much creative originality. In Europe history is everywhere and the habits of order and form are still, more or less, automatically adhered to; but the vitality of the society that once made them valid is rapidly fading. And so the writers travel by a kind of instinct of self-preservation; they move, as Lawrence said of the Pilgrim Fathers, simply 'to get away'.

Fundamentally, then, it is his pervasive sense of society that sets James, as a traveller, apart from our time. I suggested that all his details resolve at some point into concepts, and that he himself seemed to justify his wanderings by the degree to which they helped him define his own inner world of values. But in his art these values were always tested in the realm of social intercourse. He is, in fact, a novelist of manners, in the sense that manners, when they cease to be mere formulae, can become the expression of the most deeply felt human values. This has two rather different effects on his travel essays. The first is that when he set out to catch in words the essence of a place, he always finished by conveying less of its appearance than of its implications; by conveying, that is, a sense of the civilization it produces and of the peculiar forces it exerts on the social imagination. It is for this reason that most of these essays were written for American readers. Having more or less defined the failings of the American scene – 'You feel around you, with irresistible force, the eloquent silence of undedicated nature – the absence of serious associations, the nearness, indeed, of the vulgar and trivial associations of the least complete of all cities of pleasure' – James went on, through the endless variety of his travel sketches, to describe the depth and complexity of civilization he needed as a writer; to give, in short, the reasons for his self-imposed exile.

The second effect of this social filter through which all his impressions passed was to make every scene, to an extraordinary degree, seem peopled. Not that 'characters' proliferate, as in a Dickens novel, with warts on their faces, tricks of speech and idiosyncrasies of dress. But then, neither do physical details of place. James was accurate without giving any great impression of being painstaking; he never described each last curlicue on the façade. Instead, he caught the spirit of his chosen places by transforming them, literally, into people: a city, for James, was always *she* rather than *it*. London, Paris, Venice, New York became in themselves protagonists in a drama in which James was the other hero.

I implied earlier that there is a disconcerting impartiality about James's use of material that appears at times very like callousness. At first sight, it is as though he treated the London poor as if they were as much or as little useful for his purposes as the London churches. He seems interested but not much bothered. This impression is, in fact, not quite accurate. James may have described the unemployed with little of the sympathy and certainly none of the indignation that would be expected of him today:

> The neighbourhood has been much purified of late, but it still contains a collection of specimens – though it is far from unique in this – of the low, black element.

In itself, poverty was faintly distasteful. It became significant for James as a darkening trait in one of the greatest characters he ever created: London. And it is a trait of which, when he passes judgement on his heroine, he has taken better account than one had expected:

> And yet I should not go so far as to say that it is a condition of such geniality to close one's eyes upon the immense misery; on the contrary, I think it is partly because we are irremediably conscious of that great dark gulf that the most general appeal of the great city remains exactly what it is, the largest chapter of human accidents.

His vision has suffered the same sense of restrained shock as when, in *The American Scene*, he discovered that his account had to face not only antipathetic standards of wealth, power and progress, but also the more poignant indignities of Ellis Island. The event becomes, to use the habitual phrase, the creative shock of recognition.

I began by saying that the travel sketches were something more than an essential part of James's artistic development; they are also a complement of the novels. They speak eloquently for those mute background forces which James, in the refining process of his imagination, left understood. The novels do, of course, have a number of beautiful evocations of scene; Professor Zabel quotes some of them. Yet James is, I think, one of the last novelists one would think of if challenged to produce a list of the great masters of description. The human intensity of his imagination seems so very much more potent. Indeed, one of his greatest triumphs, *The Awkward Age*, owes much of its power to the manner in which all description has been rigorously pruned away. Yet however much or little he described, the cities and countryside of James's Europe are continually present in the novels. Like Banquo's ghost at the party, they are forces which, unseen and unmentioned, thread themselves into the plots and dictate to the protagonists the feelings and actions possible to them. James has been accused, for example, of a certain perversity at the end of *The Portrait of a Lady*. The charge is that by making Isabel Archer return to her husband and her great brooding house in Florence, he was doing dirt on the passion and style he had given her. The excuses are obvious enough: the child, her sense of responsibility to her own choice, her acknowledgement of her own arrogance. But there is also the pressure exerted by the place itself:

> Your sense of the fineness of the finest [villas] [wrote James of Florence] is of something very grave and stately; your sense of the bravery of two or three of the best something quite tragic and sinister. From what does this latter impression come? You gather it as you stand there in the early dusk, with your eyes on the long, pale-brown façade, the enormous windows, the iron cages fastened to the lower ones. Part of the brooding expression of these great houses comes, even when they have not fallen into decay, from their look of having outlived their original use. Their extraordinary largeness and massiveness are a satire on their present fate. . . . I don't know whether it was the appearance of these stony old villas, which seemed so dumbly conscious of a change of manners, that threw a tinge of melancholy over the general prospect; certain it is that, having always found this note as of a myriad old sadnesses in solution in the view of Florence, it seemed to me now particularly strong.

There are phrases in this that might, without any significant alteration, be used of Isabel herself. And one can at least say that once she had thrown in her lot in that particular way with that particular place, the rest was inevitable.

It is the same with *The Ambassadors*, though with a rather different effect. Paris and its surroundings are brought to life with such love and imaginative energy that I find it hard to know who, in fact, is the hero. If Strether's final renunciation seems to me more trivial than tragic, that is not because I consider a life-sentence to a New England provincial town to be a fate less savage than James suggests – it may well be – but because France herself has been endowed with such a glow of life that Strether is, in comparison, hardly interesting.

Professor Zabel's excellent collection of essays in *The Art of Travel* provides yet another proof of the wholeness of James's creative effort. He analysed the two great poles of his work, England and America, with the same vividness, moral insight and persuasive humanity as he brought to bear on his novels. Apparently, a number of the essays were originally intended to be journalism. All one can say, in the face of what was actually written, is that James succeeded, as always, in bringing the trivial form up to the level of his own intelligence. And he was, after all, one of the most intelligent men who has ever written.

The Kenyon Review, 1959

D. H. Lawrence*

Every time a book on Lawrence is published, someone or other is insulted. And there have been, so far, over 800 books on the man. As for the articles: no one, to my knowledge, has ever counted them up. Qualified and unqualified, admirers and detractors, everyone who met him sooner or later says his say about Lawrence. His personal myth has absorbed nearly all the interest; friends, enemies and general reading public, his work, his theories and his life itself, have suffered for it.

The myth is simply that of genius: 'they were always telling me I had got genius, as if to console me for not having their own incomparable advantages'. Lawrence was right; the label 'genius' was a sleight of hand which spared the *littérateurs* the trouble of taking him, not seriously, but directly. For the popular fiction of a genius is, after all, always of a creature apart, someone imaginatively unpredictable, whose insights, for all their uncanny depth, are never much concern of ours. In Lawrence's early days, when the Russian fever was raging, genius meant Dostoevsky, with his queer, strained intuitions into the nature of hysteria, disintegration and the Slavic soul. By most counts, Lawrence was quite as alien: he was a miner's son who wrote brilliantly without the 'inestimable advantages' of a Public-School–University education; he offended the respectable by running away with a married woman; he offended class distinctions because the woman was also a Baronin; he pooh-poohed Bloomsbury-Cambridge intellectualism ('He sniffed. "Have you ever seen him

* Edward Nehls, *D. H. Lawrence: A Composite Biography*, 3 vols. (Madison: University of Wisconsin Press, 1957–9).

in a bathing dress?" he asked. "Poor Bertie Russell! He is all Disembodied Mind!" '); he was technically original, yet had no hand in the American-Irish experimentalism; he lived off his writing without ever being beholden to the literary world; two of his most important novels were banned and his paintings were almost burned by the police; in his later years he was the prey of cultists and middle-aged vampires; the critics, to a man, misunderstood him. 'No one', said E. M. Forster, 'who alienates both Mrs Grundy and Aspatia can hope for a good obituary press.' It has taken over thirty years for some kind of balance to be restored. If the mark of genius is alienation and lack of intelligent recognition, Lawrence is the genius to end them all.

The bickering ghosts have at last been laid by Mr Edward Nehls, whose huge work, *D. H. Lawrence: A Composite Biography*, is at last complete. It is an extraordinary and original piece of literary history, perhaps the most creative thing of its kind since Lowes's *The Road to Xanadu.* Mr Nehls has gathered up every scrap of evidence about Lawrence. He has sifted biographies, memoirs, fictional portraits, broadcasts, diaries, letters and essays. He has unearthed new letters by Lawrence, a fragment of an unpublished novel, photographs, and a mound of new material about 'Miriam', including one of her stories. He has gone round to everyone who ever met Lawrence and wheedled reminiscences from them, following Lawrence from his childhood – 'The people of Eastwood', announced one of the miners, 'do not make a fuss over him' – to New Mexico and Australia. He has transcribed the Parliamentary backchat about the various bannings, the scandalized headlines and scandalizing muck-spreading of the journalists. He has even ploughed through the obituaries. To all this he has added a huge glossary of the lives of everyone who ever had anything to do with Lawrence, a bibliography and a list of major first editions. Mr Nehls himself has kept scrupulously out of the picture. The vast welter of material is linked by Lawrence's own account of his life, as he told it in his letters. But the massive coherence and thoroughness of the work is entirely the editor's. No doubt Lawrence would have hated it, but I think Mr Nehls, in his devoted, scholarly way, has a touch of genius himself.

His greatest step towards fairness and balance is in winkling comments from the non-professionals. For Lawrence never got on with his fellow-writers. The older ones he suspected of condescension – 'let them learn decent respect' – with young admirers he was patient but over-borne – 'you know what a depressing effect admirers have on me – I want to die'. But with his contemporaries the cycle of friendship was depressingly regular: mutual enthusiasm; then gradual disillusionment as Lawrence worked down to the bedrock of disagreement; in the end, he would crystallize his antagonism in fiction. The friendship would rarely survive publication, and hardly any of his 'friends' resisted the chance of paying him back after he was dead. The only professional writers to come out with clean slates are Catherine Carswell, Rhys Davies, E. M. Forster, Aldous Huxley and, in his grudging way, Richard Aldington.

So it is the non-professional writers who restore the balance. They have no axes to grind, no scores to pay back, and above all no public personalities to maintain. They describe Lawrence as a man rather than as a butt for their own private intensities. For each opinion on one side Mr Nehls has dug out someone who said the opposite; and the opinions range from the colour of his eyes to the colour of his politics.

The contradictions, of course, have their place. There are four stages in Lawrence's 'savage pilgrimage'. The schoolmaster who appeared in the office of *The English Review* was still a bit of a 'mard-arsed kid': literary, priggish (*The Trespasser* is an intensely priggish variation on the theme of romantic free love) and ambitious for a mythical two thousand a year. 'He was a terrific snob,' said Rachel Annand Taylor, 'he was definitely a cad, yet . . . he was touching, he was so artlessly trying to find his way.' But the prig didn't survive his mother's death. He went off with Frieda and found himself having to face the responsibility not only for her carelessness but for her immense freedom and sense of life. By writing *Sons and Lovers* he fought himself clear of his lacerating mother-love and was free to move on to his most original work, *The Rainbow* and *Women in Love*. But the war started, *The Rainbow* was banned, and the police chased him from Cornwall. In *Women in Love* an exotic darkness is setting in; Dr Leavis called it 'jargon'. It was heightened by his steady lack of impersonal, intelligent criticism. The third stage, the wander years, began at the end of the war. When Lawrence broke with England, he broke with form. Compared with his earlier novels, *The Lost Girl* and *Aaron's Rod* are haphazard in their development. The further Lawrence went from his English roots, the more his cults, the dark gods and blood consciousness grew. In

Kangaroo, *The Boy in the Bush* and *The Plumed Serpent* the prophet is continually getting the upper hand of the artist. The final stage came when Lawrence returned from Mexico. It was a period of new lucidity, when the imminence of his death sharpened his sense of life till it hurt. He wrote his calmest, most tender novels, *Lady Chatterley's Lover* and *The Virgin and the Gipsy*.

In the whole cycle, his life and his work interact continually. There is small difference between his imaginative prose style and his letters; and the letters, apparently, sounded exactly as he spoke. The man, in Lawrence's case, was the style. It is this that made for the uncanny hold he had over people. It had nothing to do with the cult of alien genius. All that weight of prophecy, the discipleship of those battling, vindictive women, the nagging about the dark gods, blur the main issue: Lawrence's genius was a kind of personal spell he cast over everyone he met and everything he wrote.

What now seems prophetic about him is not the prophecies but his carelessness, a certain iconoclastic vitality, toughness, gaiety and common sense that kept both him and his work alive. He was, above all, a free man and, despite his occasional bursts of class-consciousness, he seems now classless. Perhaps the oddest thing about Mr Nehls's three volumes is the amount of time spent wrangling about how much, how little, or simply if, Lawrence was a gentleman. It colours both physical descriptions of the man – 'He was the type of the plumber's mate who goes back to fetch the tools' (David Garnett) – and critical judgements – 'Scholars and men of the world will not find much inspiration in these novels. Lawrence opened a little window for the *bourgeoisie*. That is his life-work' (Norman Douglas). It is all about as wise and meaningful as the U–non-U controversy. Lawrence was neither a gentleman nor an upstart because he judged success in terms of human and artistic integrity, not in terms of position. He said so himself, in an autobiographical fragment, discovered by Mr Nehls:

> In 1915 *The Rainbow* was suppressed for immorality – and the sense of detachment from the bourgeois world, the world which controls press, publication and all, became almost complete. He had no interest in it, no desire to be at one with it. Anyhow the suppression of *The Rainbow* had proved it impossible. Henceforth he put away any idea of 'success', of succeeding with the British bourgeois public, and stayed apart.

The trick of birth, temperament and censorship which pushed him outside the society of his time has made him in some way typical of ours. (The censorship, incidentally, was helped out by the artistic as well as the legal guardians of the country, as Frieda's younger daughter points out:

> I sent a telegram therefore to Osbert Sitwell, who was in London: 'Discobole, Paris, propose filming Lawrence novel. May we inspect Renishaw Hall?' To this he replied, 'If you refer banned book *Lady Chatterley's Lover* your request gross as it is libellous'.)

Like Lawrence, the artist in contemporary mass-society is foot-loose, self-sufficient and, in a way, threatened – Lawrence worked under the shadow of his illness; the modern artist works under that of total war. He is more concerned with the roots of his personality than with his conforming social shell. The details, too, fit: from doing his own housework to the slangy irreverent style, which now reads more naturally than all that fine, sensitive writing that was once called Style.

'All you young writers', he once said, 'have me to thank for what freedom you enjoy, even as things are, for being able to say much that you couldn't even hint at before I appeared. It was I who set about smashing down the barriers.' By and large, he was right. And now Mr Nehls has got rid of the final barrier: the recriminations, apologies, enthusiasms and malice that make up the myth of Lawrence. Now, perhaps, after thirty years' bickering, we can let the man rest in peace and get back to what matters: his work.

The New Statesman, 1959

Ronald Firbank*

Firbank's novels have been done no good at all by the Firbank myth. That coddled, wealthy *flâneur*, the darling of the Sitwells, who started writing under the influence of the Yellow Book, flourished at the Café Royal and died at the height of the twittering twenties, is a depressing period piece. And each new fragment of the myth makes him seem the more insufferable: the squirming, giggling shyness, the gossip, the absolute snobbery, the neurotic preciousness and drunken Catholic homosexuality; he seems to be in the most tiresome tradition of English eccentricity. An air of aesthetic deliciousness still clings to him in our own time: Sandy Wilson made *Valmouth* into a musical; John Betjeman called him 'a jewelled and clockwork nightingale singing among London sparrows' (oddly enough in *The Daily Herald*); even Anthony Powell, in his Preface to *The Complete Ronald Firbank*, prescribes reading him in bed 'against a pile of pillows' and warns sternly against the pangs of commitment or similar literary maladies. Of course, Firbank is not responsible for what has been written about him; but a man is judged, as they say, by the company he keeps.

Not all of the company, however, has been lightweight. E. M. Forster took Firbank seriously enough, and Edmund Wilson called him 'the poet of the *fou rire*', tracing his lineage back to Congreve and Jonson. And now that his tics have at last become simply a part of the history of taste and manners, one can see why. Firbank emerges as a curiously impressive writer – scarcely inspiring, perhaps, but of considerable subtlety and originality. Contrary to the

* *The Complete Ronald Firbank* (London: Duckworth, 1961).

myth of the indolent amateur living off his unearned income and his connections, he seems to have been a writer of surprising dedication. *Vainglory*, his first serious novel, was written in two years of almost total isolation in Oxford at the beginning of the First World War.

To immure himself in a university town may have been an odd reaction to a major disaster, but it was, at least, single-minded and typical of him. In a way, all his work can be read as a kind of uneasy acknowledgement of the tensions that run just below the level of social chatter. He had, in fact, briefly sounded his characteristic note before *Vainglory*, in *The Artificial Princess*:

> 'Tell me, Sir Oliver,' she demanded, 'have you ever been to Greece?'
>
> 'More than once,' Sir Oliver dryly replied, 'I even married, *en secondes noces*, a Lesbian. . . .'
>
> 'A native of Lesbos? Just fancy that!' the Baroness marvelled, apprais-ing a passing débutante, a young girl in a mousseline robe of palest *Langue de chat*.
>
> '*Née* a Demitraki.'
>
> 'A demi what?' the Baroness abstrusely twittered, blinking at the intermittent lightning in the sky.

All the Firbank ingredients are in that: the faintly absurd, perverse jokes and misunderstandings and, at the same time, a sense of ominous unease. At the critical moment in nearly all his novels, the sky flickers with summer lightning. There is always the impression of a storm raging just beyond the limits of his own elegant world.

Except by the remotest implication, the storms, of course, are nothing as grand as the international and social upheavals which were going on around him. They are storms in the head, fine-drawn *crises de nerfs*. Nerves, in fact, were his genius:

> The gardens looked almost heroic in the evening light. If the statues, that lit the sombre evergreens of the walks, did *not* suggest Phidias, they did, at least, their duty.
>
> 'When the birds fly low, and the insects turn, and turn,' she said, 'there's rain!'
>
> Lady Castleyard closed her eyes.
>
> 'I like a storm,' she murmured, 'particularly at night. Sometimes one can catch a face in it – somebody one's been wondering about, perhaps, or who's been wondering of you. And one meets in the explosion.'

The writing is economical and the invocation precise. But what is being invoked is nothing exotic; Firbank's lush, moody overwriting occurs extensively only in *Santal* and *Valmouth* – his *Brideshead*

Revisited, and equally disastrous. What is being invoked is, instead, the neurasthenic. In their bright way, Firbank's novels have more in common with Eliot's 'A Game of Chess' than with the pure purple of Lawrence Durrell or, as Mr Powell suggests, with Proust or Joyce. (Occasionally, his prose does sound like one of Joyce's riper parodies, but the only stream of consciousness Firbank ever managed was that of an over-sensitive feminine socialite.)

Firbank's difficulty as a writer was to anchor his general nervousness of tone to anything as specific as a plot or a person. It is virtually impossible to distinguish one of his characters from the next; apart from the mildly offensive coon language of his Negroes, they all talk alike, think alike and behave alike. They all twitter with the same witty disconnectedness; they are all overfastidious, very bored and pained by the sexual politics they dabble in. And they all have their vague other-worldly yearnings: Mrs Shamefoot, in *Vainglory*, wants to be immortalized in a stained-glass window: Miss Collins, in Firbank's finest early novel *Inclinations*, wants Romance in the shape of an Italian count, while her elderly companion, Miss O'Brookomore, wants it in the shape of Miss Collins; Miss Sinquier in *Caprice* wants Fame on the London stage; the characters in *Valmouth* are divided equally between Roman Catholicism and the Exotic (the latter represented either by Mrs Yajñavalkya, the Negress who specializes in a kind of Voodoo physiotherapy, or by her lush daughter); the boy Cherif, in *Santal*, wants Allah; in *The Flower Beneath the Foot*, Laura de Nazianzi unwillingly transmutes her love of Prince Yousef into mysticism (we are told, in a footnote, that she eventually became a saint); Mrs Mouth in *Prancing Nigger* wants the glamour of Big City Society; Cardinal Pirelli lapses into a remarkably pious death, stark naked save for his mitre, while chasing a choir-boy round his church; most of the minor characters devote their energies to being scourged; and in the play, *The Princess Zoubaroff*, the members of the opposite sex want nothing to do with each other – the husbands go off climbing together, their wives retire to a Lesbian convent and the year-old child is sent away to school. It is the world of *The Waste Land* seen by a man who is too hopelessly involved in it to afford to be anything except amused.

Just as all Firbank's characters seem projections of the one set of jangled nerves, so the plots are barely distinguishable. Admittedly, things do happen: one person goes off with another, someone else is frustrated. And there are sudden explosions of violence; but, like those summer storms, they occur just off the page. A cathedral is struck by lightning; poor Miss Sinquier dies falling through a stage trapdoor. And so on. But each tragedy occurs between the chapters. It is like Firbank's attitude to the First World War: large-scale events may influence his work profoundly, but he would look at them only out of the very corner of his eye.

So the novels proper are carried on in a series of conversational gasps, each scene perfectly formed in itself, but each leading almost nowhere. Yet since all the works are, to use his own phrase, 'Studies in Temperament', events are not really needed. He can achieve all his effects through the pauses and flickering of polite talk. In this way, his jokes are as concentrated and as subtly maintained as his most serious efforts:

'Go to the window, Willie,' the Queen exhorted her Consort, fixing an eye on the last trouser button that adorned his long, straggling legs.

The King, who had the air of a tired pastry-cook, sat down.

'We feel,' he said, 'to-day, we've had our fill of stares!'

'One little bow, Willie,' the Queen entreated, 'that wouldn't kill you.'

'We'd give perfect worlds,' the King went on, 'to go, by Ourselves, to bed.'

. . . 'Whenever I go out,' the King complained, 'I get an impression of raised hats.'

It was seldom King William of Pisguera spoke in the singular tense, and Doctor Babcock looked perturbed.

'Raised hats, sir?' he murmured in impressive tones.

'Nude heads, doctor.'

There is no essential difference between this brilliant absurdity at the beginning of *The Flower Beneath the Foot* and the charged, yearning close of *Prancing Nigger*:

Led by an old Negress leaning on her hickory staff, the procession came.

Banners, banners, banners.

'I hope Mimi wave!'

Floating banners against the dusk. . . .

'Oh, honey! See dat lil pilgrim boy?'

> '*Time like an ever-rolling stream,*
> *Bears all its sons away;*
> *They fly forgotten, as a dream*
> *Dies at the opening day.*'

'Mimi, Mimi!' She had flung the roses from her dress. 'Look up, my deah, look up.'

But her cry escaped unheard.

> '*They fly forgotten, as a dream*
> *Dies—*'

The echoing voices of those behind lingered a little.

Both passages employ the same technical shorthand, a kind of verbal *pointillisme*, which, instead of defining the scene straight out, makes it shine through the contrasting, often clashing details.

The ability to shade the potentially tragic imperceptibly into the social and absurd was part of Firbank's gift as an artist, but it was also part of his central weakness. The persistent, underlying theme in all his work is the total, heartless disconnection of one person from another; everything is gossip and manoeuvring. Against this pervasive yet fascinating malice, Firbank evolved two defences: the first was an infinitely clever vagueness, which gave the novels their wit; the second was the attenuated moods, nerves and semi-religious languishings, which were his equivalent of a sense of tragedy. But he never finally distinguished between the two, never realized that moods only become properly serious when rooted in values as well as taste.

At this point, no doubt, Mr Powell would accuse me of priggishness. I can't help it; Firbank himself asks to be taken seriously, both for his skill and for the simple fact that the major influence on his mature work was not the Yellow Book but Henry James. *The Awkward Age* is the only novel I can think of before Firbank in which a tragedy is developed almost exclusively through the nuances of social chit-chat. But where James was always far enough outside his characters to see them dispassionately for what they were worth, Firbank was wholly at the mercy of his. All his artistic effort went into endowing them with a witty, temperamental glamour.

The Firbank myth is curiously akin to the Firbank novels. Both might have been the creations of one of James's tenser socialites. But they are the Master turned upside-down. For James, every intrigue sooner or later assumed the proportions of a monstrous perversion of morality. For Firbank, on the other hand, perversion is taken for granted as the basic moral norm. The result is an infinite, cold boredom from which the only escape is in vapours, jokes, fine moods and absurd calamities. 'Imagine the world, my friends,' says the Archbishop of Cuna, 'had Christ been born a girl!' Firbank created a world in which, apparently, He was.

The New Statesman, 1961

Dashiell Hammett*

I had better admit straight away that I find most detective stories unreadable. I haven't the knack of skimming simply for clues and the plot. So for the sake of the crossword-puzzle interest of solving the things, it never seems worth while wading through all that terrible prose, the type-casting of the characters and the inane exchange of clichés that passes for dialogue in the average Agatha Christie. On the old issue of 'Who Cares Who Killed Roger Ackroyd?' I'm on Edmund Wilson's side. With one exception. Wilson also thought nothing of Dashiell Hammett – or nothing, at least, of *The Maltese Falcon*, which was the only one he claimed to have read. I suppose he was irritated by the way Hammett was taken up by the intellectuals during the thirties: Gide, Sinclair Lewis, Robert Graves – Hammett had powerful friends.

Yet reading his complete novels in a splendid new one-volume collected edition, thirty-five years after they first appeared, he seems to have deserved them. His books tell you more about the States than many with more high-minded intentions, like Upton Sinclair's. They also have that air of moral lobotomy that seems so to preoccupy us nowadays. Above all, with their elegant plots and stripped, clean writing, they have their own unwavering kind of perfection. Only one of them fails: *The Dain Curse*, which is wandering, melodramatic, a bit silly and, with its supernatural trimmings, not at all typical. Though it was published second, my guess is that it was an apprentice work, written earlier and rushed into print only after the success of *Red Harvest*.

* *The Novels of Dashiell Hammett* (New York: Knopf, 1965).

This quirky perfection is appropriate for Hammett was in all ways an odd phenomenon: stylish, original, without a trace of the literary about him. Born in Maryland in 1894, he left school at fourteen and wandered through the usual grinding odd jobs – messenger boy, newsboy, clerk, timekeeper, yardman, machine operator, stevedore – finally landing up as a private eye for the famous Pinkerton's Detective Agency. He served as a sergeant in the First World War, but it ruined his health and for some time after he was in and out of hospitals. Though he never fully recovered, he went back to Pinkerton's until the vast success of his novels (four of them were made into films) gave him his freedom. The whole of his collected works was published in the space of five years: *Red Harvest* appeared in February 1929, *The Dain Curse* six months later, in February 1930 came *The Maltese Falcon*, *The Glass Key* in April 1931, and *The Thin Man* in January 1934. According to his friend Lillian Hellman, who has written a brief foreword to this collection, he started another novel but never finished it. For the last twenty-seven years of his life he published nothing. He was a sergeant again in the Second World War and did not die until 1961.

It is a curious history: a lifetime's literary output which did not begin until he was thirty-five years old and had already finished when he was forty; obscurity before it, silence after. It is almost as if he weren't interested in writing as such, only in making his fortune; and when that was done he retired, as though from a business. Yet that explanation clearly won't do when faced by the purity and concentration of his style. Nor will the classical Freudian line: the laconic, tough-guy hero – who was utterly Hammett's invention, however much he has since been copied – was a compensation for his own failing health. The books are neither that simple nor that self-satisfied, and have to do with a good deal more than toughness.

They also have little to do with conventional detective routine: crime, complication of suspects and clues, and final neat solution by the omniscient, omnipotent sleuth. In Hammett's books the actual finding of the murderer is almost by the way. When Nick Charles does a particularly slick bit of summing-up at the end of *The Thin Man*, his wife gets the last word: 'That may be,' Nora said, 'but it's all pretty unsatisfactory.' Hammett seems to have felt that way too. As often as not he gets the straight who-done-itry out of the way early and then goes on to something else, or at least to further, casual who-done-its which add up to something else. The crime puzzle matters less than the mentality, the habit of crime. Even in *The Thin Man*, which is smarter, more deliberately sophisticated, and also more conventional than the rest (its hero, like Hammett himself, has already made his pile and given up sleuthing), the main interest is its view of New York just after the crash, with its nervy, slanderous parties, sporadically violent speakeasies, disintegrating boozing and permanent hangovers. It might have been written by some sour-mouthed Scott Fitzgerald who was never for a moment taken in by the dizzy glamour of it all.

But his best novels, *Red Harvest* and *The Glass Key*, are not really detective stories at all. They are political; they are about what happens and how it feels when the gangsters take over. *Red Harvest*, for example, is set in an ugly Western mining town which is virtually owned by one man:

> For forty years old Elihu Willson . . . had owned Personville, heart, soul, skin and guts. He was president and majority stockholder of the Personville Mining Corporation, ditto of the First National Bank, owner of the *Morning Herald* and *Evening Herald*, the city's only newspapers, and at least part owner of nearly every other enterprise of any importance. Along with these pieces of property he owned a United States senator, a couple of representatives, the governor, the mayor, and most of the state legislature. Elihu Willson was Personville, and he was almost the whole state.

That ironic acceptance of how things are dictates Hammett's tone and pervades the whole story, however savage it becomes. Willson has had trouble from the Wobblies; to break their strikes he has imported gunmen. But the hoods have found the pickings too good to leave, and gradually they have slid out of his control. So Willson reluctantly allows a private eye in on the act. He, the narrator, is forty, overweight, thick with booze, and more or less without principles.

With a kind of blank cunning, like a good poker-player, he sets the gangs against each other. There are twenty murders before the place is finally tidied up. Only one is a normal 'mystery', and that is cleared up early. The real interest is in the effect of all this carnage on the narrator:

> 'This damned burg's getting me. If I don't get away soon I'll be going blood-simple like the natives. . . . I've arranged a killing or two in my time, when they were necessary. But this is the first time I ever got the

fever. . . . Look. I sat at Willson's table tonight and played them like you'd play trout, and got just as much fun out of it. I looked at Noonan and knew he hadn't a chance in a thousand of living another day because of what I had done to him, and I laughed, and felt warm and happy inside. That's not me. . . . After twenty years of messing around with crime I can look at any sort of murder without seeing anything in it but my bread and butter, the day's work. But this getting a rear out of planning deaths is not natural to me.'

This has less in common with Agatha Christie than with *The Revenger's Tragedy*. The killings are not a game or a puzzle or a joke. Instead, they are at one with the obsessional, illicit drinking, the drug-taking, the police beatings-up – all casual symptoms of prevailing corruption.

You have only to compare this with factual histories of prohibition and its legacy (see *Murder, Inc.*, 1951, by Burton B. Turkus, Assistant D.A. of New York) to see that Hammett exaggerated nothing; indeed, he may even have toned down the realities. Yet his massacres are intriguing neither as social history nor because they cater so nicely to our sadistic fantasies – as do his imitators, in descending order from Raymond Chandler to Mickey Spillane. The fascination of Hammett's writing is that it makes the killing somehow different: accepted, habitual, part, as he says, of 'the day's work'. It has the ordinariness of real nihilism. And this makes him seem peculiarly close to us, though we now accept violence on a grander scale and expect our politicians not to be owned by gangsters but themselves to behave like gangsters.

God forbid I should foist any large moral significance on thrillers dealing mostly with American small-town politics. But Hammett has a genius, and part of it lies in his ability to make corruption seem normal without ever quite endorsing it. His heroes have all undergone that brutalizing which Lawrence called 'the breaking of the heart'; and obscurely they know it. Hence the conventional barriers are down between the goodies and baddies. Those laconic, wise-cracking investigators may see all, know all, and handle themselves with startling confidence, but they are essentially no better, no worse, than the crooks they outwit. The narrator in *Red Harvest* becomes 'blood-simple'; Ned Beaumont, in *The Glass Key*, is an underworld figure, henchman of a political boss; Sam Spade in *The Maltese Falcon* and Nick Charles in *The Thin Man*, in their controlled, cynical, alcoholic ways, both qualify as psychopaths. All are liars when it suits them, all are indifferent to murder, all are marginally corrupt. They win out only because they are more able, more canny and, above all, more thorough-going with their contempt. Such toughness makes them seem impregnable, but it is also a burden. At moments, fatigue and distaste for themselves comes over them like a sickness. It is as though the habitual violence pulled them psychically apart and they then had to reassemble themselves through booze and cunning and patience. You can sense Hammett's own illness through all that hard-boiled glitter.

It is his steady refusal to expect anything beyond the immediate, and usually rather nasty, situation, or to presume on any values anywhere, that makes for the curious distinction of his style: the wit, the flair for essential details, the suppressed, pared-down, indifferent clarity. His achievement is to have evolved a prose in which the most grotesque or shocking details are handled as though they were matters of routine, part of the job. Granted, Hemingway's simplicity was devoted to much the same end and was capable of far greater subtleties; but it was also a deeply literary device, almost dandified at times, something he had learned the hard way from Gertrude Stein. Hammett, too, was a writer of considerable deliberation and skill, but he made his taut style, like his ear for gangsterese, sound as though it were something he had come by in the grind of being a Pinkerton's agent. He seems less to have evolved his style than to have earned it.

Maybe this is what makes him so sympathetic. At the moment, the serious arts are faced with gloomy choices: either they are tense with despair at the confusion of all the values on which they were traditionally based, or they are anxiously – and suicidally – scrambling aboard the pop wagon. Dashiell Hammett, who had no cultural pretensions at all, provides a hard-minded alternative: his books have artistic concentration without literariness, they achieve their purity from their absence of values. They are meticulous, witty, authentic and utterly nihilistic. It may not be high art, but it is a relief.

The Spectator, 1966

Norman Mailer's *An American Dream**

Norman Mailer's last book, a collection of essays and occasional pieces, was called *The Presidential Papers*. It was offered as a kind of corrective to the late President. From it, the theory was, Kennedy might learn something of the psychic realities of the States, something to offset the great mass of predigested facts which was his official daily diet. The idea was not quite as off as it sounds, for Kennedy – a Harvard man like Mailer, not much older, and with a gossipy interest in the cultural world – was the only American president who might really have read a book of this type, however quizzically. What was off, however, was something never explicitly stated but sharply present in the tone of the writing: a continual, irritated buzz of implication that Mailer was not so much advising Kennedy as competing with him, and that the book was a way of setting out his qualifications for the boss's job.

An American Dream is Mailer's presidential novel. Kennedy appears in the first sentence and reappears just before the climax ('Kelly returned. "It was Jack," he said to me. "He said to send you his regards and commiserations . . . I didn't know you knew him." '). In between are dramatized some of the qualities needed for the making of an Existential President. Rojack, Mailer's hero – university professor, TV personality, ex-Congressman and war-time hero – is alive to his impulses and accepts the risks of acting them out; he is responsible to his buried madness. In one chapter he murders his wife with considerable satisfaction and then, with slightly less, elaborately buggers her German maid. Sleeplessly, he

* Norman Mailer, *An American Dream* (London: André Deutsch, 1965).

dispenses orgasms to lost girls and knock-out punches to their dispossessed lovers. He cons the police, squares up to the underlings of the Mob, and tests on his nerves the seductions of suicide, gambling and physical daring. He also has a little thing going for him in extra-sensory communication, is in vague touch with the spirit world and has muddled thoughts on God and the Devil – mostly the Devil. All this, it is implied, has given him his skill in riding the power circuit of big money, political influence and smart espionage. When Mailer talked at the Mayfair Theatre the other night he referred a number of times to the Sexual Revolution. I think he fancies himself as its Trotsky, and this novel is his way of showing that he is qualified and ready for the job. His party will be the Hipocrats and his slogan, 'Psychopaths of the world unite, you have nothing to lose but your cool'.

The trouble with *An American Dream* as a novel is precisely that in it Mailer *has* lost his cool. The tone is hectic, sometimes raucous and, above all, anxious. You would never guess from it that Mailer has written the most alive and intelligent prose of his generation, a style in which his swarming ideas and insights, imaginative depth and intellectual pressure work effortlessly together, making *The Naked and the Dead* the finest book to come out of the war. He still has his moments:

> She was bad in death. A beast stared back at me. Her teeth showed, the point of light in her eye was violent, and her mouth was open. It looked like a cave. I could hear some wind which reached down the cellars of a sunless earth. A little line of spit came from the corner of her mouth, and at an angle from her nose one green seed had floated its small distance on an abortive rill of blood. I did not feel a thing. Which is not to say nothing was happening to me. Like ghosts, emotions were passing invisibly through the aisles of my body. I knew I would mourn her on some distant day, and I would fear her.

He is trying to catch the present sensations as they come and chart them as they sink down into the psyche, to watch, as it were, the present reverberating into the future. But that fine control that used to distinguish Mailer's prose has gone: the sentence about the 'sunless earth' is romantic rhetoric, half-digested *Kubla Khan*, whilst poor, dead Deborah's snot is there merely to shock. It doesn't; it only undercuts what he says about not feeling a thing, since the reader is clearly intended to feel so much.

To shock, in fact, is the book's chief aim. But the shock works on two levels, one superficial and more or less frivolous, the other serious. Frivolity first: just as Rojack is continually making physical dares with himself – with drink, with sex and with suicidal situations, such as walking round the parapet of a skyscraper – so Mailer seems to be daring the American public to be outraged, daring *Esquire* magazine, who serialized the thing, to refuse it, to cut it, to protest. But it can't be done; in America everything is acceptable, everything a success; the book has already made him half a million dollars. This accounts for that shrill edge of frustration, like a naughty child with a swampingly permissive parent. It is the stylistic parallel to a curious, undiscussed thread in the narrative: the fact that Rojack's father-in-law, Kelly, has slept with all the girls – including his own daughter – whom Rojack so strenuously makes in his wanderings. Hence the sexual exhibitionism – Mailer writes as though he had just invented the orgasm – has about it a compulsive desperation that flows pure from infantile sources: as who should say, 'However omnipotent and overpowering Daddy is, you *shall* take notice of me'.

On this simple level, the sexual revolution has already taken place. Since *Lady Chatterley* went on the best-seller list it has been possible to write frankly about any kind of sex, however complex or perverse. Nobody really cares what people do with each other in bed; after all, it's harmless, it's been done and said before, and it's not political. Yet it can, in a devious way, become an instrument of politics: the sex novels and titillating films, the unchanging, bogus psychologizing about mutual orgasms, all those empty, smiling faces and mass-produced bosoms looming from every billboard and TV screen, are the new opiate of the masses. So the more sex a book has the less it basically offends those blank, 'totalitarian' forces which Mailer fears are running American life. When Kennedy went to the White House Mailer wrote, 'America was faced with going back to its existential beginnings, its frontier psychology, where the future is unknown and one discovers the truth of the present by accepting the risks of the present; or America could continue to go on in its search for totalitarian security.' Rojack, I suppose, was created as an urban embodiment of this frontier psychology, a man whose life depends on being true to his present truth and risking his obscurest instincts. To insist on him as a superman with a phallus as big as the Ritz is merely a distraction.

Essentially, he is a post-Sexual Revolution hero. His athletic promiscuity is interesting only for its lovelessness. With Cherry, the nightclub singer, he works up a little strained feeling, with Ruta, the German girl, he finds self-congratulation, and with Deborah, his wife, a piercing, vindictive hatred; but with none of them is there any tenderness. It never occurs to him that sex can involve giving, trust, renewal. The theme of the book is the violence of it all; the violence of the libidinal drives, but also the violence of frustration, prejudice, power and the whole seething, envious antagonism of New York City. The best scenes are those with the police and the Negro singer, Shago Martin, where Mailer catches, almost without seeming to know it, the incredibly insulting tone of American life. In the final analysis, it doesn't matter if Rojack screws away like an automated factory; what matters is that he should sense the psychic outrage that this kind of frantic, loveless violence reeks on his self. He may be dressed up as a hero but he looks like a martyr to me.

Mailer's strength as a novelist and essayist has always been his sense of which issues are on the edge of erupting into the American consciousness. *An American Dream* was begun in September 1963. Two months later the private, bedroom violence he described was given overwhelming political expression when Kennedy was assassinated. Since then murderousness has proliferated like cancer in the States: Philadelphia, Miss., Selma and Harlem. It has status and recognition, it has class. It even has its own formal political parties and extremist platforms: the Black Moslems, the Klan, the Birchers. One of Mailer's finest pieces was his defence of hipsterism, 'The White Negro'. *An American Dream* might be sub-titled *The White Black Moslem* – written, of course, by Norman X.

Violence and schizophrenia as values in themselves is not a concept original to Mailer or America. Over here the psychiatrist R. D. Laing has, if I understand him rightly, been promoting much the same thesis: that 'madness' may give you truer and deeper insights into your own reality than 'sanity'. It is the gospel according to St Genet. Mailer, however willing, finds it a strain; madness does not come naturally to him. He is above all an intellectual: Jewish, Harvard, New Yorker. For all his sharp responses and awareness, there is always behind every word he writes a hint of theory, a force which checks, tabulates and organizes the material with an often considerable intellectual elegance. The grand, controlled madness of Dostoevsky or Lawrence's absolute certainty of intuition are not his style. He is too cerebral and well-read ever to be able to rely wholly on his instincts; for even his present absorption with way-out experience he has formal existential excuses.

So *An American Dream* remains a political novel. It is written to shock people into recognizing the underforces that run their lives and society; it is written to change things a bit. Maybe it would have more chance of doing so if it had been dashed off less like a pamphlet, impatiently, carelessly, to do a job; not so much a way of life, more a programme. Even so, there are touches of genius about it, as there are about everything Mailer writes. It may not be the masterpiece he promised at the end of *Advertisements for Myself*, but it is a splendid fill-in on the most improbable fictional character since Moby Dick: I mean Norman Mailer.

The Spectator, 1965

Patrick White's *Riders in the Chariot**

Every so often some tough American critic takes to reproving the Novel for its lack of manners. It has neither style nor substance nor breeding; it doesn't know how to behave in society; and often, like a reluctant debutante, it doesn't even want to be brought out. Usually, the attack is directed against local talent. What can one expect, the critic implies, from such provincial upbringing? In a lecture in London in 1960, even the sophisticated Miss Mary McCarthy took this same stern view. The novel's future, if any, lay not with the Faulkners or Goldings but with the Compton-Burnetts, the Amises, or even the Snows. She sounded very despondent, as though the only abiding value of the novel was as a more artistically coherent, humanly meaningful branch of sociology. The rest is poetry. And that, everyone knows, means exoticism and purple passages, Djuna Barnes and Lawrence Durrell.

This, anyway, is the grim theory. Mercifully, it is not true. There is something between the purely social novel and the gush of poetical prose or prosaic poetry. There is, for example, the work of Patrick White. Even in his relative failures, such as *Voss*, he seems to me an unmistakably major writer who commands a scope, power and sheer technical skill which put even our more ambitious novelists in the shade. Yet he does not, by any means, fit into Miss McCarthy's scheme of things. In theory his latest novel, like some great, leisurely Russian masterpiece, takes in the whole of his society; it swings its beam right across Australia, shedding a brief light on

* Patrick White, *Riders in the Chariot* (London: Eyre and Spottiswoode, 1961).

everyone from double-barrelled aristocrats to factory-hands. But it is a narrow beam, which penetrates deeply and disperses little. Manners for White are not so much expressive of life as a caricature of it, a complicated, almost farcical excrescence:

> 'Are you a Baptist, perhaps,' she asked.
>
> 'I am a Jew,' the Jew replied.
>
> 'Arrrr!' said the lady.
>
> She had not heard right, only that it sounded something funny. Her skin closed on itself rather fearfully.
>
> All the ladies, it appeared, had paused for a moment in their breathing. They were slavering on their plastic teeth. Before they began to clatter again.

When White plays tricks of style like this he is using his wit not to pin a scene down but to evaporate it into fantasy. The images fuse sharply into each other, as in a dream. And the Australia he so lovingly plots begins to seem a country of the mind.

He has, in fact, reversed the novelist's traditional procedure: in his work it is manners and social behaviour which are dream-like; reality is all inward. He seems to see his artistic function as a matter of penetrating the hard shell of social habit until he exposes that peculiar vibration which makes each person what he is. He would draw, in short, a firm line between life and society. Society swarms around us – in most of its manifestations rather distasteful: all plastic, chrome and banging machinery – while significant life runs on in isolation below this turbulent surface, like the green, unnoticed river which flows beside Rosetree's Brighta Bicycle Lamps factory at Barranugli. Which, according to Patrick White, is where the crucifixion took place.

For *Riders in the Chariot* is, unequivocally, the story of Christ retold in terms of modern Australia. The Messiah is an ageing, ugly German refugee called Himmelfarb, an orthodox Jew and one-time university professor, whom the Nazis drove into hiding and then deported to a concentration camp. He escapes from there miraculously (and also unconvincingly, for the miracle occurs too early in the novel for one to realize that it is in order), is smuggled in a daze across Poland, peers briefly at Israel and promptly emigrates to Australia where, for the sake of humility, he takes an unskilled job in Rosetree's factory. His St Peter is a half-aboriginal painter, Alf Dubbo, who has been educated and then seduced by an Anglican pastor, has drifted from town to town, from whore to whore, is syphilitic, tubercular, gentle, speechless and able to communicate only in his strange, obsessive paintings.

Then there are two Marys: Mrs Godbold, a slow, massive mother of swarms of daughters, with a genius for simplicity and unselfish love; and Miss Hare, 'fox-coloured', epileptic and slightly mad, who communes with the lives of plants and animals and leads a haunted life in a vast, derelict Victorian folly called Xanadu, built by her drunken father who, when she was a child, had drowned himself in a rain-butt while she looked on. There are also two devils, Mrs Flack and her familiar Mrs Jolley, who was once Miss Hare's housekeeper. They live together in a nice little suburban home, all raw brick, good plumbing, blue eiderdowns and plaster goblins. Both have secretly done for their husbands, and both now live, with stomachs rumbling, off the lives of other people. Their instrument is Mrs Flack's illegitimate son, Blue, whose mindless, brute beauty is the personification of everything White hates in Australia. Finally, there is a Judas, the factory-owner and Catholic convert, Harry Rosetree, born Haïm ben Ya'akov Rosenbaum; he begins like one of the bumbling heroes of Dan Jacobson's *Price of Diamonds* and ends hanging from a dressing-gown cord in his tiled and glass bathroom.

Nothing very much happens: the lives of the four main protagonists are told in rather clumsy flashbacks and then the inevitable tragedy is briskly played out. The Jew is crucified at Easter by a gang of drunken workmates led by Blue. Of course, it is all a joke, all Australian matiness. But a few hours later the Jew, attended by his Marys, dies of a heart-attack brought on by the horseplay. Shortly after, the abo paints his great work, 'The Deposition', and dies of TB, Rosetree hangs himself, Miss Hare disappears for good and Xanadu is torn down. Only Mrs Godbold solidly remains.

In outline, the work sounds humourless and apocalyptic. It is not, and for a simple reason: *Riders in the Chariot* is no more a symbolic novel than Joyce's *Ulysses*. The author, that is, is not constantly chivvying one to read significance into trivia by insisting on some buried treasure of meaning which the diligent reader must dig out. He is not writing cheap and selling dear. For White is a myth-writer not a symbolist. In this, he is in the same camp as Sidney Nolan: both are artists of extreme technical sophistication, both have devoted themselves to the creation of coherent but expanding imaginative worlds, and both are obsessed by the vast, hard emptiness of the

Australian subcontinent. Given this unyielding background, there seem to be only two ways of doing creative work: the artist either sticks doggedly to the facts as he knows them, and so remains provincial, like Howells in nineteenth-century America; or, like Melville, he populates the country for himself by absorbing it into his imagination and re-creating myths for it. So Nolan has his Ned Kelly and Mrs Fraser, his Leda and the Gallipoli paintings, which are his version of the *Iliad.* White, in his turn, has re-created Adam and Eve in *The Tree of Man*, Odysseus in *Voss* and now, in *Riders in the Chariot*, Christ.

Myths have a simple advantage: they are known. This does not mean that the reader is hypnotized by the booming of an archetypal, Jungian ground-bass. White, anyway, is far too deliberate a writer to allow this to happen. *Voss*, for example, partly failed because one can't respond to a voyage of discovery when it is described with the static mannerisms of a late-Jamesian house-party. If *Riders in the Chariot* does not suffer from this nervousness of style and is closer to the fine simplicity of his masterpiece *The Tree of Man*, it is still a very cunning and elaborate piece of work. But because the myth is known, its framework leaves the artist free to explore the unknown; and it gives his tentative discoveries a base and logic they might otherwise lack. White may not write novels which are poetic in the hepped-up, modish sense, but he does use the form to explore territory usually reserved for poetry. His novels, that is, are powerful and valid only to the degree to which they reflect an inner reality.

This is particularly true of his latest book. Its four main characters are joined less in fact than in imagination: at the emotional centre of each of their lives is the image of the Chariot. To the learned Himmelfarb it is the Chariot of Redemption, partly from Ezekiel, partly cabbalistic; for Mrs Godbold it is love; for the abo it is the imaginative magnificence and certainty which, until just before his death, he can never quite express in paint; and for Miss Hare it is the blinding, frightening approach of one of her fits. But for all of them it is also, most passionately, the sunset:

> Before he could answer, she exclaimed:
> 'Look!'
> And was shading her eyes from the dazzle of gold.
> 'It was at this time of evening', her mouth gasped, and worked at words, 'that I would sometimes feel afraid of the consequences. I would

fall down in a fit while the wheels were still approaching. It was too much for anyone so weak. And lie sometimes for hours. I think I could not bear to look at it.'

'There is no reason why you should not look now,' Himmelfarb made an effort. 'It is an unusually fine sunset.'

. . . The Chariot itself rode straight and silent, both now, and on the clouds of recollection.

So the novel is possessed by the idea of luminousness. Nearly all the important scenes take place at sunset; one hears continually how the light lay, glowed and shifted. Yet each time it seems to reflect inwards. Limpidly, the details of every scene appear not for themselves but as projections of an inner landscape. The theme of the novel is, in every sense of the term, illumination.

Though the characters are connected in theme and, cursorily, in action, they scarcely seem to touch. White speaks once of the 'extraordinary non-relationship' between the Jew and the abo. It is true of them all. Each is adrift in his own isolation; though each may brush the others fleetingly with words, though each may share common glimpses of the Chariot and of good and evil, they connect only in the mind. For the rest, they are left with the blank fact of what is, for Dubbo, 'his unconvincing, to himself always incredible, communal existence'. This lack of a rooted sympathy between one person and another leads to lapses: Himmelfarb's Jewishness, like Daniel Deronda's, is too sanctimonious; Mrs Godbold's simplicity is, in the end, sentimentalized; there are passages of heavy overwriting which show that White's disciples, when they come, may well be appalling. Yet even though the behaviour of those outside the still centre of beatitude is less a comedy of manners than a stylized, roaring farce, this in itself can become a strength:

Then, as people will toss up the ball of friendship, into the last light, at the moment of departure, and it will hang there briefly, lovely and luminous to see, so did the Jew and Mrs Godbold. There hung the golden sphere. The laughter climbed quickly, out of their exposed throats, and clashed together by consent; the light splintered against their teeth. How private and mysterious, and beautiful it was, even the intruders suspected, and were deterred momentarily from hating.

When they were again fully clothed in their right minds, Mrs Jolley said to her companion:

'Do you suppose she comes to him often?'

'I would not know,' replied Mrs Flack, though it was obvious she did.

'Tsst!' she added, quick as snakes.

Mrs Godbold had begun to turn.

'See you at church!' hissed Mrs Jolley.

'See you at church!' repeated Mrs Flack.

Their eyes flickered for a moment over the Christ who would rise to the surface of Sunday morning.

Then they drew apart.

I can think of very little as subtle and concentrated as this that is being written in either form, prose or poetry. Patrick White may have tried to evoke, in his latest novel, the whole of Australian society and have succeeded in projecting only a multiple image of his own isolation, but it is an image of great beauty.

The New Statesman, 1961

6

CRITICISM

The Limits of Analysis

I intended to call this essay 'A Paraphrase of Heresy'. But a tour of the New Criticism is no longer necessary. In scholarly company Criticism (with a capital C) is no longer a fighting word. *The Explicator*, which began, in the best tradition of scruffy little magazines, as a revolutionary battlefield, all war cries and fighting footnotes, has become just another scholarly paper. Yesterday's critics have become today's contributors to the *P.M.L.A.*

What, in short, has happened in the last thirty-odd years is not that the old Dry-as-Dusts have disappeared, but simply that they have been replaced by Dry-as-Dusts of another style. Perhaps this was inevitable; the pressures of academic life sooner or later bring everything down to plain method. For method is impersonal, almost an abstraction. It reduces to clear teachable elements the huge complexity of disciplined response and choice which the reader otherwise needs to re-create for himself each poem. Method, of whatever brand, is always easier to teach than discrimination. The scholars substituted for the work of art the multitudinous details of its background; the critics replaced it with the details of their own technical process. Landscape or physiology? Either way the life of the work is hardly touched.

Granted all this is old hat. Granted, too, the technical revolution was necessary. In *Practical Criticism* I. A. Richards demonstrated blindingly enough that undergraduates who were, in theory, both specialists in literature and, the reputation of Cambridge being what it is, sophisticated representatives of their breed, were simply unable to read. The subsequent critical revolution restored at least that *sense of analysis* without which good criticism is impossible. For the sense of analysis is a token of sanity in all the varied critical fringes of literature. It guarantees that each judgement, each detail of interpretation, each generalization, is based on observation and argued from it. The critic is not simply exploiting his sensitivity in order to rewrite the poem in his own simpler terms. For example:

> . . . that miracle of the summer air, airy and glittering as the nets of the summer light and early dew over the strawberry beds – a poem so airy that it might have been woven by the long fingers of the sylphs in their dark and glittering Indian gauzes, floating like a little wind among the jewelled dark dews on the leaves of the fruit trees – this flawless poem. . . . Et cetera, et cetera.

The subject of that, believe it or not, is *The Rape of the Lock*. This is, of course, not criticism at all; it is simply a literary travelogue of a kind that no one now bothers with, apart from a few elderly members of literary circles and poetry societies scattered here and there in the interior. 'Fine writing' has been left to the light essayists; it is no longer the final criterion of the excellence of critical prose. Back in 1930, in the first chapter of *Seven Types of Ambiguity*, William Empson wrote:

> Critics, as 'barking dogs', . . . are of two sorts: those who merely relieve themselves against the flower of beauty, and those, less continent, who afterwards scratch it up.

The scratchers have carried the thirty years since then. Criticism has ceased to be a questionable skill – a self-conscious parading of sensitivity had gone a long way to destroy such residual respect as the non-specialist still had for the art – it has become instead an arguable one. Its opinions can be challenged on the evidence produced, its reasons are susceptible to other reason. There is no longer an impassable barrier between being sensitive to poetry and being intelligent.

There is, however, a difference between being intelligent and simply using one's wits, and a difference again between the latter and the mere fitting of a ready-formed technique to whatever material appears; a difference, in short, between a sense of analysis and analysis as an end in itself. Without a sense of analysis no good criticism is possible, although there might well be good critical theory. On the simplest level, the sure touchstone of a critic is the maxim: 'By his quotations shall ye know him.' The influence of

Matthew Arnold and T. S. Eliot, for instance, is as much in what they quoted as in what they said. The critical case remains unproved without exact lines to back it up. And it is impossible to smell out the quotations without a peculiarly shrewd idea of the weight and mechanics of the language; without, that is, a sense of analysis. So it goes back as far as good criticism, as far at least as Dryden. Until the appreciators moved in, the question was simply the extent to which the analysis was put down or left implicit.

But now, in the time of the dissectors, the question is of the use it is put to. Consider, for example, Doctor Johnson on the famous lines of Denham:

> *O could I flow like thee, and make thy stream*
> *My great example, as it is my theme!*
> *Though deep, yet clear; though gentle, yet not dull;*
> *Strong without rage, without o'er-flowing full.*

> The lines are in themselves not perfect; for most of the words, thus artfully opposed, are to be understood simply on one side of the comparison, and metaphorically on the other; and if there be any language which does not express intellectual operations by material images, into that language they cannot be translated. But so much meaning is comprised in few words; the particulars of resemblance are so perspicaciously collected; and every mode of excellence separated from its adjacent fault by so nice a line of limitation; the different parts of the sentence are so accurately adjusted, and the flow of the last couplet is so smooth and sweet, that the passage, however celebrated, has not been praised above its merit. It has beauty peculiar to itself, and must be numbered among those felicities which cannot be produced at will by wit and labour, but must rise unexpectedly in some hour propitious to poetry.

The analysis has embroiled the doctor in comments about the function of language that are both misleading and wrong-headed: 'If there be any language which does not express intellectual operations by material images, into that language they cannot be translated.' 'There is, of course,' Professor I. A. Richards tartly replied, 'no such language.' But although Johnson's conclusions may be faulty, his reasons are not. The analysis is there only as part of a genuine critical response: the feeling that the lines are better than anything Denham, on the evidence of the rest of his work, could ever reasonably have been expected to do. That is why the doctor devotes his last sentence to explaining the mechanics of the poetic fluke – which has, at other times, been called inspiration. He analysed, in fact, because he was unable to believe that a poet as undistinguished as Denham could turn out lines so good that were not also faulty. The analysis is there to serve the purpose of the judgement and, like the generalizations, is dictated by it.

The difference between this and New Critical analyses, is not that the doctor is wrong and the analysts, on the whole, are right; it is instead that Johnson is, to use the fashionable word, *organic* and they are not. And he is organic – his analysis, generalizations and judgement are all part of a single process – because his concern is, first and last, with the poetry. He writes what I would call primary criticism; criticism which, as rationally, deliberately and lucidly as possible, gives a sense of what the poetry is like. This means it describes not only the mechanics of the verse, the interaction of the various complex elements, meter, imagery and the rest; it also judges the work and sets it down within some scale of values. The values may never be set out formally, but they are everywhere implied in the critic's tone, reasons and choice of works.

Secondary criticism, on the other hand, is concerned more with its own processes than with the work of art. This makes for a queer unrelatedness between its major and minor premises, its generalizations and local analysis. For example, off and on for seven years I have been working on a book on the Metaphysicals, yet in that time I have never once come across a seventeenth-century Metaphysical poem that fits Professor Cleanth Brooks's definition:

> The Metaphysical poet has confidence in the powers of the imagination. He is constantly remaking his world by relating into an organic whole the amorphous and heterogeneous and contradictory. Trusting in imaginative unity, he refuses to depend upon non-imaginative classifications, those of logic and science.

It is an odd statement in itself; it becomes odder when you remember Donne's open, steady contempt for aesthetic values unrelated to the more active, sceptical intelligence; but it is oddest of all as a critical response to the extraordinarily stringent, dialectical movement of Donne's verse, the continual pertinacity of his argument. Now that we have got over the shock of the conceits, it is remarkable how small a part, in cold blood, they contribute to the effect of Donne's work, and how subordinate they are to the remorseless and insistent logical movement. They are themselves part of the world of 'logic and science'. If anything, they are there as a kind of aesthetic disinfectant: to prevent the work from sounding too 'poetical'. Professor Brooks, in fact, is generalizing not from Donne's poems but from Eliot's essays on the Metaphysicals. And Eliot was more concerned to find traditional precedents for Symbolist devices than to define, in any disinterested way, a particular seventeenth-century style. There are, after all, only two ways in which a poet can criticize his own work: the first is to rewrite it later, which was the way of Crashaw, Wordsworth, Keats, Tennyson and Yeats; the second is to pretend that you are writing about someone else, which is what Lawrence did with the novels of Hardy, and what Eliot did with the Metaphysicals. There is nothing in the least questionable about Eliot's practice. But it is odd that Professor Brooks should have made the same mistake after so painfully picking apart so much seventeenth-century verse.

The reason is that the business of secondary criticism is to show above all how neatly the machinery can be set in motion and the wonders it can perform with such slim material. Fundamentally, this great rumbling of critical engines seems to me to be covering up a certain nervousness. It is as though the analysts were unsure of the value of the work they discuss, and so had instead to affirm at every point the soundness and verifiability of their method: 'Poetry', they seem to say, 'may be marginal, antisocial nonsense, but we can at least write about it as thoroughly and unsentimentally as if it were the latest A.E.C. report.' I once read a paper by a professor of philosophy designed apparently to spread the message of the New Criticism to his colleagues. Its subject was the method of Professor Brooks and its title was a paradox: 'Criticism without Evaluation.' The theme was roughly that positive philosophers could now begin to respect criticism since it had at last been purged of all personal taint. The analysts had reduced the skill to 'the explication of the various constituents of the work of art. . . . And because they have correctly understood the organic character of these constituents, they have stressed in their critical exegeses the functional role of the various constituents.' By this token, the business of the critic is no more personal than that of the analytical statistician, or even, perhaps, that of the positive philosopher himself. The logical inconsistency of the position hardly matters (Who is to choose which elements to stress? Who is to decide about the primacy of the 'organic character' of a poem? And so on. The personal elements are not so easily exorcized.) What is odd is the fact that Professor Brooks never, to my knowledge, tried to correct the interpretation. Of course, no one is to blame for his admirers; but, as James said of Gautier's essay on Baudelaire, 'One must, in some degree, judge a man by the company he keeps. To admire Gautier is a mark of excellent taste. But to be admired by Gautier we cannot but regard as somewhat compromising.' Similarly, Professor Brooks, no doubt, would never have voluntarily gone out so far and precariously along the limb. But there he is.

He looks odd there because he is above all an educationist. His achievement is to have reduced the immensely complex discoveries of modern criticism to formulas and methods simple enough for the needs of university freshmen. And this, after all, is something. But it is something rather more than is suggested by his philosophical protagonist. For by reducing criticism to impersonal descriptive analysis he has reduced the critic to the status of grammarian, who teaches literature, or literary analysis, simply as a useful way of 'training the mind'. Literature, in fact, dwindles to a kind of dead language, like school Latin and Greek, justified only by the degree to which it supports the pedagogical technology. We are back, by another way, to the position Robert Graves found in Oxford after the First World War:

> At the end of my first term's work I attended the usual college board to give an account of myself. The spokesman coughed and said a little stiffly: 'I understand, Mr Graves, that the essays that you write for your English tutor are, shall I say, a trifle temperamental. It appears, indeed, that you prefer some authors to others.'

At Oxford, where the methods of analysis have still hardly penetrated, one-third of the syllabus for a Bachelor of Arts degree in English is made up of Anglo-Saxon, Middle English and Modern Philology, a less daring method still of ensuring some element of 'mind training'. Both brands of professor, in short, distrust literature. For the English it is merely so much gentleman's relish, one of the amusements of gracious living, like port and six-course dinners, never to be defined or discussed, only to be surrounded, for professional purposes, by a few well-chosen facts.

The American methodologists, on the other hand, seem to distrust literature for precisely the reasons Englishmen like it: for its accretion of triviality. They seem afraid that some successful ad-

ministrative pragmatist may one day demand straight out, 'What is the *use* of all this poetry? And why do you, a grown man with a college education, devote your life to it?' The reply to this is simple: 'If you can ask those questions, you couldn't even begin to understand any answer I gave you.' But the analysts never make it. Instead, they first make their position worse by insisting on the absolute independence of aesthetic criteria from all others; they then, in a kind of triumphant reversal, show how their peculiar brand of critical automation produces organization men who are shrewder, less sentimental, more analytically wary than those who come out of any other education mill. The best mechanical grooms for the mechanical brides are the products of the most rigorous aesthetic technology. It is for this reason, I suppose, that academic critics insist on a vocabulary of technical terms that never at any point touches those used naturally of human behaviour. The discipline must be invulnerable, uncorrupted by life. And it doesn't matter a jot, apparently, that literature *is* human behaviour crystallized into its finest, sharpest, most translucent form.

They are, of course, hardly fair on the students whom they subject to this technology. For the undergraduates, presumably, have come to literature for education, not for mere technique. That is, they have come to have their own judgement and experience developed, measured and affirmed by vital contact with what Matthew Arnold called 'the best that is known and thought in the world'. The professor who fails to encourage this kind of creative response shelves his responsibility as a teacher and becomes merely a specialist.

Teaching, however, is not my subject here. The critic, either as a professor or as a man of letters, has other responsibilities: to himself and to his position in society. Fundamentally, the fault of *merely* technical analysis is much the same as that of *merely* appreciative criticism, for all that one exploits a method, and the other a trick of sensitivity. Both are too easy; both, essentially, are at best middlebrow. The sensitives, of course, have never pretended their work had any truck with intelligence. The case of the analysts is less obvious. It is not so much a question of the complexity of their work – most of them know how to attain at least the appearance of considerable difficulty – it is a question of attitude. For the complexity of the analysts is simply a matter of technique. They go at the work of art, explicate it fold upon fold, for the sake only of their method. The process is mechanical and is judged, like any other technology, for its usefulness and efficiency.

Genuine criticism, on the other hand, is never, in any obvious sense, useful. For it is not concerned with conventional values. On the contrary, its value depends precisely on the distance it keeps from the conventional. Everyone knows that the function of criticism is to serve literature; but it does not follow from this that criticism is therefore servile. What the professor is in theory, the critic is in practice: an intellectual. He is, I mean, someone to whom ideas are emotionally important, who responds to experience by thinking for himself. This, I take it, is what makes Donne the first properly intellectual poet. The intellectual thinks by virtue of what he is in himself, not because he happens to know the accepted technique. It is the business of the pedagogues to be useful, but it is the business of the critics to be lucid. Perhaps this is what Matthew Arnold meant in his essay 'The Function of Criticism at the Present Time': The course of literary criticism, he wrote, 'is determined . . . by the idea which is the law of its being; the idea of a disinterested endeavour to learn and propagate the best that is known and thought in the world, and thus to establish a current of fresh and true ideas'. In his 'disinterested endeavour' to come to terms with the nature of a work of art, the critic also extends and substantiates his own values. The essence of his job, in fact, is judgement. The artist creates his own moral world out of his intuitions into the nature and significance of his experience; the critic does the same out of his intuitions into the nature and significance of the work of art. Both are concerned with a morality that is continually flexible and continually open to fresh impulses. Both are also concerned to make their intuitions, of no matter how obscure a nature, as lucid as possible. For it is lucidity, not complexity, that is the final token of intelligence and honesty.

The two essential elements of primary criticism, then, are judgement and intuitive pertinacity. The business of the intellectual is to be true to his own lights, not to find excuses for popular tastes. He can safely leave conventions to the administrators. The one demand that can be reasonably made of the critic is that he be original. In the last analysis, it doesn't matter if he is right or wrong, bigoted or generous, narrow-minded or catholic, provided he says his own say, gets his own feelings straight and sets up his own standards for inspection and, if necessary, for disagreement; provided, that is, he creates his own moral world with as much intelligence as he can muster. And this is the most fundamental form of commitment; it is not a matter of political dogma or accepted standards, but of the life of the man linking creatively with the life of the work. Apart from the artist, the literary critic is perhaps the only intellectual left who is concerned more directly with life than with abstractions. Hence he is an intellectual in the proper sense of that term: not just a man with an adroit, well-trained intellect, but a man who is qualified above all by the subtlety and depth of his human intelligence. That, as I understand it, is what Eliot meant when he disposed, offhand, with the whole problem of critical method: 'The only method', he said, 'is to be very intelligent.'

The American Scholar, 1959

Cinema*

For the two worst years of my life I was theatre critic for the *New Statesman*. On the average, I saw three shows a week, often five, sometimes more, and remember from all that welter only two occasions with pleasure: Olivier as Coriolanus, Mostel as Bloom. The rest is a vast and miserable smudge of boredom. At the end of my two years' sentence I took a vow never voluntarily to go to the living theatre again – except to see friends perform, or for money. Yet since childhood I have gone quite as often to the movies, still do, and can see no possible reason to stop. It is not a question of quality: at one point I developed a passion for bad films; it took me a long time to come, reluctantly, to the conclusion that bad films were not as good as I thought they were. Instead, it is a question of the kind of response the movies elicit.

Theatre-going is, above all, a social act, involved with booking in advance, dressing up, and eating some unspeakable and expensive meal. You go, as Eric Bentley once remarked, for the company of the actors. You sit there in the half-light, sharply aware of them as people much like yourself, knocking themselves out to amuse you, fallible, anxious, often a bit pathetic. It takes the genius of a Mostel or an Olivier to go through that social barrier into the realm of compulsive illusion.

Yet even a second-rate movie can enter that world effortlessly. The cinema has, after all, all the conditions working for it. It is informal,

* John Howard Lawson, *Film: The Creative Process* (New York: Hill and Wang, 1964); John Russell Taylor, *Cinema Eye, Cinema Ear* (New York: Hill and Wang, 1964); Kenneth Macgowan, *Behind the Screen* (New York: Delacorte, 1964).

casual, private. You sit passively, in total darkness, eating chocolates, while the stuff of dreams – the primal image of love, the fantasies of violence, loss, and anguish, magnified beyond all imagination – is acted out before you, usually in black and white, the colour of dreams. It is the art of utter illusion, as purgative as a successful psychoanalysis, and far, far cheaper.

I exaggerate, of course. Yet the cinema, as Gorky noticed as early as 1896, has a curious knack of stirring things up:

> It seems as though it carries a warning, fraught with a vague but sinister meaning that makes your heart grow faint. You are forgetting where you are. Strange imaginings invade your mind and your consciousness begins to wane and grow dim.

This ability to disturb you obscurely yet profoundly is stronger in the cinema than in any of the more formal contemporary arts. It is also often stronger in good 'commercial' movies than in most deliberately 'art' products. It is stronger, that is, in the films of Nicholas Ray than in those of Satyajit Ray, in *Shane* than in *Alexander Nevsky*, in Rossen's *The Hustler* than in Bresson's *Pickpocket*. The reasons, I suppose, have something to do with the stars, the expensive professionalism and the relatively simple points made within simple frameworks. Despite themselves, the dream-factories have turned out not so much dreams as myths for the commercial mass societies. Cooper and Fonda, Brando and Newman, Garbo, Dietrich, Monroe and Karina enter into some almost chemical relationship with the camera which, with only minimal encouragement from the script, can embody all that floating sense of isolation, displaced violence, yearning and mobility which runs under all our over-stocked, domesticated lives. By simply trying to gratify and glamorize our fantasies, the movies end up by defining them, re-creating them for us in new terms.

The paradox is, then, that the closer a movie seems to stick to conventions and reality, the more freely it circulates in the fantasy world. That is where the protagonists of *avant-garde* abstract or 'pure' cinema go wrong. They unchain the art from the clichés of the commercial story and obligatory popular appeal only to tie it ever tighter to the director's exclusive, carefully defended subjective view of things. The results may be very brilliant, intriguing and original, but they are most often curiously unmoving.

Style for its own sake and the preoccupation with technique, in short, are as much a distraction in movies as in any other art. When, during the worst period of Stalinism, Eisenstein was unable or unwilling, or both, to cope in his art with the society around him, he lapsed into the mildly allegorical grand opera of *Ivan the Terrible*. He presented not a creative interpretation of the world but the more trivial spectacle of himself as Great Stylist. For Eisenstein, as for most of the Russians, style always meant skill, drama and invention in purely visual terms – a question of camera angles, cutting, montage. This is the inheritance of their great days in the silent beginnings of cinema, when each new technical discovery changed the language and possibilities of the art. In Europe, where the glamour of literature is still strong, style often means dialogue: witness those slightly self-indulgent scripts of Prévert and Pinter. In Hollywood, style often means simply the star; then the film becomes a vehicle for boosting the vanity of its principal actor, as in Brando's *One-Eyed Jacks*. But in the really successful movie, style is all of these things and none of them. That is the cinema's peculiarity and uniqueness. It is neither a way of merely looking at things nor of merely saying things; it is a way of being in things. It makes the eyes see, the ears see, the mind see. It is, to use the appropriate cliché, a totally existential art.

This uniqueness is the burden of John Howard Lawson's muddled, illuminating, maddening book, *Film: the Creative Process*. Lawson insists that the cinema is not theatre, not fiction. Instead, it is a product of what he calls 'the audio-visual imagination' which, using images and sounds as its basic elements, works with its own special rhythm and structure. He feels that cinema, alone among the arts, can set its heroes meaningfully and critically into action at the same time as it defines and criticizes their environment. As a Marxist, this cheers him and fires his enthusiasm; like Lenin, he believes that cinema is the great socialist art, a new opiate of the masses perhaps, to stir them, teach them, form them. Lawson has all sorts of qualities working on his side to make him seem sympathetic: that enthusiasm, for example, and his determination to worry away at the problems of movie-making until they reveal their specialness; the fact that he has already written the definitive book on script-writing; above all, he was black-listed, stood up to the House Un-American Activities Committee, and still apparently sticks by his Party principles. Like a tired old trout, the bourgeois liberal in me rises to the bait. But I can't swallow it.

It doesn't matter that his history of the cinema is absurdly slanted. Russia becomes *the* dominant force and everything else is downgraded accordingly: *The Blue Angel*, for example, is dismissed in four lines; Hollywood, after Griffith, Chaplin and Stroheim, is written off as utter decadence; even the Poles, who have emerged in the last few years as major film-makers, are given short revisionist shrift. Granted the Russians in their time did marvellous things; but that time, like their great creative outburst in literature, was over by the end of Lenin's New Economic Plan; and that coincided roughly with the advent of sound. So he makes it seem as though artistically the cinema has advanced little in the past thirty-five years. More important, behind his critical evaluations of works – not, at best, particularly original – are all the old glib clichés of Marxist propaganda: the positive hero and social optimism, the emergence of the masses and the death of capitalism, even the chestnut about *The Tempest* being a critique of colonialism. And these platitudes poise a glum query over the rest: if he is *that* second-hand and naïve in his basic premises (and I'm not saying Marxist premises are necessarily naïve; just his use of them), how much are his other insights worth? Oddly enough, they are worth a fair bit. Lawson is excellent on the specialness of the cinematic imagination and its distance from all the other arts, on the rhythm of film-making and the means by which conflict, climax, resolution and meaning are created in audio-visual terms. The hints are many, vivid and often go deep; but I'm not sure that they add up, as he obviously wants, to much of a theory.

I'm even less sure that they need to. Theories were needed early on, when the possibilities of turning a low pop entertainment into a high art form were slowly being realized. Yet even the theories of Pudovkin and Eisenstein are less interesting than their practical analyses of how they actually got the effects. This is true of all the performing arts. There is only one convincing theory of tragedy – Aristotle's – and nothing at all for Shakespeare, particularly from his time; even Dryden, fifty years later, didn't get far. The method, instead, is practice and example. Once the cinema can be taken for granted as a separate art in its own right, there are no longer any theoretical rules; there are only good and bad movies. And the approach to them is by way of criticism, not theory.

This is where John Russell Taylor comes in. His *Cinema Eye, Cinema Ear* is a set of purely critical studies of six leading contemporary film-makers: Fellini, Antonioni, Buñuel, Bresson, Hitchcock,

Bergman, plus shorter things on the New Wave boys, Godard, Truffaut and Resnais. These men have only two things in common: excellence in their different ways, and the ability to take the art of film utterly for granted. For them, says Taylor, 'the film was as natural a means of self-expression, as much a part of the habitual furniture of their world, as painting or writing or music or architecture . . . [they] seem to me to create directly in terms of film, to wield what . . . Alexandre Astruc called the "*camera stylo*", the camera as a fountain-pen.' For Astruc, that meant 'that the cinema will break away little by little from the tyranny of the visual, of the image for its own sake, of the immediate anecdote, of the concrete, to become a means of writing as supple and subtle as that of written language'.

The degree to which Astruc's predictions in 1948 have come true is implicit in Taylor's book. There isn't a touch of theory or prophecy in the whole performance. He treats each of his chosen masters as artists working in an achieved medium, using it for their own special ends, each with his own special quirks, each making his statements in his own special way. His analyses are detailed, witty, detached, and – despite his occasionally overbland urbanity; he doesn't write for *The Times* for nothing – remarkably intelligent. He writes, in short, like a critic who doesn't have to justify the status of the art; he simply has to get his values and judgements right. Since he is one of the more reliable film critics in London the judgements are mostly good; by which I mean I agree with him, except for his fashionable over-evaluation of Hitchcock and his unfashionable under-evaluation of Resnais. He is excellent on the greatest of modern masters, Buñuel, and on Fellini and Godard, he puts Bergman sympathetically but firmly in his place, and makes startlingly good cases for those two old master bores, Bresson and Antonioni.

But there is one vital cinematic element that Taylor ignores in his cool discriminations: money. Of his group only Buñuel and Hitchcock have been men of the commercial cinema all through their careers, though Fellini has recently graduated to it. The rest keep their artistic control by filming rigorously, though relatively, on the cheap. Without that safeguard the merchants step in, delegating authority and responsibility to producers, editors, script-writers, camera-men, stars; the director has then to do his cynical damnedest to mark the end-product with his own personal signature. Yet cash is a potent ingredient in the cinema, not only because the film is the most expensive, technological and corporate of the modern arts, apart from architecture, nor because all those telephone-number sums add to the popular glamour of everyone concerned in the business. For the average Hollywood man cash is a fact in the final criterion of excellence.

No one, for instance, could be more average than Kenneth Macgowan, who produced in Hollywood from 1932–46, and then lorded it over film studies at U.C.L.A. for ten years. *Behind the Screen* is his amiable, low-brow history of the industry, interesting because it totally and uncritically accepts the hard currency standard of values. For him, the two major problems of the art are: cajoling the public and side-stepping the tax-man. Otherwise, a film is as good as its gross. As a history, his book is as dull as cold toast, but it packs in a good many fascinating facts about the financial structure of the big studios – who, even in their decline, still reckon in millions – and about the strange financial gags pulled by the stars: Elizabeth Taylor was paid $1,750,000, plus a hefty cut of the profits, for her absurd performance in that greatest of all absurdities, *Cleopatra*.

Everybody knows how deadening the cash nexus is: how good films get watered down and bold projects made timorous; how the taste of the ignorant slobs who run things runs things (one of them said of Hays: 'He is one of us. He is folks.' So much for the cinema as folk art); how *Kitsch* and violence become industrial products, and universal vanity buries all. All that is common knowledge, and if it wasn't already, there is now Fellini's *8½* to prove it. Yet I wonder if there aren't positive sides to all this stupidity. First, the vast investments and intricate technical proliferations of the big studios ensure nearly always a certain professional perfection. Second, out of their need to filter their art through or around the meat-headed merchants who put up the money, the more imaginative and original directors have developed a certain healthy toughness of attitude. It is partly cynicism, but it is also partly moral hardness. Combined with that complete professionalism, it can produce a specifically adult sense of reality – even if that reality is often violent and corrupt – a feeling for the inescapable brute facts of urban life, which keeps at bay the more fey self-indulgences artists are heir to. (Of course, I am not referring to the professionals in sentimentality, nor to directors like Tony Richardson, who have made a successful commercial gimmick out of borrowed artiness.)

Apply that hard adult realism to those continually evoked myths and deep fantasies and you have the curious worldliness and intense imaginative realism of the best films. Macgowan points out that seventy-two per cent of movie-goers are under thirty, fifty-two per cent under twenty. Maybe the final art of the movie is to inspire in an adolescent audience the myth of being grown-up.

The New York Review of Books, 1964

Ken Tynan*

Kenneth Tynan 'came floating down from Oxford', as he puts it, just before I swam up there. He had, already, I quote again, 'sailed broad-bottomed' across the Atlantic when I embarked on my short, unhappy voyage as drama critic for this magazine. And I had sunk noiselessly beneath the waves before he hove into sight again. So we are ships which have never passed on first nights. I can write fairly objectively of this selection from his work, and I do so, let me say it straight away, with admiration and a certain compassion. For drama criticism is a grinding job and Tynan does it extraordinarily well – better, in fact, than any contemporary theatre man in this country. He knows the stage inside out, loves it with ardour even when – or particularly when – scourging it most; he is a clever writer and, within limits, he is serious.

The trouble is: those limits. They are partly inherent in the nature of the job, partly in the nature of modern drama. First, then, the job. In England, at least, theatre criticism is almost exclusively journalism, most of it dashed down smoking hot within minutes of the curtain fall. And even if the critic is lucky enough to write for a weekly, he usually has only a couple of days in which to brood on the subject, and by then, as like as not, a couple more plays have intervened. His business, however, is not to brood, it is simply to evoke, as Tynan has it,

> exactly what it felt like to be in a certain playhouse on a certain distant night. . . . He will find readers if, and only if, he writes clearly and gaily

* Kenneth Tynan, *Curtains* (London: Longmans, 1961).

and truly; if he regards himself as a specially treated mirror recording a unique and unrepeatable event.

Now Tynan is a very sensitive mirror indeed, but he reflects more than impressions of plays and actors; he shines also with the popular image of the stage itself. And unlike the cinema, the theatre is still a deeply middle-class fashionable occasion – no matter whether its excuse is Pinero or Brecht. At the moment, the fashion is left-wing and anti-establishment, but the same old social dance goes on: all that advance planning and posh clothes, the warm light ales and demonstrative giggling in the intervals, the bad and pricey restaurants after. You don't just drop in to the theatre; you are involved in a smoothly planned social expedition. Naturally, the glamour of the evening and of all those famous, gossip-column creatures up there in the spotlights rubs off on the critics. They, like their quarries, must be personalities; they too must provide the public with a performance on a performance. They must be 'brilliant', full of jokes and parodies and bitchiness, very much on the inside.

Of this cosmopolitan, green-room style, Tynan is a real master. His puns and jokes may be too many, but they are often genuinely funny ('the Coward–Gielgud axis . . . the *derrière-garde* of the profession'); he knows exactly how to re-create the swarming life of a production and has a wicked gift for catching a player where it hurts – Vivien Leigh as Cleopatra, for example:

> Taking a deep breath and resolutely focusing her periwinkle charm, she launches another of her careful readings; ably and passionlessly she picks her way among its great challenges, presenting a glibly mown lawn where her author had imagined a jungle. Her confidence, amazingly, never flags.

He has, too, that chameleon quality which is essential to good journalism: he catches uncannily well the tone and preoccupations of the societies he haunts. In England, at the moment, he is New Leftish, on the Continent rather more Marxist, in the States a' babbled occasionally of Zen Buddhism. And it is all sustained in the same elegant, aphoristic style.

On these terms Tynan is excellent, and this collection of ten years' articles is remarkably stimulating. But the terms themselves are constricting. Like some shining suit of armour, they make a fine show, a fine noise and a fine defence, but they are hard to move about in; for they are created, first and last, for destructive work.

This would be all very well if Tynan had remained where he began, 'in love', as he says, 'with the theatre of fantasy and shock'; a theatre, that is, fit for heroes to strut in. But during the last decade he has grown up. The cult of heroes has given way to politics. This seems to have happened around 1956 when, under the double influence of Brecht and Suez, he underwent an almost Pauline conversion to Socialism. He emerged disenchanted with what in Russia they were calling 'the cult of personality', and convinced that the theatre could be a means of influencing people, of presenting ideas and life as we live it. All well and good. But there was a difficulty: though Tynan may have changed his beliefs, his style – the product of a long, hard, eminently successful apprenticeship – remained the same. He may have begun to think Socialist but he continued to write Tory.

This Toryism, of course, has nothing to do with what he says, it is simply a question of how he says it:

> The theatre of mindless farce and meaningless melodrama is unknown [in the U.S.S.R.]. One would like to see a Western theatre organized on Russian lines without Russian ideology; but without some ideology or other the theatres would never be built and the organization never imposed.
>
> I was revolving these things in my mind as my plane rose, bearing me away from the shashlik territory, across the *boeuf Stroganoff* belt into the Schnitzel country. I landed for a while at Prague – sour word, which rhymes with nothing. . . .

I have left out no subtle linking passage. The shift from ideology to gastronomy is immediate, complete and, more important, quite in key with the tone of the piece as a whole. It is as though Tynan inhabited a world in which *haute cuisine* and politics were equal and interchangeable. I don't know how much this helps dignify his attitude to good living, but I know perfectly well what it does to his politics: it makes them appear superficial, slick, too easy by half. Obviously it is encouraging that the best of our drama critics supports most of the best causes. Equally obviously, Tynan can't be expected to write dully just because he has otherwise aligned himself with the New Left. Nor can he be expected, in a weekly column, to work out the complexities of his political position with much delicacy. But he might reasonably be expected to give an impression of knowing that the complexities exist.

He suggests in the Preface that his taste has developed over the decade. The process seems to be less a development than an abrupt switching of the points: a flick of the wrist and suddenly Tynan was steaming off in a new direction. And he dragged with him wagon on wagonload of new presuppositions: that Brecht was, without qualification, the greatest dramatist of the age, that Osborne and Delaney spoke definitively for all the young in England, that colonialism is automatically brutal, unilateral disarmament the only possible hope, and so on. All of them are serious, arguable causes. But Tynan seems to have received them ready-packed at the goods depot and never bothered to pry into the crates for himself.

Compare this with the kind of development which takes place in, say, Edmund Wilson's collection of reviews, *Classics and Commercials*, and the hollowness of theatrical procedure becomes clearer. Because he writes on books Wilson is not forced to be as relentlessly bright as Tynan. Yet he is bright enough. And under the glitter is a steady pressure of argument. Where Tynan merely records or asserts, Wilson works out his perceptions gradually, subtly and without any flagrant *parti pris*. Similarly, Wilson's massive, easily-worn reading is the product of real intellectual curiosity, a framework in which his intelligence can operate at constant pressure; with Tynan, on the other hand, it might almost be possible to chart, article by article, the books he has dipped into that week; he seems a bit of an intellectual name-dropper.

Yet the fact that he gives the impression of caring for anything outside the theatre, of having read anything but plays and actors' memoirs, of having any political position to defend, makes him a looming exception in the drama world. For the limitations of the art he serves are even more blinding than the style he is forced to employ. At one point, he remarks that 'no Englishman since the third decade of the seventeenth century has written an acknowledged dramatic masterpiece'; the English theatre, he continues, is in fact the creation of Irishmen. True enough; but I would put it more strongly: since the death of Ben Jonson the intellectuals and the theatre in this country have had no truck with each other. What Tynan calls 'the Irish conspiracy' has chiefly contributed great cleverness, flashing rhetoric and one cult of personality after another. But these are all qualities of the surface. Any centre of mature, developing intellectual life is lacking in the English theatre. This is not so on the Continent, where they still have an elaborate and responsible *dramaturgie* created by professionals unrepentantly devoted to the theory and development of the drama. So Europe breeds its Brechts and Stanislavskys, while Britain labours to produce – whom? The answer, I'm afraid, is Guthrie and Littlewood.

The blank fact is that the British intelligentsia – by which I mean not some fashionable in-group but a whole class of people who are involved in using ideas, the arts and sciences to make sense of their lives – go willingly and often to the cinema but hardly at all to the theatre. And they are stopped not just by the boring social rituals involved but by the deadening lack of urgency and pressure, by the sense that still, despite the Osborne–Pinter breakthrough, nothing really *matters* in contemporary British theatre. Issues may now be raised but their treatment remains fixed at superficial effects. As for thinking, our preconceptions can do that for us; and if the preconceptions are the right ones, the audience is expected to cheer uncritically. The spectacle of an artist moulding ideas and forms to fit precisely the shape of his original experience will be submerged – if it ever existed – in rhetoric and self-advertisement.

Granted the theatre is a highly specialized art, involving not one artist but several: author, director, actors, designer, lighting expert. Granted, too, that the work these men produce has its own specialized forms and rules and logic quite other than those of the rest of literature; Gordon Craig, who should have known, once announced to Tynan that 'literary men . . . are intruders, despoilers of the purity of theatre as a separate art'. But in England this specialization, when it gets into print, seems to produce not its own discipline but a mystique. Even when a critic sets out with enormous talent and the most high-minded intentions he always seems to end up with the glamour of show biz.

This is a genuine pity, for the theatre has changed a good deal in the last decade and Tynan has been a powerful instrument in changing it. An appeal to the old drawing-room-comedy, expense-account ethos is no longer any guarantee of success; rather the reverse, as a long string of West End flops has proved. It is now possible for serious themes to be aired in plays which take account of the tensions and discomfort of modern life. Indeed, kitchens and commitment have become almost as essential ingredients for success as french windows and frivolity used to be. But there is a stage beyond this: a creative and experimental milieu which is not wholly at the mercy of the popular press!

If this could be achieved, as it sometimes is on the Continent, then writers like Osborne and Pinter might be able to be as intelligent and meticulous in their public pronouncements as they are when doing original work for the stage; the best young directors might be given the money and time to develop their own schools, styles and theories, without endless commercial chivvying; and critics like Tynan might be able to write at full stretch, using all the great professional knowledge they command, without feeling they must endlessly cajole their readers with wisecracks.

Meanwhile, like Auden's Prospero,

I am very glad I shall never
. . . have to go through that business again,
The hours of fuss and fury, the conceit, the expense.

The New Statesman, 1961

John Berger*

John Berger's attack on Picasso has been given the full treatment of weekend publicity: a spread in a colour supplement, three-quarters of an hour of Sunday evening television, immediately followed, like some political manifesto, by discussion on BBC-2; there was gossip, indignation and applause long before the thing arrived in the bookshops. In short, it has had the whole controversial works. This is ironic, since Berger blames part of what he calls Picasso's 'failure' on the alacrity with which the master has played along with the corrupting mass-media. Yet it is also inevitable, for Berger has produced a kind of mass-medium book: Lenin's maxim, 'Patiently Explain', adapted, as it were, for television. His style is easy, intimate, deliberately provocative and resonant with slightly displaced feeling (I'll come back to that); he often makes his points by a simple movement from picture to picture, as though leaving the linking argument to the play of the camera; he writes as a public personality – a relief after so much anonymous prose – and one who has the best interests of his audience at heart. All this is as it should be, for his subject is a painter who has himself been transformed into a major personality. As Berger says, 'His name is known to those who could not name their own Prime Minister.' Picasso has taken his place with Freud, Einstein, Churchill, Kennedy, Hitler and Stalin – he is part of modern history. You don't have to know anything about art to know about him. So the publicity that has accompanied

* John Berger, *The Success and Failure of Picasso* (Harmondsworth: Penguin, 1965).

Berger's book is based on the Oedipal relish we all feel when a giant is cut down to size.

Granted, it's high time someone pointed out the failings. Picasso has reigned unchallenged on a serious level, at least since the last war, nearly since the first. He and his work are surrounded by a continual barrage of obsequiousness: there are adulatory movies and memoirs, and intimate records, like expensive, souped-up family albums, fascinating yet somehow pointless; there are dozen upon dozen of marvellous picture-books with inert commentaries. He reigns, as Berger says, 'like a king', progressing with his court, his baggage and his buffoons through his châteaux and villas (he has as many elegant properties scattered across France as the average millionaire has Picassos). Everything he does is taken with owlish seriousness. His admirers may talk lovingly of his jokes, but are reluctant to admit that they are often in doubtful artistic taste. Yet since 1917, when he collaborated with Cocteau and Diaghilev in *Parade*, he has often been mixed up with occasional *frou-frou* that has nothing to do with his genius. He has encouraged the flattering myth of himself as the eternally young, eternally creative, eternally potent and mysterious genius; he has encouraged the potters of Vallauris by his casual doodling on ceramics (he uses them like sketch pads). Unlike most geniuses, he has never dried up; but although he has gone on working relentlessly, he has inevitably had periods when he has produced nothing of great importance.

Berger hammers all this home remorselessly enough. If he is sometimes unfair, it is, he makes you feel, more in sorrow than in anger. If he is sometimes downright misleading – in suggesting that Picasso has produced nothing of real seriousness since 1944 and largely wasted the 1920s (how about the variations in 1921 on *The Three Musicians*? Or the crucial and superb *Three Dancers* of 1925?) – well, he is misleading in the service of a theory. It is a Marxist theory of the inexorable corruption of the arts in a competitive bourgeois society, where the standards are cash and fame. According to Berger, Picasso began as a prodigy and only developed beyond that ambiguous virtue in two isolated periods: first, during the spell that began in 1907 with *Les Demoiselles d'Avignon*, and continued through the days of pure Cubism when he collaborated with Braque and writers like Jacob and Apollinaire; this ended with the First World War; second, from 1930 to 1944, when the combination of a peculiarly deep and satisfying affair, plus the Spanish Civil War and the Nazi occupation of France, released a second creative outburst.

Why these two periods above all others, apart from the fact that any theory that didn't account for *Les Demoiselles* and *Guernica* is plainly inadequate? The answer lies in Berger's Marxist view of History, Progress and the Artist's Position in European society. As he sees him, Picasso, a permanent exile from his native Spain, erupted into cosmopolitan France as 'a vertical invader' (the phrase is Ortega y Gasset's). That is, despite his middle-class intellectual family, he drew his psychic strength and habits from the primitive, violent, self-stultifying, anarchic Spain of the late nineteenth century. Thus he has always been isolated from the intricate society of his adoption. However sophisticated his techniques, his genius lies in his direct, intuitive contact with his unmodified, unsocialized instincts; it is sensual, a-social and intensely subjective.

Picasso, then, has been doomed to perpetual isolation, a deprived, deified millionaire. Only twice has he broken out of this claustrophobic freedom: once as a Cubist, once under the spell of his affair with Marie-Thérèse Walter. Berger has an ingenious theory of Cubism as 'the only example of dialectical materialism in painting', fusing 'Courbet's materialism' with 'Cézanne's dialectic':

> The Cubists created a system by which they could reveal visually the interlocking of phenomena. . . . Cubism is an art entirely concerned with interaction: the interaction between different aspects: the interaction between structure and movement: the interaction between solids and the space around them. . . .

This, he feels, somehow fits in with Faraday's and Maxwell's conception of the electro-magnetic field, with Planck's Quantum Theory and Einstein's Relativity, with Niels Bohr's theory of complementarity and Heisenberg's Uncertainty Principle. All centre on the idea of the indivisibility of nature; mysteriously, ineluctably, the world connects up. Similarly, Marx's view of the historical inevitability of socialism is a kind of political Quantum theory, based on a belief in the indivisibility of mankind, despite the class system. Hence Cubism, Marxism and post-Newtonian physics are all of a piece throughout.

It is a clever idea, if you don't push it too far. But its connections with Picasso's Cubism are tenuous, particularly since Berger allows him small share in the formal achievement. By painting *Les*

Demoiselles he simply and unwittingly 'provoked' the style; it was Braque who saw the formal possibilities. What Picasso got out of it, and what made him suddenly flower into major art, was a social connection:

> He became part of a group who, although they did not formulate a programme, were all working in the same direction. . . . It was . . . a period of inner certainty and security. It was, I believe, the only time when Picasso felt entirely at home.

Picasso, that is, in his life more than in his paintings, was demonstrating the indivisibility of the art-world.

Berger makes a curious connection between all this and Picasso's second blossoming. When he was obsessed with Marie-Thérèse Walter he was the reverse of 'part of a group'. Instead, his theme became what Berger calls 'the marvellous shared subjectivity of sex', 'a preoccupation with physical sensations so strong and deep that they destroy all objectivity'. In short, he lost his sense of isolation a second time in his sexual absorption with a woman.

There is, I think, something fundamentally tricksy about this argument. It is a question of tone. As a critic, Berger has a considerable impressionist gift for re-creating the sense of a picture; he is also clever, though conventional, in his handling of Marxist dialectic. But in both activities he employs a constant excess of feeling. The feeling, I mean, is a personal mannerism which exists over and above the subject. This is parodied in his, to me, unfortunate television manner, which I find cloying and over-intimate, as though seduction were the better part of communication. In his writing this is held more in control; but the excessiveness is still there. For all his brilliance, Berger is a sentimentalist, and what he sentimentalizes above all is the ideal of solidarity. So it makes sense that Picasso's genius should flower most for him only when working with a mutually supporting group of artists or when involved in a mutually satisfying love-affair. For, as Berger describes them, there seems no essential difference between the lover's 'marvellous shared subjectivity of sex' and the Marxist's 'true fraternal sense of solidarity'. In these circumstances, revolutionary 'fraternity' sounds oddly like Eisenhower's 'togetherness'.

The confusion would hardly matter if Berger didn't make it central to his criticism of Picasso's achievement. He allows him his genius, his integrity, his despair, but he flails him for his lack of a 'subject'. To Picasso, exile and 'vertical invader' of a society he is indifferent to, nothing is given, everything has to be mined painfully out of his own self. This is partly true, and it is in this process that Picasso foreshadows the whole internal migration of modern art, as it is driven to the periphery of mass culture, rewarded, praised but 'alienated'. Hence, though Picasso's genius may be characteristic of our time, Berger feels it is wrongly so. And this, perhaps, says more about Berger's criteria than Picasso's genius, for only relatively minor artists like Léger and Siqueiros seem to fill his bill. Yet, paradoxically, of all modern masters, Picasso comes closest to Berger's ideal, largely because he is, above all, a maker of statements. Unlike the abstract painters, he is rarely more than marginally concerned with colour. His greatest works, like *Guernica*, are in black and white – the colour of print, the colour of statements. Indeed, one of his crucial contributions has been to develop Cubism away from its formal, rather intellectual beginnings and use it as a direct expression of reality as he understands it. So where Berger damns many of Picasso's distortions as 'absurd' he could equally easily see them as social comment. When Picasso parodies Velazquez's *Las Meninas* he is showing what has happened *now* to all that calm and dignity and sense of order: it has become disjointed, distorted, colourless, ludicrous, violent. This is applied Cubism, Cubist social criticism.

But Berger won't allow this:

> In front of *Nude Dressing her Hair*, we never get beyond the violence that each part does to the next. No emotion develops because it is short-circuited by shock. . . . A woman's body by itself cannot be made to express all the horrors of fascism. But Picasso clung to this subject because, at the moment of fear and crisis, it was the only one of which he felt certain.

At this point the 'absurdity' comes home to roost on Berger himself. Following the fulfilled sensuality of the Marie-Thérèse paintings, Picasso expresses his rage against 'the horrors of fascism' in *Nude Dressing her Hair* by doing violence to all the values he has previously so beautifully created. He has given 'the horrors of fascism' precisely the emotional reality which that tired cliché lacks.

Yet I suspect that, for all his cleverness and insight, Berger fundamentally prefers the clichés of the Marxist view of history and brotherhood to Picasso's shocked and original vision. The reason is not because he is immune to new ideas – he is full of them himself – but because he is a sentimentalist. And the essence of sentimentalism is to reduce – or inflate – all feelings to one comfortable commonplace. So though he cuts helpfully through much of the nonsense surrounding the master, he leaves the genius of the man untouched. It lies in the certainty of Picasso's intuitions, and his refusal to put in their place any prefabricated answers, however reassuring, however theoretically impeccable.

The Spectator, 1965

Yvor Winters*

There are two kinds of critic: the professional and the amateur. Of course, I am using both words in their literal, not their derogatory senses. The amateurs are those who love literature for its own sake. The printed word and the effort of writing inspire in them a devotion which is very close to awe. For them criticism is a matter of selection and arrangement, like floral decoration or stage lighting, to show off the work to its best advantage. They will find something good to be said for every work, no matter how trivial. Now these amateurs may seem professional; they may be sunk in writing up to their ears – as dons with the most rigorous standards of scholarship or as literary journalists haunted by the weekly need to be lively on the subject of dead books – but by their judgement shall ye know them; or by their lack of it.

The professionals, on the other hand, are those who are vowed to the job by a kind of act of faith. They make their living out of literature in the true sense, which is not a question of cash but of moral habit. In short, they use literature to build up for themselves a world of values. Inevitably, they don't like much, for in all viable moralities the elect are, of necessity, few. So their work is devoted to keeping up the standards, always with an intellectual passion, sometimes with a certain savagery. Like old-fashioned doctors, they believe that blood must at times be let to preserve the health of the system. In England, the foremost professional critic is in this sense F. R. Leavis; in America, he is Yvor Winters.

* Yvor Winters, *In Defense of Reason* (London: Routledge and Kegan Paul, 1960).

In Defense of Reason has taken a long time to reach us. It is made up of three independent but related books: *Primitivism and Decadence*, an analysis of modern American poetry, was first published in 1937; *Maule's Curse*, on the classical American novel and its intellectual tradition, appeared in 1938; *The Anatomy of Nonsense*, on American critical theory, came out in 1943; the complete collection, with an additional essay on Hart Crane, was published in the States in 1947. It is a pity that the book has been so long on the way, for original ideas spread their light before them; a number of Winters's suggestions have become fashions and he has not been given credit for them. He was, for instance, the first man to debunk Eliot's claims to classicism by showing how his theories descend straight from the late Romantics; he attacked the vagaries of neo-Symbolism and the craze for Laforguian irony (which he blandly equated with 'careless writing'); he praised Melville, James and, with reservations, Stevens, Crane and Hawthorne, long before any of them had become cult-figures. All this he had writ large in the thirties and early forties. We are just catching up with him.

But Winters would wish to base his ultimate reputation less on his originality or on the profundity of his insights than on his ability to produce a system that works. He has a rage for order and is fierce in proportion to an author's lack of it. He calls himself an absolutist, which means he demands nothing less than everything:

> It will be seen that what I desire of a poem is a clear understanding of motive, and a just evaluation of feeling; the justice of the evaluation persisting even into the sound of the least important syllable. Such a poem is a perfect and complete act of the spirit; it calls upon the full life of the spirit; it is difficult of attainment, but I am aware of no good reason to be contented with less.

Stated briefly, with such massive and ironic Johnsonian certainty, there is no arguing with Winters. But principles, particularly when they concern the enormous complexity of artistic and moral judgement, are better left brief or implicit than explained. The critic creates his audience and his context more by his intellectual tone than by spelling things out. Leavis, when challenged to define one of his terms, would, I imagine, prefer to point to a work of art than to launch into abstractions. Winters, on the other hand, is determined to have everything down in black and white. The results are often less flexible and profound than his practice:

> The artistic process is one of moral evaluation of human experience, by means of a technique which renders possible an evaluation more precise than any other. *The poet tries to understand his experience in rational terms, to state his understanding, and simultaneously to state, by means of the feelings which we attach to words, the kind and degree of emotion that should properly be motivated by this understanding*. . . . The 'intensity' of the work of art, which is different from the intensity of crude experience, lies in this: that what we call intensity in a work of art is a combination of the importance of the original subject and the precision of the judgement; whereas that which we call intensity in life is most often *the confused and therefore frightening emotion* resulting from a situation which we have not yet had time to meet and understand. . . . [My italics]

The business of the poet is to know himself: by his art he makes clearings of sanity in the encroaching jungle of experience; and because of his skill, these clearings are more lucid, more precise, more generally meaningful than those of other people. His method, for Winters as for Wordsworth, is that of 'emotion recollected in tranquillity'.

So far, so good – or almost so good. The flaw is in the first sentence I italicized. Winters makes it sound as though the *rational* understanding always came before the poem rather than during the process of writing, or even after it; as though each poem were accreted round a separate pearl of wisdom. He also implies that there are rules for the degree of emotion proper to each subject. It sounds more like a Renaissance than a modern theory. What he is describing, I suggest, is less the act of poetry than the act of criticism.

It is easy to see why. Like Winters, I too dislike obscurantism and the cant of blind inspiration. I am all for poets knowing what they mean. But knowing is not a clear-cut business. In the twentieth century, to be intelligent does not mean simply to be rational. It means the ability to make one's reason supple and subtle enough to include the irrational without being overwhelmed by it. The physicists have long worked with this element of irrationality, which they call entropy, the measure of chance or probability. In other terms, the whole of Freud's work was devoted to showing how irrational desires and fears run deep and compulsively below the most rational motives. The irrational, in short, is a vital element in modern reason.

When Winters, however, calls his book *In Defense of Reason* he really means it. He is not only Johnsonian in style; like the Doctor, he believes absolutely in the power of rational common sense. Because he is a peculiarly fine critic, his logic is always instinct with feeling, but he seeks to reduce everything to its terms. It doesn't always work. Eliot's importance, for example, has nothing to do with his Symbolist tricks and obscurity: instead it is in the way he worked out for our time a language in which great formal intelligence combines with great psychological depth, in which the rational and irrational meet and illuminate each other. But Winters will have none of him. He opts instead for the totally rational. And that means Robert Bridges, Adelaide Crapsey and Elizabeth Daryush, 'the finest British poet since T. Sturge Moore' – 'that sheep', Yeats called him, 'in sheep's clothing'.

It is perhaps the least distinguished 'great tradition' any important critic has produced. Yet although Winters has deliberately set his face against American modernism, his choice is not dictated by mere perversity. Like Zeno with his arrow, he is in a logical quandary: Winters admires above all sureness and clarity of moral choice; therefore he is against the experimental because it attempts to cope more or less directly with 'the confused and therefore frightening emotion' of unregulated experience; therefore he makes a virtue out of the traditional which 'endeavours to utilize the greatest possible amount of the knowledge and wisdom, both technical and moral . . . to be found in precedent poetry. It assumes the ideal existence of a normal quality of feeling'; therefore he chooses Bridges & Co. The flying arrow does not move; the great poets are the consolidators, not the transformers of art. For all his originality, Winters is, by force of logic, profoundly reactionary.

Yet this taste for clear logic and moral certainty is also the strength of his criticism. His method is to combine literary insight with the history of ideas. Lucidly, stringently, he builds up the world of ideas and beliefs in which his authors wrote. He then goes through their works showing how the ideas were transformed and coloured by the writers' sensibilities. It is a kind of paraphrase done from the inside, so that at the moment of defining what a work of art says, Winters is defining how it feels:

> [*The Awkward Age*] is a tragedy of manners, in which no genuine moral issue is involved, but in which vague depths of moral ugliness, especially in Vanderbank, are elusively but unforgettably suggested. Vanderbank is a creature through whose tranquil and pellucid character there arises at the slightest disturbance of his surface a fine cloud of silt,

of ugly feeling far too subtle to be called suspicion, but darkening his entire nature and determining his action.

It takes a major critic to combine that degree of aesthetic understanding with so firm and pervasive a judgement.

So in the end, his tight, restrictive moral system seems not only justified but necessary. He is a man of acute moral instincts with no strong moral system to which he can instinctively adhere. Although he deeply understands the New England tradition, he is not part of it. He belongs, apparently, to no organized church. So he is left with his belief in literature, his logic and his considerable ability as a writer (he is also a distinguished poet). From these he has erected, by Johnsonian reasonableness, a moral and literary tradition of his own. One may not agree with it, but it is impossible not to admire his skill, his courage and the superb criticism it has enabled him to write.

The New Statesman, 1960

Norman Podhoretz*

In one of the most intriguing essays in an immensely intriguing collection, Norman Podhoretz sets out to defend 'The Article As Art':

> Why should the magazine article, of all things, have become so important and fertile a genre in our day? Why have so many writers . . . found it possible to move around more freely and creatively within it than within fiction or poetry?

His slightly anti-climactic answer is that the article chimes with our taste for the functional, as in architecture or painting. But clearly there is more to it than that. The article is a short-term form in a time when the value of long-term efforts seems none too high. It offers instant cash, more or less instant reputation and, at best, instant controversy. It is also, in New York, a projection of the intense, caustic arguing which continually rumbles away in that intellectual jungle where everyone knows everybody else, and the knives are sharp and busy.

Podhoretz is an expert in knocking criticism: witty, subtle, ironic. Reading him in full cry – against Faulkner or Mary McCarthy or the Beats – is a sharp aesthetic pleasure, like watching a good athlete on form: the intellectual muscle is all there and all being used, with no holds barred, no false pieties and everything working for him. On his day, Podhoretz, as they say of Skegness, is so bracing. Yet it

* Norman Podhoretz, *Doings and Undoings* (London: Rupert Hart-Davis, 1965).

turns out that literary criticism isn't quite what he means when he talks of 'the article as art'. In the introduction to *Doings and Undoings*, he writes off his earlier, more exclusively literary essays as the work of someone who is now a stranger to him, adding:

> What I mean, then, in saying that for me literature is not an end in itself is that I look upon it as a mode of public discourse that either illuminates or fails to illuminate the common ground on which we live. . . . I write as a participant observer of the culture for whom the novel is one form of discourse among many, and not necessarily the most valuable.

What concerns him at the present, then, is not the work of art as such but the cultural and political situation it reflects: what we do, what we think, what we are, and the forces that make us so. Partly, this shift of focus is a symptom of Hack's Fatigue, the disease all reviewers suffer from sooner or later: an utter boredom with literature as the beginning and end of wisdom. Heaven knows, Marianne Moore had the root of the matter in her poem on 'Poetry': 'I, too, dislike it: there are things that are important beyond all this fiddle.' Partly, too, it reflects a change in environment from the Eisenhower–McCarthy days when Podhoretz began writing, the days of comfort, prosperity and fear, when the intellectuals, cosily provided for in their universities, opted out of everything that didn't directly concern their relatively narrow specialist functions. But by the time Podhoretz was about thirty and was fully coming into his own as a writer, Eisenhower had been replaced by Kennedy. The intellectuals were rallied to, or behind, Washington and it seemed possible that their brand of tensely sceptical criticism might even influence those who were governing the country. For not only did Kennedy take an amused, sophisticate's interest in the highbrow magazines, but, thanks to the grace of his sheer presence and style (though not always his policies), the business of politics seemed, for the first time since Jefferson, not entirely hypocritical and sub-literate. Hence the intellectuals were often tempted to deliver themselves of their own State of the Union Messages.

Yet when Podhoretz defends the article as 'functional', something beyond all this seems to be involved: I mean a specifically Jewish anxiety about the value of one's work and the tradition one should be in. This anxiety is very much present in the writing of the three cultural heroes whom he acknowledges: Lionel Trilling, who was his teacher at Columbia, and Isaac Rosenfeld and Robert Warshow, both of whom died prematurely in their thirties, leaving behind some brilliant articles, some less satisfactory creative work and a pervasive influence. With all of them the question of what one is and how one behaves *vis-à-vis* society emerges from every discussion, no matter how literary its overt intentions. I suspect that this is linked somehow to the Old Testament and Talmudic concern with secular moral order. Lacking a belief in an after-life, Judaism is, after all, *the* worldly religion: it centres on patriarchal authority and the intricacies of family piety; its ten commandments are a social code. At the core of it all are twin concepts of respect and responsibility. And this puts a great weight of justification on the gifted Jew, a disturbing certainty that talent, cleverness and success are not in themselves enough; one must also contribute to and maybe alter, however little, the moral climate in which one lives.

Clearly, Podhoretz has felt all this keenly, more so perhaps because, whilst at Columbia, he also attended the Seminary College of Jewish Studies, where young rabbis are trained. Though the rabbinate was not his style, as Trilling's most gifted student a teaching job in a university would have come automatically. Yet that, in the early fifties, seemed too restrictive and comfortable a solution. As an outstanding critic, a more glittering chance on *The New Yorker* appeared. Finally, he turned that down in order to edit *Commentary*, the American Jewish Committee's excellent highbrow magazine. His choice, in short, was for a public function in the Jewish intellectual world.

It is as editor of *Commentary* that he has come into his own and written his most ambitious 'articles as art'. The problem is to know to what extent his rather grand position has changed or distorted his freedom of judgement. His two latest articles are particularly relevant: one on Hannah Arendt's book on Eichmann, the other on the Negro problem. Both are highly personal, committed, passionate and deliberately provocative; yet for all their bravura I find them curiously unsatisfactory. It is not simply that I disagree radically with his conclusions – to provoke disagreement is, after all, one of the functions of a fighting article – it is a matter, rather, of *how* he says his say. Consider, for example, the rhetorical question that ends the Arendt piece:

> The Nazis destroyed a third of the Jewish people. In the name of all that is humane, will the remnant never let up on itself?

Leaving aside whether or not the appeal is justified (I don't think it is), there remains the question of whom it is made to. Not, I think, to his peers in the Manhattan gang – whom he ironically calls 'Everyone-I-know' and who took sides with a vengeance in the Arendt affair – but to the Jewish middle-class community as a whole: to all those Long Island doctors, philanthropic businessmen and psychoanalysts with cultural leanings – wealthy, adjusted, assimilated, complacent.

Now, I personally believe that in matters of real intellectual conscience one can't finally appeal to such people because the answers and assent one gets from them, however enlightened and liberal, will be in the last analysis middle-brow, philistine. Ultimately, they don't want to know. I also believe that Podhoretz is perfectly aware of this. After all, he fought his way out of the Brooklyn jungle by sheer talent; he owes no one anything. And as editor of the most influential Jewish magazine he is in a unique position to shake his readers' more comfortable pieties. His talent has made him an eloquent spokesman for his generation. It would be a pity if it were to trap him in the false position of moral guardian of the Community Chest. *Doings and Undoings* is a brilliant collection of essays, but it made me uneasy.

The Spectator, 1965

Never on Sontag*

Anyone who had only seen Susan Sontag on *Monitor* or read about her in *Time* would probably imagine a kind of New York Brigid Brophy: a lady, that is, with an eye firmly on her shock-appeal and paradoxes – though cooler, perhaps, and more hip than any British-made product. *Against Interpretation* will change that image. Flashiness is not Miss Sontag's *forte*; her essays are careful, tightly argued and often rather heavy; she has a taste for abstraction, a wide, easy knowledge of philosophical background – she read and taught the subject at university – and that slightly ponderous prose style which usually goes with philosophical debate. Her characteristic note is one of unremitting seriousness.

Given the appropriate subject, she can be very good indeed: lucid when expounding the intricacies of Lévi-Strauss; sharp and knowledgeable about George Lukács, and not at all impressed by his cult reputation; positively tender about Pavese, 'the exemplary sufferer', and elegiac about the clash in Camus's work between genuine 'moral beauty' and 'inexhaustible self-perpetuating oratory'. She also has a brilliant analysis of the 'puzzling thinness', the whimsy and pretension of Ionesco, of the way Hochhuth's *The Representative* manages to be moving despite the flabby language and clogged structure, and of the oddly effective manner in which science fiction movies express contemporary anxieties. In short, with traditionally serious, highbrow subjects she has all the qualities of an excellent critic; she is intelligent, perceptive, clear and impressively well informed.

* Susan Sontag, *Against Interpretation* (London: Eyre and Spottiswoode, 1967).

But there is a hitch: her main interest has, apparently, shifted from the intellectual life, in its relatively pure and abstract forms, to the goings-on of the very latest *avant-garde*. However good she may be at it, she is, as her title announces, 'Against Interpretation' and all that implies – with its psychoanalytic overtones – of close analysis and patient attention to ideas. All she now cares about is the aesthetic surface of art, its gestures and style. I can see her point: we have all had our bellyful of dogged, line-by-line New Criticism. Even if we hadn't, the *avant-garde*, particularly in New York, is now impervious to the old critical techniques, since it is deeply involved in intellectual fringe activities: in the various manifestations of commercial cinema – Western, gangster, science fiction and blue – in drugs, near-pornography, pop music, happenings, advertisements, comic strips, TV. In short, *avant-garde* reality is now defined by a world of urban junk. To cope with all this a critic needs a good deal of speed and appetite and, above all, flexibility.

These are precisely the qualities in which Miss Sontag is weakest. Not that she isn't open-minded, liberal and, more important still, seemingly impervious to whole universes of boredom: on the evidence of these essays, she must have sat through enough bad movies and wan happenings to rupture the iron digestion of an ostrich. But stamina, like patriotism, is not enough. There is also a question of tone. *Avant-garde* art is able to absorb all sorts of extra- or infra-artistic material because it is cool; that is, it maintains towards all phenomena a witty, highly pragmatic detachment. In contrast, Miss Sontag's tone is too earnest, too unchanging. Whether she is discussing *Anthropologie Structurale* or *The Invasion of the Body-Snatchers*, Weiss's *Marat/Sade* or Smith's *Flaming Creatures*, her solemnity never wavers. Granted, the point she is making is that there is much to be said for many conventionally despised forms; but she makes it in a way that cancels the discovery and the pleasure:

> If art is understood as a form of discipline of the feelings and a programming of sensations, then the feeling (or sensation) given off by a Rauschenberg painting might be like that of a song by the Supremes. The brio and elegance of Bud Boetticher's *The Rise and Fall of Legs Diamond* or the singing style of Dionne Warwick can be appreciated as a complex and pleasurable event. They are all experienced without condescension.

The Rise and Fall of Legs Diamond is, admittedly, an excellent film. But to talk of its 'brio and elegance', as though it were a Haydn quartet, is, precisely, a form of condescension. The only difference between this and more usual modes, is that she is condescending as much to her non-swinging audience as to the movie.

It also means that she goes to the cinema in a special, effete way. This is particularly obvious in her long essay on Godard's *Vivre sa vie.* It is a film she regards, rightly I think, as a masterpiece. So in defiance of all her critical principles, she painstakingly interprets the thing, elucidating its levels of complexity, its conception of freedom and responsibility. Her justification comes two thirds of the way through: 'The whole of *Vivre sa vie* may be seen as a text. It is a text in, a study of, lucidity; it is about seriousness.' My first reaction to that statement is that she is talking about some other film altogether. *Vivre sa vie is* serious, *is* beautiful, but it is also funny, destructive and a bit flip. This is typical of Godard, whose irony is always two-edged, as is inevitable in a man who can make such cool and canny art out of an obsession. The image of this obsession is the marvellous Anna Karina, and he deals with her partly in dead earnest, partly by jokes and partly by a stylishly disguised murderousness (at the end of this film he has her casually shot down). It seems to me that an account of a Godard movie that altogether misses the wit is dictated by an utterly inappropriate critical response, a tactlessness close to insensitivity.

Miss Sontag would probably justify this in the name of what she, approvingly, calls 'excruciating seriousness'. A less rosy way of putting it would be 'lack of humour'. God forbid I should accuse her of being short of that bland metropolitan knowingness; there is quite enough of that in London, without going to New York for it. What she does lack, however, is a degree of self-irony. Consider, for example, her discussion of Jack Smith's homosexual blue movie, *Flaming Creatures.* She begins by describing 'the close-ups of limp penises and bouncing breasts, the shots of masturbation and oral sexuality'. Two pages later she writes:

> One can easily doubt that a certain piece of footage was indeed intended to be over-exposed. Of no sequence is one convinced that it had to last this long, and not longer or shorter. Shots aren't framed in the traditional way; heads are cut off; extraneous figures sometimes appear on the margin of the scene. The camera is hand-held most of the time, and the image often quivers. . . .

Believe it or not, she isn't being funny. The context makes it clear that this isn't an elaborate exercise in *double entendre*: the footage is film footage, the sequences film sequences, the shots film shots, and the hand-held camera really is a camera. The enormous possibilities of what she is saying never strike her, I suppose, because of her curiously unyielding earnestness. Anything she can discuss becomes, by definition, ultimately serious and therefore inviolable to irony. In another essay she is plainly embarrassed to admit that she sometimes laughs at happenings.

This embarrassment is, I think, a dominant motive in her famous 'Notes on "Camp" ', which has become a guidebook for swinging highbrows. Like Marshall McLuhan and Leslie Fiedler, Miss Sontag has done a great deal to show how the minority arts now spill over significantly into the realm of mass culture, and how pop products can often be skilful, exciting, compelling. Her theory of 'camp' seems intended as a vindication of all this. In fact, it is the reverse. It is a counsel of despair, as who should say, 'Rubbish and boredom are unavoidable; since we must live with them, we might as well find ways of enjoying them.' Miss Sontag's solution is 'camp', 'the discovery of the good taste of bad taste'. The core of her essay is an amusing, perverse compilation of exaggerated, artificial, corny phenomena which, despite themselves, exert a certain awful charm: *King Kong*, *Swan Lake*, Jayne Mansfield, Flash Gordon, General de Gaulle. An equivalent English list would include, *inter alia*, Paul Johnson's *London Diary*, Kingsley Amis on Vietnam, Tony Richardson movies, George Brown and, or course, Miss Sontag on *Monitor*.

As a party-game, like the 'U–non-U' craze, 'Camp' has immense, albeit rather 'camp', possibilities. But as a serious element in Miss Sontag's view of things it hides a wealth of uneasiness. It is as though she felt she had to justify her enjoyment of things lowbrow by a sophisticated double double-take which proves that, in the last analysis, what is terrible is good, since boredom is the only interesting emotion left. To the pure all things are pure. 'Camp', 'the sensibility of failed seriousness', is an equivocal form of condescension by one whose seriousness, whatever else, has never failed.

By aestheticizing the world and her responses to it, Miss Sontag somehow manages to anaesthetize her anxieties. Well and good. But in doing so she is implicitly denying her whole defence of *Lumpen* culture. After all, a vital pop art like cinema creates its own standards, which are different from those of the traditional arts, yet powerful enough not to need highbrow patronage. Robert Warshow, the most brilliant of film critics, once wrote:

> One cannot long frequent the art cinema or read much of the criticism which upholds it without a sense of incompleteness and even of irrelevance. Really the movies are not quite that 'legitimate' – they are still the bastard child of art, and if in the end they must be made legitimate, it will be a changed household of art that receives them. . . . I have had enough serious interest in the products of the higher arts to be very sharply aware that the impulse which leads me to a Humphrey Bogart movie has little in common with the impulse which leads me to the novels of Henry James or the poetry of T. S. Eliot. That there is a connection between the two impulses I do not doubt, but the connection is not adequately summed up in the statement that the Bogart movie and the Eliot poem are both forms of art. . . . It must be that I go to the movies because I am attracted to Humphrey Bogart or Shelley Winters or Greta Garbo; because I require the absorbing immediacy of the screen; because in some way I take all that nonsense seriously.

This relatively simple human distinction is one which Miss Sontag has yet to make. Being so firmly 'against interpretation', she compensates by over-aestheticizing, by reducing everything to the same sophisticated surface. In her ideal world a swinging audience will get the same *frisson* from 'the beauty of a machine or of the solution to a mathematical problem, of a painting by Jasper Johns, of a film by Jean-Luc Godard, and of the personalities and music of the Beatles'. It seems to me to be an elaborate way of selling both cultures short at once.

The Spectator, 1967

American Critics*

The World's Classics volume of *American Critical Essays* is, in a way, a melancholy sight for an English critic: not, certainly, in appearance – with its positively jaunty pink and grey jacket – nor in size – it could profitably have run to a second volume – but simply in the standard of the work. It supplements the quite extraordinarily unrepresentative collection of American criticism published in the same series in 1930; it is also, says the blurb, a companion to the volume of English criticism World's Classics brought out last year. It is here the melancholy strikes. One might as well call the Matterhorn a companion mountain to Snowdon. The sheer bulk of serious, complex, concentrated and detailed American criticism is not matched in this country. For our major generation we have Eliot (since Harold Beaver does not count him among the Americans), I. A. Richards (though he is mysteriously chosen for the other side), F. R. Leavis, William Empson, Wilson Knight and F. W. Bateson. Against them Mr Beaver can line up, among others, R. P. Blackmur, Allen Tate, Yvor Winters, Edmund Wilson, Lionel Trilling, Alfred Kazin, F. O. Matthiessen, Robert Penn Warren and W. H. Auden – among others. And behind them are all the important critics Mr Beaver hasn't chosen at all: no Kenneth Burke, no John Crowe Ransom, no Francis Fergusson nor W. K. Wimsatt; none of the Chicago Aristotelians nor semantic analysts; scarcely any of the younger critics – no R. W. B. Lewis, nor Marius Bewley, no J. W. Aldridge, no Joseph Frank nor Randall Jarrell. The roll-call is

* *American Critical Essays, Twentieth Century*, selected by Harold Beaver (London: Oxford University Press, 1959).

long and intimidating, for American criticism is, in its way, one of the great impressive achievements of modern literature.

Of course, the Americans have all the advantages: they have huge benevolent foundations to give them money; they have high-powered seminars, summer schools and conferences to listen to them; above all, they have space. There is virtually no journal in England that will pay a critic for a long, detailed essay on a literary subject which, by the editor's lights, is considered neither 'contemporary' nor 'of general interest'. If an English critic wants to write at length he must publish in the States: in *The Kenyon*, *The Partisan*, *The Hudson*, or *The Sewanee*. But then there are not many English critics who seem interested in that kind of extended work: *Scrutiny* foundered, presumably, from lack of new contributors, not lack of support; and *Essays in Criticism* rapidly turned, with occasional exceptions, into Essays in Scholarship. Most English academics stick to literary history, an admirable job, but one more concerned with background than judgement. Hence evaluation has largely to be done within the limits of critical journalism. Instead of the great quarterlies, we have the weeklies.

Now literary journalism has its advantages: it must be clear, to the point and readable – which does not necessarily mean vapid. But good art is long, and space short. One can state themes, hint at complexities, but rarely analyse them and still less follow where they lead. Moreover, part of the reviewer's job is to tell the readers whether or not they should buy the book. What of the good books with which he disagrees and the bad books which are on the right side? Without room to make the proper qualifications, he succumbs, as often as not, to paralysis of choice. At a lower level, there is an even more deadly disease, sheer fatigue: with deadlines looming and the 'phone ringing, the writer by-passes the difficulties of critical judgement and settles for usable material – trends, attitudes, striking lines and phrases. Unlike Homer, the continual surprise of critical journalism is not that it sometimes nods, but that, considering the conditions in which most of it is written, it gets anything said at all.

Critical journalism hardly exists in the States. (Edmund Wilson is its only major exponent, and he has considerably more space and vastly more intelligence than the rest of us dream of.) One can read through *The New York Times Book Review* for months on end without realizing a bad work has been published. The serious critics make their living on the universities circuit. So they have a different function: they may or may not be teachers, but they are always Intellectuals in Residence.

Perhaps this is as it should be. Modern criticism was made necessary by modern poetry. Its aim was to elucidate work that was concentrated, allusive, difficult and new. But the major critic was also the major poet, T. S. Eliot. His interest was not to develop a handy technique of analysis; that was a job for the pedagogues and codifiers. Eliot, when he was not working out his preoccupations as a poet, was concerned to raise the general level of critical discussion. The old gentleman-of-letters clichés – that 'rare gift for a haunting phrase' and the like, that aura of 'fine writing', those invocations of 'verbal magic' – had created a block to the understanding; sooner or later, they landed all criticism with its head into a blank wall of speechlessness. Housman's final criteria of poetic excellence were, he admitted, purely physiological: a bristling of the skin, a piercing sensation in the pit of the stomach, a shiver down the spine.

Eliot replaced all this with a sentence: 'the only method', he wrote, 'is to be very intelligent.' From this the whole New Criticism developed. All its strategies and techniques, its ambiguity, irony, symbolic action, intension and extension, texture and structure, were simply so many ways of ensuring that the reader be intelligent: that he read closely, think as well as respond, reason and argue instead of merely asserting. In America, the twenties was the decade of great creative activity. The thirties was a time of criticism, when the creative discoveries were analysed and established. The achievement of the great generation of American critics was to ensure that literature was once more available to sophisticated discussion.

The popular image of the New Critics, where it exists, is of so many cold-blooded analysts examining with powerful lenses and clinical neatness the delicate secrets of verse; and, of course, they murder to dissect. Yet little of this kind of niggling gets into Mr Beaver's collection. Admittedly, it is not wholly representative; the editor has more a taste for critical biography than literary dialectic and this does not do full justice to the range of American work. Nevertheless, analysis, for the best American critics, is always a starting-point for a journey to somewhere else.

From our point of view, for example, the most curious essay in the book is Allen Tate on 'The Man of Letters in the Modern World'. He begins unexceptionally enough:

> To keep alive the knowledge of ourselves with which the literary arts continue to enlighten the more ignorant portion of mankind . . . to separate them from other indispensable forms of knowledge, and to define their limits, is the intellectual and thus the social function of the writer. Here the man of letters is the critic.

Yet within a page or two the writer is no longer the practitioner of one discipline among many, he has become responsible for the whole of society, its corruption, its decay, its appalling misuse of power:

> If [he] . . . is aware of more, he is able to do less, than the politician, who does not know what he is doing. The man of letters sees that modern societies are machines, even if he thinks that they ought not to be. . . . While the politician, in his cynical innocence, uses society, the man of letters disdainfully, or perhaps even absent-mindedly, withdraws from it.

What is curious about this charge is not its truth, but the fact that it can be made at all. When Dr Leavis, for example, criticizes contemporary literature his attacks are based on a steady rejection of contemporary society, as though the measure of his integrity were his refusal to participate in the rat-race. For his American counterpart, this would be the measure of his guilt. Because the critic knows literature, he knows man; hence his responsibility extends directly and continually from writing to society. If the individual is being overwhelmed by mass-society, it is the critics, not the politicians, nor the corporations, nor the Madison Avenue boys, who are to blame. 'If a nation's literature declines', wrote Pound, 'the nation atrophies and decays.' The critics, with their painfully acute awareness of language, have become the intellectual guardians of the national conscience.

The reason is, quite simply, that in the States literature – and largely modern literature, since American writing begins where the Oxford syllabus used to end, around 1830 – has replaced the other humanities as the major cultural discipline. So the kind of moral and intellectual discriminations which used to be the business of the philosophers and theologians have been taken over by the new humanists, the critics. It is they who must continually discriminate among the Protean shapes and functions of man. Hence when the Rockefeller Foundation wanted a cultural report on Europe and the Middle East, and the State Department wanted to send a distinguished non-political emissary to Japan, they both chose a literary critic, R. P. Blackmur. And the article he published in *The Kenyon* on the latter trip was concerned with the function of the American intellectual abroad, not with the dissemination of American literature.

The Japanese, apparently, gave Blackmur the title of 'Sage', not critic or writer. They had a point. For the foreigner one of the more surprising things about the best American literary men is the breadth and thoroughness of their reading. An Englishman who could move almost as effortlessly in philosophy, political theory, sociology and psychology as in literature, would be a phoenix among critics. In America, he could hardly lay claim to a really serious reputation without that equipment. The specialist training provided by knowing about literature and deploying the complex techniques of analysis is only the entrance ticket to a much larger arena of discrimination where all the forms in which behaviour and language mingle are put to the test. And this, since the time of Plato, has been the traditional function of the intellectual. It is certainly as much in the tradition of Coleridge and Matthew Arnold as it is of the great generation of American critics. We might do well to revive it here.

The New Statesman, 1959

R. P. Blackmur, 1904-65*

Richard Blackmur had all the major critical gifts in profusion: intelligence, knowledge, range and, above all, a superlative sensibility. Despite that, he remained a rather shadowy figure, and a lonely one. His students idolized him, yet always from a slight distance. Though he was patient and approachable, he paid them the ambiguous compliment of never condescending. His oblique, elliptical, probing talk, which proceeded by unexpected analogies and difficult jumps, was the same for his undergraduates as for his friends. As often as not, it left them tantalized and a bit baffled. Of course, they also felt flattered, since through him they graduated for a while into the free and adult world of letters; and this inspired devotion. Yet it was never possible to be anything as simple as a disciple of Blackmur. What he had to give was not so directly usable. His style, for example, was so peculiarly his own – though I suppose he had developed it, in an idiosyncratic way, from Henry James's prefaces – that no one else had the conviction or natural intricacy to maintain it. A few tried but the results were invariably inflated and rather silly. His subtle intellectual temper and tautness of mind were simply a brilliant example, something not to be copied but, at best, to be aspired to.

Though he called himself a 'Tory anarchist' and had a lordly taste for good food and expensive hotels, he was also radically unconventional. J. W. Aldridge once remarked that Blackmur's learning was so profound as to seem positively saintly. Yet it was wide and detailed

* R. P. Blackmur, *A Primer of Ignorance* (New York: Harcourt, Brace and World, Inc., 1967).

in a way utterly remote from that of the standard post-graduate footnoter. Regular scholars disliked him for the way he knew the work of, say, St Augustine or Dante or Vico as intimately as the things he was supposed to know about, like modern poetry. He induced in pedants a curious frustration and envy, which they thinly disguised as disdain. After all, he had never taken a university degree. His formal education finished when he graduated from Cambridge High and Latin School. He continued it in his own time and style while working at the Mandrake Bookshop and attending lectures at Harvard. In his restrained way, he was a bohemian figure in those days, a poet and something of a dandy. He was also a regular contributor to and associate editor of one of the most brilliant and influential of all American little magazines, *Hound and Horn*.

He stayed free-lance during the late twenties and most of the thirties. After his first critical collection, *The Double Agent*, was published in 1935, when he was thirty-one, the Guggenheim Foundation supported him for a couple of years. But it wasn't until he had published a volume of verse (*From Jordan's Delight*, 1937) and a second book of criticism (*The Expense of Greatness*, 1940) that he was finally invited to a university. Princeton brought him into their Creative Arts programme in 1940; he stayed there, on and off, until his death in 1965.

Yet even in Princeton he seemed isolated. He had almost nothing to do with most of the bland and heavy scholars who ran the English Department; those who rallied to him were younger, livelier and mostly without tenure. For the rest, his closest friends came from other departments, like Modern Languages or Music, or from the Institute for Advanced Study. The rumour is that it was in order to bring together these different friends with their different interests that he thought up and organized the Christian Gauss Seminars in Criticism, which turned out to be the brightest intellectual happenings in Princeton. In the impromptu parties he held after each seminar, surrounded by people who liked and admired him, and whom he trusted, Blackmur would expand and relax. White-haired, round-stomached and benign, a highbrow Father Christmas, he would argue in fierce, sidelong bursts and with obvious enjoyment, far into the night. He had a curious, attentive way of holding his cigarette between his third and fourth fingers, which made him seem continually poised for some unanswerable question.

I have the impression that during the last four or five years of his life, as he got iller, the loneliness tightened around him. He was divorced in 1951 and the beautiful little house he had built for himself in the late fifties never seemed quite full enough, despite the piles of books and papers, and the friends and students continually dropping in; despite, too, the garden which he tended with love. He had always over-valued England for all those Jamesian subtleties the place no longer has, and his year there in 1961–2 was a sad let-down. He was the first literary man to hold the Pitt Professorship at Cambridge. But although Christ's College welcomed him and made him a Fellow and the University gave him an honorary M.A., the English Faculty, rapt as ever in its rancorous in-fighting, more or less ignored him; his lectures were too hard for the undergraduates and were sparsely attended. When I saw him in London, in the beige gloom of the Park Lane Hotel, he seemed bleak and disappointed.

In the end the loneliness got into his writing. His work had always been difficult, but the difficulty of the later essays was radical where that of the earlier work was simply one of adjustment. He had from the start the writer's equivalent of absolute pitch: he knew the precise weight and vibration of every word, and his insights into these faint modulations controlled what he had to say. Yet once you had tuned into this very high frequency the discriminations were clear, graspable and rather witty. Despite his New Critical principle of never making a statement he couldn't prove from the text, he tenaciously used literature for purposes of his own, purposes, as he put it, 'of reaching understanding of the grounds of action and of finding a frame for decision, or alternative decisions'. In short, he always recognized with peculiar intensity the crisis of modern letters: the need to write within a firmly understood framework of values at a time when no such framework exists – or can, at least, be generally assumed. So he built up his values bit by bit, by his loving, unbiased attention to the work of art and his endless awareness of the resources and reverberations of language. Meticulously, fastidiously, he seemed to re-create each poet's work from the inside out, without ever losing that assured core of detachment of a critic who knows what he knows.

Even in his earlier essays Blackmur the critic and Blackmur the poet were never far apart. His poems – now out of print and terribly hard to come by – have the tautness and inturned power that is typical of his achievement everywhere. And as he developed, his prose gradually grew closer to the autonomous creative world of his poetry. He ceased to be satisfied with writing about other men's work and became more and more preoccupied with larger, more general themes: with the function of the arts, the function of the intellectual and, above all, the function of reason in the context of the insistent irrationality of the modern arts.

These problems haunt *A Primer of Ignorance* – a posthumous collection of his essays edited by his friend Joseph Frank – and wholly dominate the opening section, his 1956 Library of Congress lectures, 'Anni Mirabiles, 1921–1925: Reason in the Madness of Letters'. I imagine he intended these lectures as a kind of critical *summa*, since they centre on his own acknowledged masters – Eliot, Yeats, Joyce, Mann, Gide – and on the new shifts in emphasis peculiar to this century:

> The anarchy of our artists is in response to facts as well as in evasion of facts. The two great external facts of our time are the explosion of populations and the explosions of the new energies. The two great internal facts of our time are the re-creation of the devil (or pure behaviour) in the place of authority and the development of techniques for finding destructive troubles in the psyche of individuals.

In these lectures Blackmur was using criticism as a means to provisional and empirical wisdom; from his experience of the modern arts he was evolving techniques for coping with the new and almost impossible strains of experience generally. Elsewhere in the book he was also deliberately using the impact of foreign cultures to define, and refine, his own deeply American sensibility. His ambition, as I see it, was somehow to write into these essays the terms of his own identity, as a novelist or poet defines his own self with each new work.

The result was a mass of insights and formulations of enormous subtlety. Yet it would be dishonest not to add that much of it is often almost impenetrably difficult. For an example at random:

> It is the writhing of actual knowledge under these malicious techniques that makes choice and purpose and taste so difficult, uncertain, and fractious. We tend to relapse from all human creation back into almost pure momentum (in analogy to pure sensation), with all our activity becoming mere sports on the movement of inertia. Thus it is we seem to manipulate for manipulation's sake and find the *acte gratuite* a liberation when it ought to be a warning, an explosion when it ought to be a play,

a gesture, a feint. It is thus that we *become* our problem when we ought to exemplify some effort at the solution of it. We become, in Dante's language, the War of the Journey without active knowledge of the War of the Pity. It is the two Wars that need the Muses; either, taken solely, puerilizes man.

The initial insight is clear enough but, impelled by Blackmur's sidelong logic of analogies, it gradually takes off into some opaque inner world where you can only stumble hesitantly, a long way behind.

God knows what the audience at the Library of Congress made of this. But I suspect that Blackmur himself may not have cared much by then. At some relatively late point in his career he seems to have come to the conclusion that however flattered his audience may have felt to be treated as his equal, they never really understood what he was getting at. So he decided simply to write at the highest pitch of which he was capable, and let the audience go hang. The more his influence seemed indirect, his position to one side and his loneliness complete, the more oblique his writing became. Perhaps that is what he implied when he adopted Montaigne's motto: 'Epecho: I will not budge, I will suspend judgement.'

Maybe it is this which accounts for the underlying sadness of *A Primer of Ignorance*. All that purity and concentration and effort are somehow without much hope; it reads like an epitaph on a tradition. Certainly, the times and the styles were already changing before he died. He belonged to a period of high cosmopolitan sophistication in American culture which is now in eclipse. For the moment, the fashion is for what he called 'that easiest of all reservoirs, spontaneity', and the influence is with the tradition of 'the barbarians', Whitman and Pound. He recognized this and didn't much care for it.

The last time I saw Richard Blackmur, briefly in Princeton the year before he died, he seemed ill and preoccupied. But his intellectual fierceness and relish had not changed, nor had his oddly silent personal kindness. He was a profoundly original writer, an intensely private man, a great friend and, in his own words, 'a hospitable intellect'.

The Review, 1967

7

VARIETY

New York

To most people New York is not really a city at all; it's a state of nerves, an excitement. It doesn't, after all, even look real. When you first see it – steaming in from the Narrows or driving in from the airport – it hangs just above the horizon like an hallucination, white, slender, remote. That, you feel, is what the cities of the future will look like. And suddenly, the future seems enormously desirable.

Yet by the time the boat is finally docked or the bus has emerged from the Midtown Tunnel, all those elegant, seductive towers have disappeared utterly. They are so big you can no longer see them; only their weight presses in on you, their vast shadows and stoniness. The rest is chaos: noise, diesel fumes, filth, restlessness. The future seems more harsh and unforgiving than you would ever have expected, and also very much more tatty. It is like marrying some great beauty and finding yourself bedded down with a madwoman. From then on, every time you see New York shimmering away through its haze in the distance, your pleasure is qualified by a curious sense of loss.

Perhaps the hardest thing is to understand that all the dirt and din and callousness, and the bullying, driven quality of life there are the real source of the city's attraction. If the beauty of the place exists only at a distance – from across water, from Central Park, from the air – its power, on the other hand, is everywhere: in the drama and ostentation of the buildings and the casualness with which they are knocked down and put up again; in the equally casual, almost

* V. S. Pritchett, *New York Proclaimed*: photographs by Evelyn Hofer (London: Chatto and Windus/Heinemann, 1965).

habitual violence (500 murders a year compared with London's forty); in the speed and impatience of everything. Even the litter and tawdriness are expressions of its careless go-ahead: obsessively driving on into the future, New York leaves a wake only of broken rubbish. It is a city of complete indifference. You don't properly live a life there; rather, you are dominated by the place; it runs you and you run off your nerves.

It would not, at first sight, seem to be V. S. Pritchett's style of town. He is, after all, one of the last genuine humanists. I think him also one of our best literary critics – though he keeps his standards so high while performing so regularly that we tend to take him for granted – and his strength is a nose like a truffle-hound for precisely that distinguishing scent which gives each author his individuality. He writes about books with a quickening awareness that makes you feel you have met each of them personally. His humanist flair is for the quirky, idiosyncratic life of each work and his humanist fault is that he is sometimes too humane: he makes too many allowances, as though loath to hurt the feelings of some poor, dead author or deader book.

As a travel-writer, he works in much the same way: nosing out just that humanizing oddity which gives a place character. It is all tolerant, witty, intensely personal; cities become people and Pritchett elegantly performs the introductions. The companion volume to *New York Proclaimed* was his book on London; both have the same brand of statuesque photography by Evelyn Hofer, as plush and formal as a mortician's parlour. But *London Perceived* is a work of love; it reads like a forgiving and rather nostalgic novel about his parents.

New York, however, is not easy to love and even less easy to humanize. Pritchett succeeds best from the outside; for him, the place is most human before the ship docks:

> These buildings are beings, and they move. The Chrysler glides northwards and the Empire State moves graciously south; soon all are changing places in a millionaire's waltz, slow and silent, male and female, exchanging the light in their eyes, the touch of roof and penthouse like the touch of passing hands.

Thereafter, nothing quite seems to live up to that moment of slow-motion grace. He goes over Manhattan Island in a helicopter, he goes round it in a boat, he goes into its ramshackle history in detail and assiduously visits most corners. Yet you have the impression that he never gets to like the place much. He is intrigued, fascinated, appalled, but never touched by it.

The fault is partly the city's. It is peculiarly resistant and deadening to personal oddities. The Bowery may swarm with derelicts and the whole town with madmen, but there are few eccentrics. No one has the leisure or the patience to cultivate mere scattiness. There are no comfortable halfway houses on the road to the mental hospital. You get on or you go under. Most get on with depressing thoroughness. Even to be a down-and-out is a career of a kind: 'You graduate in dereliction. You put in a twenty-four-hour day of internal fantasy-making in your studied rejection of the New York norm.' It is the same at the other end of the scale: the monstrous deep-sea goings-on of the millionaires at the turn of the century – Pritchett chronicles them with relish – were done with a single-minded and aggressive ostentation which, in a lower-income bracket, would have been certifiable. Being rich is as much an activity as being a bum; both are impersonal, in the way madness is impersonal.

This impersonality has, I think, something to do with the lack of a past. Murray Kempton has suggested that each successive wave of immigrants becomes American by a process of parricide. By cutting yourself off from your family and its traditions you cut the roots to Europe. Americanism is a quality of the future. You take to it only the most portable personal baggage: energy, ambition, passion, nothing as cumbersome as a set morality or accustomed habits of life. Even the inherited skills are disposable. New York, for example, has almost the only thriving Jewish peasantry the Nazis left; it also has an Irish peasantry probably not much smaller than that of Eire. But both are now urban peasantries, streamlined to another pace, another function. Their roots are in the future, which is not quite the same as being rootless, since it validates the most bull-headed ambition. It is the same with the architecture. There is only one thing more bewildering than the size and style of the buildings that are going up and that is the speed at which they are coming down again. The whole town, like the way of life, seems provisional. Pritchett's image of Manhattan Island as a ship is accurate; the place is on the move, steaming relentlessly from an impossible present into an improbable future.

It takes an immense effort to maintain your individuality against this flood-tide of progress. The Americans have, in an unprecedented way, exploited their beautiful continent. But in New York the city is exploiting the Americans. If the intellectual life there is more talented and vigorous, more absorbed and absorbing than in any other country, that is partly because the place itself won't let up. It winds you up daily in work and you wind yourself down nightly in drink. The key is a sheer vitality – vitality, that is, without much human particularity. Even spring is different: not the tentative, fragile convalescence after winter that it is in England, but a sudden, brutal surge which lasts a couple of days and then slips blazing into high summer.

Only in Greenwich Village and Harlem does the pace seem easier, the living more casual. Characteristically, it is on these that Pritchett is at his best. The Village, with its Fulbright Grant bohemianism, is no longer very stirring. It is the place where the near-artists and sad protesters can expand a little and shed their silliness before the advertising agencies or universities claim them. 'It is', as Pritchett says, 'rather touching.' For Harlem, however, he falls flat. He knows the dangers, or says he does; certainly, he had been warned. Equally certainly, he sensed the mounting pressures, since he discussed them at length with Negro intellectuals. But the tone of the place is too seductive: 'Quite simply people *live* there. They pass the time.' The style is the style he likes, so he interprets the place in terms of the places he likes: Southern Europe, the Caribbean, South America. When Ralph Ellison called his fine novel *Invisible Man* he was implying that to the whites all Negroes are alike, all invisible. For Pritchett, on the contrary, the Negroes seem to be the only New Yorkers he properly saw. Suddenly, he is caught up in small, affectionate details; oddities flourish; he is at home, the humanist restored. Even the politics take on an amiable Left Book Club air.

It is a moving and startlingly generous chapter. But the events of the last year have shown it to be not quite accurate. Negro forbearance is a positive virtue which Pritchett greatly admires, but it is a virtue which has grown out of a century of passivity. In its turn, passivity, particularly in New York, readily turns murderous. It is the underclasses, the put-upon, the outcasts – at their worst like Oswald, at their best like the Negro marchers – who finally explode. And there is an undercurrent of continual anger in New York which not even the most forbearing escape in the end.

It is as though the whole city were one great expression of power.

The skyscrapers express it one way, the poverty another. The dirt, the rush, the rudeness, the manic, concentrated lives and what Pritchett calls the continuous 'shindy' are all expressions of a kind of abstract power. It is a city that runs instinctively to violence and extremes. That is why it is so endlessly stimulating: it enables you to get in touch with the power in yourself which, with luck, encourages work rather than megalomania. Henry James called it an 'invented' city; certainly, it gives you the energy to invent yourself in the same way as it seems to be continually inventing itself. But if the centre of active power is shifting slowly north from the downtown skyscrapers to the Harlem slums, God knows what strained, harsh future is now being dreamed up for the place.

The Spectator, *1965*

Bird in the Hand*

No generation has been more conscious of itself than the one now emerging in the sixties; none has worked harder at defining itself, been more encouraged in the effort, and done so in less compelling ways: by endless interviews, vague pronouncements, inarticulate, though often cheerfully dramatic, protests; it has been continually reborn in the findings of the market-research boys and now promoted in the well-meaning but rather sloppy pop sociology of Charles Hamblett's and Jane Deverson's *Generation X*. Granted, its emergence is a little premature. Generation X is still in its teens and no one expects teenage art, however sincere, to be any good. Even giants of precociousness like Donne and Keats didn't properly get going until they were in their early twenties; a Rimbaud comes once in a civilization. But with the new lot there is peculiarly little to get hold of: not a sniff so far of an embryo-Waugh or proto-Auden or baby-Amis; someone, that is, who can get down what they feel in forms that persist beyond all the fuss of publicity and personality-mongering. What they have instead is the Beatles.

Though the Beatles make, it seems to me, a most seductive and original noise, their huge fame and attraction depend less on their music than on them – on their unfooled, nihilistic, bubble-pricking ability to take care of themselves despite all the big-time glamour. At the Royal Command Performance or the British Embassy in Washington they still behave as though they might at any moment

* Charles Hamblett and Jane Deverson, *Generation X* (London: Anthony Gibbs and Phillips; Tandem Books, 1964); Michael Braun, *Love Me Do* (Harmondsworth: Penguin, 1964).

be held answerable to one of those unimpressed toughies they were brought up with in Liverpool. They are not so much natural as wary, they have less a sense of humour than a sense of reality about the people whom they finally have to face and get through to. They also have a marvellous sense of show biz.

These qualities have persisted despite all the nonsense. And the nonsense is overwhelming, as Michael Braun demonstrates in his sharp little report on a spell with the Beatles, *Love Me Do*. The screaming, the frenzy, the rushing around in special planes and special trains, the fantastic security arrangements, avalanching finances, spending-sprees, celebrity-baiting, success-plotting (who's where on the National Charts?) and the sheer, blind exhaustion come across nicely from Braun's dead-pan, sub-Lillian Ross account. You may never be shown the Beatles at the moments of depression, uncertainty or utter desolation which follow the great hurrah, but neither do you see them throwing temperaments or showing off their power. When they overdo things, they horse around too much, forcing the jokes and anarchy. It may not be all that inspiring, but it is as handy and unvicious a way as any of asserting their contempt for the social-financial thing.

Yet their contempt, alas, does not make them free of it. It must be intensely frustrating for them that their zany individualism itself has been taken over and transformed into a kind of marketable product. That, rather than sheer musical superiority, is what gives them their commercial edge over the rival groups. After all, at their public performances, as someone has said, they are like all good children: seen but not heard. So it is their personal flair itself that has been processed and pre-packaged. Braun has dug out a splendid photograph of the Beatles in their early Hamburg days, before that 'Young-Brother-Is-Watching-You' image was created. They look like any other working-class lads: leather jackets, jeans, winkle-pickers, bristling haircuts and an edgy, attacking air. It seems that before they could be sold to the public they had to be smoothed down, rounded out, made elegant and topped off with those lush, bisexual hairdos that so send the little girls. Now they seem softer, sweeter, more winsome than they were – younger, somehow. They have been made into public playthings; someone waved a magic wand and the Teddy-boys were transformed into Teddy-bears.

Much the same is happening, I think, to Generation X. All that attention and publicity isn't a sign of any unexpected surge of public concern with the problems of adolescence. The interest is strictly financial. Since the teenagers are multitudinous, relatively wealthy and want to be amused, they form an enormous potential market for consumer rubbish. So if, like the Beatles, they can be reinvented in commercial terms, they can also be exploited.

In a curious way, Hamblett and Deverson's collection of teenage statements about themselves, by simply being too long, too repetitive, too formless and often too pious, ends by being reassuring. It appears they haven't yet been sold on their own image. They are still bugged by the same old muddles, worries and distrusts as we all had: total resentment of the older generations and total determination to have done with them all; total certainty that wisdom begins with them, plus an equal but opposite nervousness about how little they really know; hatred of growing up, of losing their wildness and sense of the present; fear of compromise, of being caught and tied to a job or a girl. In short, they are oppressed by the prospect of having to take out a mortgage on their freedom.

So we have been there before. Even the Mods and Rockers have their forbears: in snobbier pre-war circumstances they were called Aesthetes and Hearties. But Generation X has one distinct advantage over its predecessors: it is freer – financially, sexually, religiously, morally, even geographically. They are no longer obsessed by class distinctions, and intolerance is out – at least among themselves. Despite those seaside battles, there is an odd streak of gentleness in their creed:

> 'Teenagers – the enlightened ones – have a common hate,' writes a middle-class girl. 'They have an absolute obsessional hatred of colour and race prejudice. . . .'

Though this relative freedom from prejudice is part of their larger freedom, we don't hear much about it. The only teenage quality that really seems to fascinate the outraged public is their apparent sexual freedom. From Quintin Hogg to Paul Johnson, from the TV vicars to David Holbrook, the denunciation of that is unanimous. It strikes me as utter hypocrisy. It is also inaccurate: despite those screaming Beatle fans, Generation X is no more sex-conscious than any previous set of teenagers.

No one could be more obsessed by sex than the average public school boy, shut up in his monastery nine months of the year. But for him sex means masturbation fantasies or furtive, guilt-ridden perversions. The modern teenagers simply go to bed together. This may produce all sorts of difficulties – illegitimacies, abortions, premature marriages, premature disillusion – but at least the kids try to face them, however inadequately. I can't believe that the rest of us have gained much by postponing them. My own generation, for instance – ten at the start of the war – grew up too late: solemn as owls in our austerity teens, soberly intense in our twenties (remember the Movement?), and a good thirty before we achieved delinquency, or had it thrust upon us. Yet when this happened there was no lack at all of socially accepted ways of expressing it. After all, in its sexual mores London is a frontier town – as wide open as Anchorage in the Gold Rush. Its promiscuity makes most other capitals – New York, Paris, Stockholm, even Warsaw – look like seventeenth-century Salem. And I am not referring to Bohemian circles, which tend to be drably domestic, though unmarried. On the contrary, the smarter the set, the freer and less particular the sex. 'Can you blame a bloke for trying to get birds?' asked a Mod who had fought in the Battle of Margate. The Battle of Profumo was fought with the same war cry.

The French, who are supposed to know about these things, have an adage: *Si jeunesse savait, si vieillesse pouvait.* But between the two is a group who both know and can, and they now seem to be calling the social tune. The best and most disturbing interview in *Generation X* is with a young, pretty and very expensive society whore – whisked abroad during the Profumo crisis – who remarked:

> There's so much hypocrisy in London society, so much social bullshit, that the ponces are bound to flourish. I tell you, as a girl who has made her way in these social circles, I'm part of a daisy chain that stretches from Whitechapel to Kensington Gore. That's not counting the scores of stately homes in the shires.

So the real difference between the middle-aged and teenaged generations is less a question of morals than one of tone – and there the teenagers have the edge. Someone once said that after a certain age men talk about sex and think about money. Conversely, the teenagers talk about sex and think about love. They may go after the birds, but they are all hoping that the next one will turn into Miss Right. Older ornithologists know that if Miss Right does appear she is bound to be hand-in-hand with Mr Wrong.

All adolescent revolt is an attempt to reshape the world out of an obscure understanding of their own incompleteness. Like the Beatles, Generation X has foisted the blame squarely on the stale old shams – social, sexual, racial. They may be as unsure as the rest of us were, as anxious, in some areas as frustrated, and probably no more rebellious at heart. But they are certainly freer, more careless, more independent, less bothered by rules and conventions. If they can go through their delinquency and come out on the other side, they might manage to build a more wholesome set-up than our own lot have done. Of course, there is an equal chance that they will go full circle and become terrible prigs. But if they don't, the prospects are cheering.

The Spectator, 1964

Oxford

If my childish revolt against the religion of my country had not stripped me in time of my academic gown, the five important years, so liberally improved in the studies and conversation of Lausanne, would have been steeped in port and prejudice among the monks of Oxford.

Gibbon wrote that at the end of the eighteenth century. I doubt if there is much in modern Oxford which would make him change his mind, though now he would probably have found his Lausanne somewhere in the United States. Granted the monks are no longer quite so monkish. Most, sometimes to their own surprise, are married and live in considerable elegance: all *House and Garden* colour schemes, Swedish furniture and gleaming kitchens. The plumbing is now more efficient and closer to hand. Otherwise, not much has changed. The port is still excellent and the prejudice remains. Not that it often manifests itself in distasteful ways. In public manners the mild, gentlemanly ideal still prevails. The open rancour of something like the Leavis–Snow controversy could, they say, never have been seen at Oxford; in comparison the Taylor–Trevor-Roper exchange seems temperate and technical. Common-room feuds are kept to the common-rooms; only rarely do they broaden even into the kind of public farce which accompanied, for example, Mr Macmillan's election to the Chancellorship. The glaze of polite, well-fed caution is more or less unbroken. Nobody sticks his neck out; after all, practically nobody cares enough to do so. Issues come and issues go while those Oxford spires dream on forever, unperturbed by the smoke fuming from the practical spires of Cowley.

For Arts undergraduates, a good deal of the University's appeal, hence its influence, comes from this vast, complacent courtesy. The freshman suddenly finds himself treated as a more or less responsible human being – which, after most English schools, is something of a shock. He becomes his own task-master. Between the middle of his first year and the end of this third, there are no exams to bedevil him. No one forces him to go to lectures; the wiser tutors, in fact, encourage him not to. Provided he turns out his weekly essays, he can do as little or as much work as he pleases. Six months of the year he is not at Oxford at all. In the more civilized colleges the gates are now not closed until 3 a.m. He even, at last, meets girls. There may not be enough undergraduettes to go round, but the art and secretarial schools do their best to make up. The college servants, most of them old enough to be his grandfather, call him 'sir' and about half the shops in Oxford exist to see him elegantly dressed. If the result is cloaks, velvet waistcoats and an air of high sartorial melodrama, who cares? Who even notices? He is left on his own. If he is capable of it, he has the chance to grow up – preferably before the Day of Judgement comes in the Final Examination Schools.

This sense of *Zuleika Dobson* absurdity, like the affectations, competitive talk, cinammon toast and awful sherry, is an integral part of the Oxford thing and has its value. When it is all over the undergraduate may be prepared for nothing in particular – except perhaps the Civil Service Examinations – but he has got a good deal out of his system. He has wasted, at least, quite enough time; he has shed, at best, a few prejudices; he may even have acquired a little specialized knowledge. It is, anyway, one style of education. No one could accuse Oxford of raw-boned practicality. It has never set out to produce technologists and only recently has it paid much attention to its many distinguished scientists. The standard of its chemistry and mathematics may be high, shining new physics laboratories may be going up, but the University's reputation and main interest remains in the humanities and their worldly cousin, politics.

Yet perhaps it is the huge success of its alumni which helps debilitate Oxford. Since the children do so startlingly well in the great big outside world, the parents can sit back confirmed in their habits. They can even, in their fantasies, imagine that they too are part of that world. Anxious illusions of metropolitanism make the place seem more provincial than is strictly necessary. It is, after all, very close to London, scarcely more than an hour by train or car. Dons regularly trot up there to do their stuff on television or the Third Programme. But this in itself does not constitute an influence; perhaps it only makes the lack of it more surprising. For the mountain now comes more and more rarely to Mahomet, and All Souls is no longer quite the out-of-town club for top people it used to be. Too often it manages to give the impression of being less absorbed in real issues than in delicate connoisseurs' problems such as who did what to whom in *Lady Chatterley's Lover*.

It is this curious mixture of gossip and pedantry which, more than anything else, isolates the University from the rest of the country. Its causes seem not so much lost as totally unimportant. Even the undergraduates seem a little uneasy. For, despite its style of education, Oxford is no longer a finishing school for gentlemen. Since the modification of the means test, all but a tiny fraction of the students receive one kind of government grant or another. The meritocracy, in short, is there in force and it has brought with it different values, different expectations: above all, a certain urgency which makes it impatient with the tradition of port and prejudice. Jude is no longer obscure but his new mixture of nervy, throw-away seriousness still keeps him in a world apart from Oxford's mellowness. So a fellowship now seems less a rare prize than a life sentence. The bright graduates tend to drift away to livelier new universities, or to America, or to situations where to be productive is not necessarily a stigma.

For 'publish and be damned' is still the motto of most dons, as though to put into print a challengeable opinion were somehow dangerous, like going naked into the common-room. In the English Faculty, for example, a certain amount of discreet, scrupulous scholarship may get done and even published. But criticism – intellectual work based on personal judgement – is scarcely ever seen. The lone and unhappy exception is F. W. Bateson, who also edits Oxford's one attempt at a critical periodical; and he has no college fellowship and has never examined in the Final Schools. In place of the intellectual discipline of criticism the students are forced into the compulsory tedium of philology. They order these things better in more strenuously taught subjects like History and Greats. But in general common-room society does not encourage the setting up and analysis of anything as chancy as personal values.

The analysis of personalities, however, is another matter entirely.

Oxford thrives on gossip, denigration and a carefully cultivated amateurishness of approach. Yet even its cliquiness is archaic and sets it apart from the rest of contemporary intellectual life. That paranoid fantasy – admittedly more prevalent at Cambridge than at Oxford – of a metropolitan literary racket which runs things on the basis of personal relations, shuts out talent and assures jobs and good reviews for the boys has no longer much basis in fact. It is, instead, a projection on to the Metropolis of the way in which the less principled and efficient faculties are run. All this is typical of the dons' creed: the whole world is just old Oxbridge writ large.

No doubt the glamour of the place and the dons' easy, opulent-seeming life encourage this trance of self-admiration. But the mystique of the degree is an even more potent force. It is also self-perpetuating. Generation after generation of undergraduates arrive at Oxford intent on one of two ideals: a Blue or a First. As like as not, they will have had years of schooling at the hands of men who just failed to get one or the other. For three years they will then be taught by tutors who have been given their jobs simply by virtue of their performance in Finals. The First begins to seem like an absolute criterion of human excellence. Heaven knows how many people have gone down in a state of more or less permanent depression because they feel that they have been weighed in some ultimate balance and found second- or third-class. Yet if you attain that elusive First, what in fact have you got? The answer now is just an ordinary degree in a world in which degrees are becoming increasingly ordinary. 'Glamour' may originally have been derived from 'grammar', but they are no longer synonyms. It is, however, an all-important part of Oxford's intellectual mystique to believe that they are.

This is implicit in the University's extraordinary indifference to graduate studies. Although over eighteen per cent of the students – 1,604 out of 8,802 – are doing advanced work, only three small colleges are entirely devoted to their needs. And of these, the immensely wealthy All Souls would probably resist the imputation, since it fancies itself less as a graduate college than as an exclusive intellectual club, a kind of Oxford Athenaeum, whose membership includes only one scientist. As for the other two advanced colleges, Nuffield and St Antony's, both are the creations of private benefactors. The rest of the graduate students have to squeeze into the no man's land between the undergraduates and the dons. According to a recent unofficial survey – organized, significantly, by a student of Nuffield College – they are a vastly dissatisfied group. They lack status: unless they are graduates of Oxbridge or Trinity, Dublin, they are treated, governed and gowned like ordinary undergraduates. They lack any special facilities or even social life: there is no graduate centre, and very few colleges provide graduate common rooms or even accommodation: most researchers live isolated in shoddy digs on the outskirts and eat at Oxford's unspeakable cheap restaurants. They don't even share in that student–tutor intimacy on which Oxford rightly prides itself: if a graduate is lucky and insistent, he may see his supervisor twice a term; usually he is neither.

Since the D.Phil. regulations demand 'an original contribution to knowledge', the student is forced to spend his years in a tiny, unaired corner of pedantic boredom. And if he finally gets a degree – though well over fifty per cent of the art students fail – he will probably find that he has committed what amounts to a social-academic blunder. A doctorate is considered slightly infra dig. Not many of the dons have anything more than an M.A. Jobs too often go on Schools results, charm and skill in that specialized brand of spinsterish chat which dominates the High Tables. In the shadiest quarters the correct High Church affiliations will also help.

No doubt the University would reply that aspiring Doctors of Philosophy come there at their own risk. Oxford has never claimed to be much interested in post-graduate studies or qualifications. Its business is with undergraduates and the training needed to get a good Oxford B.A. is sufficient for anyone except the purest scholar – for whom, anyway, room can always be found. The place functions, in short, not as a training-ground for specialists but as a civilizing influence. So naturally it takes an Oxford man to dispense that peculiarly Oxford quality. Very well. But a nagging worry remains: what kind of civilizing are they up to? And even granted the cultural discipline of a genuinely excellent course like Greats, there is still a question of style. How valuable is a training in the values of a charmed circle as in-turned and self-regarding as this? Perhaps Oxford can pride itself that nothing as upsetting as the Leavis–Snow rumpus could have happened there for a perfectly simple reason: no one as upsetting as Dr Leavis would ever have got a toe in the door. Namier, for instance, had to go elsewhere.

Even when the Kraken does wake it is only to perpetuate, in one form or another, its own entranced image: in honorary degree ceremonies at which dazed notables are belaboured in Latin; or in the more publicized elections, such as that for the Chancellorship or the Professorship of Poetry, which quickly assume the massive comic proportions of a national lottery. Or it is for something like the Historic Buildings Appeal, that latest, typical lost cause. One and three-quarter million pounds was raised to restore the fabric; the money was spent and a second appeal is now threatened, while those naked, unaccommodated research students scrape along as best they may. It cost almost as much to prop up the tottering façades of Christ Church as it did to build Nuffield College. Yet there would seem, by the University's lights, no doubt about which is the more valuable undertaking. Work is only work; someone will do it if Oxford won't. But the refaced buildings shine to the greater glory of Oxford itself. The dreaming spires of tradition are now safe for another couple of hundred years.

Perhaps the University is right. In the end, the intellectual complacency doesn't matter. Oxford continues to draw the best students because only it and Cambridge offer that magic combination of social status, the tutorial system, easy living and beautiful architecture. The charm is so charming and has gone on so long. Why should it alter now? As for preparing undergraduates for the world they will eventually live in, our Redbricks can do that for us.

The New Statesman, 1963

The Poet in the University

> The proprieties and delicacies of the English are known to few; 'tis impossible even for a good wit to understand and practise them, without the help of a liberal education, long reading, and digesting of those few good authors we have amongst us, the knowledge of men and manners, the freedom of habitudes and conversation with the best company of both sexes; and, in short, without wearing off the rust which he has contracted while he was laying in a stock of learning.
>
> DRYDEN

> Then begin men to aspire to second prizes; to be a profound interpreter and commentator, to be a sharp champion and defender, to be a methodical compounder and abridger. And this is the unfortunate succession of wits which the world hath yet had, whereby the patrimony of all knowledge goeth not on husbanded and improved, but wasted and decayed.
>
> BACON

Granted that the creative writer may, and does, serve his turn as a university teacher, the questions are: How does it affect him? What sort of writers flourish there? And is it worth it? There are, we are told, no patrons left. Better to be beholden to a university than to the State; certainly better than dragging on with one foot always in the gutter. But there is a difference between living by one's writing and living by talking about it. It is rather like employing a cook to lecture on the pleasures of eating; it will probably not be good for his cooking. There have, of course, always been university wits, men like Randolph, Cleveland or Flatman, who would never pass up the opportunity of exhibiting in rhyme their intellectual talents. We have them still. But the serious writer is quite another being, and none of them seem to have stayed on at the university. Many have been through the training and never lost the mark of it; I can think of no better undergraduate poems than *L'Allegro* and *Il Penseroso*, nor any poems so good which are quite so subtly shot through with undergraduate self-consciousness. Or Marlowe, Donne and Eliot have a pointedness in their learned references which is not fortuitous. But if they can command dryness of tone they do so for variation; it does not prevail, nor is it for that that they are considered major writers. They derive their vitality, their seriousness and their range from no university.

It is the minor writers who have remained academics. Which is, I suppose, as it should be; for good minor verse does not require any large store of originality, it relies more on sensitivity and a critical knack. Much of it is poetry from poetry, the major poet has his say first, the others follow him; they are sensitive to his attitudes, they respond critically to the tone of his idiom in order to reproduce it themselves. Dr Leavis has suggested that inspiration in a minor poet often comes when he is unconsciously echoing the tone and rhythms of whoever it is he models himself on. Done in all faith it is almost an act of critical reverence, less simply it may be a vice: you may rely on someone's authority because your own resources are not adequate, or you may do so as a way of avoiding personal commitment. This is particularly the university failing. Thomas Gray, for instance, had intelligence, sensitivity, learning, tact, but lacked vitality. Matthew Arnold said 'He never spoke out', and blamed it on the time in which he lived: 'A sort of spiritual east wind was at that time blowing.' The chill, I think, was as much in the place. His vitality as a poet was sapped by academic timidity. After all, even the *Elegy* was criticized for lack of delicacy and taste and was accused of being too personal. It was easier, always, to avoid compromising himself and do nothing: 'Brandy', he wrote, 'will finish what port began.' It is the usual university remedy.

The failing is still timidity. But now the fear is lest the writer violate not so much the standards of personal decorum as those of the literary tradition. Neither Gray nor Housman, Cleveland nor Grimald taught English literature. At least they had their language to themselves; they could experiment with some sort of freedom. Not so today. The English don busies himself professionally with the best of his own literature. Its excellencies and seriousness, its subtlety and modulations are what he is constantly faced with. At the lowest level they are his job; at a higher one, they have given him his standards; by them he discriminates and urges discrimination. Then he tries to write himself. It is disheartening. He is nagged by his awareness that, say, Donne or Pope or Conrad would have done what he wants to do much better. And if he is honest – *this* is the depressing thought – he knows that so too would Davenant, Stephen Duck or Dorothy Sayers. Of course, he has an advantage: he knows where they went wrong, he knows what to avoid. Unfortunately he may know the pitfalls so well that, in order not to go wrong, he may never go at all. He can see through his own attempts too quickly, he begins to qualify almost before he has started to write, and his awareness turns in on itself. Every good work of art needs, I think, at least two things: in the simplest terms, they are vitality and something to say. The writer must have felt something and he must have thought something. In any good writing there is not only a zest, a pleasure in the act of writing and an awareness of what is involved, there is also some sort of emotional generosity which will allow the experience its full worth, which will not choke back and deny. Theory, which is what too much artistic self-consciousness gives, is the outside limits of art; it rarely makes much difference to the life within. Conrad had the root of the matter when he wrote: 'This world, even if one is tied fast to its earthy foundations by the subtle and tyrannical bonds of artistic conviction, is not such a bad place to write fiction in.' It is this sense of the world as he sees it and as he lives in it that the don may lack in his writing. He will have instead the world as it is seen and lived by whichever writer, or tradition of writers, he admires. His own attempts, he knows, fall pathetically short.

There is, perhaps, a personal risk in writing anything at all, particularly when literature, according to the Oxford syllabus for the B.A. in English, stops in 1830. What follows, or at least what has happened in our time, is still a little suspect. Scholarship has its own objective standards of accuracy and decorum, but outside these the university ideal is often little more than a cultured literary conservatism which judges writing as an agreeable, and incidental, accomplishment. By these lights any idiom which is new, probably not fully understood and almost certainly not perfected, may well seem slapdash and clumsy. The writer sets himself up as a target simply by having something to say. Perhaps his perceptions are strange or his enthusiasms misguided, but at some point he must cease from qualifying them and commit himself. Too much taste can be a drawback: Keats was often over-emphatic, so was Lawrence, so, at times, was Shakespeare. Criticism is easier, less chancy. Academic verse in this sense is critical, that is, almost never new, almost always fashionable; it tries to seem impregnable, it succeeds in being knowing, polished, learned, measured, but, as often as not, dead. Somewhere in *Ulysses* an Oxford don appears pushing a lawn-mower that goes 'Clevercleverclevercleverclever'.

Oxford has never pretended to be responsible for the failure or success – in that order – of contemporary writing. The curtailing of the syllabus is one way of showing this, compulsory philology is another. The concern, ideally, is with the assured tradition of literature. If the undergraduate wants to read what is being written now, or himself to write, he must do so as best he may in his spare time. It won't help him to his degree; the Poet's Third is an institution. What is needed of the teacher is not that he write but that he have a sense of literature; that he communicate to his pupils his feeling for the vitality of his subject. For this he must understand literature, to rephrase Mr Eliot, to the tips of his senses. Except that he may respect its difficulties a little more, it hardly matters if he dabbles in writing himself. His real business is with what is written and with re-creating his own understanding of this in the minds of others.

Things are very different in America, where the writers are firmly settled in the universities. If Mr X is introduced to you as 'the poet' or 'the novelist' you may by that token be sure that somewhere he teaches Creative Writing, with subsidiary courses on Critical Analysis and the Metaphysical Poets. On the other hand, Professor Y, 'the scholar', teaches the more humdrum things, like Chaucer, Shakespeare, Milton or Pope. It is a strong way of emphasizing that American literature is on its own and no longer dependent on English. It is also a way of showing that literature is still happening there, whilst in England the feeling is that it has happened; all we can do, as readily and as sensitively as possible, is remould our idea of the tradition in order to include whatever tiny fragment of contemporary writing seems important. While we rather preen ourselves on our great literature of the past, in America they sometimes seem still to be waiting for the major poets to arrive. It is reasonable for them to assimilate completely only those writers who can be read with an American accent: they too often discuss Donne as though he were Hart Crane; the minor and careful address themselves to Andrew Marvell. When a writer is assimilated in this way, he becomes in some obscure sense 'modern', and is therefore part of 'creative writing'. When he doesn't, he may remain a subject for intensive and efficient study, but he won't properly belong. He will remain as tenuously connected with American literature as, say, *Beowulf* is with ours.

The split between 'creative writing' and 'English literature' may be a deliberate declaration of independence, but it also undercuts critical judgements by breaking that sense of continuity which a tradition gives. It is a certain objectivity that makes for critical standards; it comes from the ability to understand and be moved by excellence however different, or even irrelevant, its idiom may appear. 'Literature' read as something quite separate from 'Creative Writing' is a dead subject. It belongs to the past and to facts, whilst the other belongs exclusively to the present, and is exciting for nothing so much as its bohemian *panache*. 'Literature' belongs to text-books, but the Creative Writer is the man who lectures to you twice a week and corrects your scripts.

It is not easy for the poets and novelists in the universities; their positions are no sinecures. They are not there simply because they, in some way, *are* American literature; they have to show others how to be so too. In the States, where far more people go to college than over here, the first aim of the universities is encouragement. The specialized scholarship and detail are left to the graduate researchers. It is often enough if the undergraduate can discover what his particular aptitudes are for. And many, of course, have a penchant for writing. Hence the Creative Writers, whose position is that of the master-craftsman with his apprentices. I feel that the results, though indubitably writing, are often not very creative. A contributor to one of those special American numbers of the *T.L.S.* called attention to the current insistence on the techniques of poetry. It is, I think, an unfortunate peculiarity. It avoids the responsibility of having something to say by concentrating wholly on the way of saying. As a rule, the reigning poet is well drilled in critical analysis; he knows what is needed to be modern; he can at will be ambiguous, ironic, paradoxical, symbolic; his transitions are always correct, but almost predictable. It is all so lifeless. He experiments from a sense of duty; he is not driven to do so because the literary forms to hand are inadequate for the new things he has to say. It is merely a proof of his mastery over his craft, almost a piece of academic research he could get a doctorate for. Of course, he is teaching a discipline and need only give the effect of art without its deeper insistence. Yet it is precisely on the depth and integrity of its insistence that the artistic effect rests, if it is to last. Method is subsidiary. According to one teacher of Creative Writing, 'Undergraduates today are beneficiaries of the lessons learned so painfully from Joyce, Stein, Pound and Henry James.' I am not sure that writers so different jumbled together only for their technique can teach anything except a painful surface obliqueness, a way of missing the point while remaining fashionable. Dull men taught craft are merely dull with aplomb, whilst the talents of the writers who have to teach it sink beneath the inflexible surface of 'art'.

I have said that minor writing flourishes at the universities because it deals with experience filtered through literature. Perhaps the writer is forced to make this remove by timidity, by an over-nice sense of decorum or simply by lack of originality; or it may be part of a technical pedagogy. It depends on whether he is teaching an existing tradition of literature or a craft. Either way, he is a middle-man to art, which a really creative artist can never be. My belief is that discrimination is worth more than technical competence. But both are a long way from originality.

The Twentieth Century, 1955

Encounter

Encounter has reached its hundredth issue and the applause is beginning to thunder in. So too, apparently, are the subscriptions: the circulation at the moment is nearly 30,000; for the special hundredth number, 33,000 copies are being hopefully printed. This, Stephen Spender writes in his 'Postscript', is over three times the popularity envisaged when the venture began in October 1953. The Congress for Cultural Freedom must be very pleased, and even one or two weeklies will be a little green at the gills with jealousy. I imagine that neither *The Criterion* nor *Horizon*, whom Spender mistakenly invokes as *Encounter*'s forbears, got anywhere near a comparable circulation.

The period, I suppose, has a good deal to do with it. There is at the moment a fashion for things intellectual, a strange epidemic which brings everyone out in highbrow paperbacks. At the airport in Wichita, Kansas, for example, the works of Dostoevsky and Faulkner are as readily available as those of Mickey Spillane. Instead of pin-up girls, *Esquire* now publishes Norman Mailer; *Playboy*, which was once the American equivalent of *London Opinion*, is taking the same thorny path. The times are serious and fashions go with them. Perhaps, too, a fair proportion of *Encounter*'s circulation is among those successful young executives who still guiltily remember their university training. They take it for much the same reason as they loudly and nervously applaud attacks on themselves at the Royal Court and The Establishment. Those who aren't worried any more take *Town* and *The Queen*. Nevertheless, 3*s*. 6*d*. a month is dear enough for a status symbol – particularly when it buys one, as like as not, 8,000 words on the economic conditions of India.

Encounter, however, usually offers rather more than that: in its time it has offered Crosland on the Labour Party, Fiedler on the *T.L.S.*, Trevor-Roper on Toynbee and Wayland Young on prostitution. Its list of bombshells is impressive. Indeed, it has cornered the English market for long, serious articles. Not that there is much competition: only *The Twentieth Century* and *The New Left Review* are contending in the same field, and both are obviously handicapped by the absence of that Ford Foundation money. So for the professional writer *Encounter* has every advantage; it offers wide circulation, good money and ample space. And since most writers are praise-seeking, avaricious and long-winded, *Encounter* automatically gets the pick of the market. The only profitable alternative is to publish in American magazines like *Commentary* and *The Partisan Review*, which are better – though often less vivacious – but 3,000 miles away.

Yet considering its advantages, the magazine's record has been at best patchy and in places remarkably poor. Its most signal failure has been in literature. In his 'Postscript' Spender refers yearningly to the contents of *The Dial*, vol. lxxiii, 5, for November 1922:

T. S. Eliot *The Waste Land*
W. B. Yeats *The Player Queen*
Arthur Schnitzler *Doctor Graesler*
Sherwood Anderson *Many Marriages*
Ezra Pound *Paris Letter*
Illustrations by Picasso, Brancusi, Duncan Grant, Adolph Dehn

To judge from *Encounter*'s literary contributions, the editorial principle has been to emulate this list without taking any risks. They have simply gone all out for big names in the apparent belief that fame and quality go hand in hand. They don't. But they do give the contents page a remarkably consistent look. *Encounter* No. 1 has some fiddling 'Pages from a Diary' by Virginia Woolf; for No. 100 E. M. Forster has dug into his bottom drawer and brought up bits of an Indian Journal. In No. 1 there is a beautiful meditation by Camus, in No. 100 some perceptive letters by Orwell. No. 1 sticks its neck out with stories by a Japanese ur-beatnik Dazai Osamu; No. 100 has a trashy one-act farce by the pure-beatnik Gregory Corso. Both, of course, have poems by Dame Edith Sitwell.

And in between the first and the hundredth issue most of the famous literary names occur.

Naturally, if a magazine is to circulate as widely as *Encounter*, famous names are essential. But there is a difference between publicity-prestige editing and the principles which guided *The Dial*. The difference was summed up in one of the latter's editorials:

> If a magazine isn't to be simply a waste of good white paper, it ought to print, with some regularity, either such work as would otherwise have to wait years for publication, or such as would not be acceptable elsewhere.

The only waiting much of the work by *Encounter*'s big names seems to have done is that long, sad burial at the bottom of the authors' barrels. *The Dial* created reputations, *Encounter* merely uses ready-made ones. Its literary side, in short, seems to lack both editorial consistency and often even taste. For every piece of serious criticism by, say, J. G. Weightman there seem to be five bits of plump snobbishness by Hilary Corke.

But in all truth, though tiny salvoes from big literary guns may help sell *Encounter*, its reputation and influence come from its political and sociological essays. Which is as it should be, since *Encounter* and its parent body, the Congress for Cultural Freedom, were chilled into being by the cold war. If neither was designed specifically as a weapon in the fight, they were both intended at least as hefty defences of Western cultural values. The magazine's first editorial made no bones about this. It proclaimed, somewhat prematurely, 'the destruction of the Marxist-Leninist creed', and continued with the startling assertion:

> The dark side of the moon may no longer be mistaken for the rising sun, but it is still there and still dark. And shadows move among us; almost too many to count and sometimes even hard to name.

I don't know whether it was Spender or Irving Kristol, then the American co-editor, who was responsible for that extraordinary outburst. It wouldn't have happened now; the paranoiac throb of genuine propaganda is rarely heard in *Encounter* these days. Its tone has grown more sophisticated, though there are still moments, heaven knows, when the light seems dark enough.

Perhaps this sudden access of urbanity was due to the arrival of Melvin J. Lasky, who is a tougher and more accomplished journalist than either Spender or Kristol, from whom he took over. Certainly, since Lasky became editor *Encounter* seems to have been run as a more severely practical journalistic enterprise than it was when it began. It has become a good deal less idealistic and a good deal more successful. Perhaps it had to be: since the Stalinist ice age began to thaw, impassioned but naïve propaganda has lost its appeal. Enough people now get behind the iron curtain for them not to be fooled by all they are told. Therefore the editors now have to create what the cold war automatically provided: the opportunity for controversy.

But the English are, on the whole, a non-political race. Unlike the French or the Germans, they rise sluggishly, if at all, to a purely theoretical bait. They will, however, talk endlessly about themselves and, rather late in the day, they have come to sociology. So the editorial function of *Encounter* seems to have been to create issues by using the techniques of Americanized sociology on contemporary British themes. In this, at least, it is both a useful and truly Anglo-American enterprise.

Encounter may not have discovered new writers or created any great literary reputations, but it must have provoked more cocktail-party conversation than any comparable magazine of our time. All the talking points are there, from U and non-U, through the Two Cultures and on up to the Meritocracy. This again may be a sign of the times: it may well be – as American critics are for ever pointing out – that a good deal of writing talent has swung away from literature and gone into sociology. But I wonder if it isn't also true that the British intelligentsia feeds on these pre-packed instant issues – most of which can be reduced, in the end, to terms of snobbery – because of a failure in 'the moral imagination'.

The phrase is Leslie Fiedler's and it comes from his notorious essay on the Rosenbergs. Agree with it or not, his piece had undoubted qualities: it raised genuinely urgent issues and dealt with them logically, unsentimentally and with passion. I imagine that, in effect, we were being treated in this essay to an inside view of a parochial New York battle: that is, Fiedler was using the Rosenberg case largely to air his own annoyance with the over-ripe liberal humanism which is worshipped around Columbia University, and which was fairly represented in *Encounter* by Lionel Trilling's humourless defence of *Lolita* as – God help us – a great love story. My point, however, is simple: among the best of the American intelligentsia a trivial domestic quarrel as often as not expands into something really important and can provoke a radical self-criticism which, by its very exacerbation, both demands considerable intellectual effort and can bring about a truly 'agonizing reappraisal' of values. One feels that the best American writers mean, and are vitally exercised by, what they say.

In comparison, their English counterparts mostly speak in what a writer in *Commentary* recently called 'the bland, wistful tone of the British Left nowadays'. They are clever and polished, but they don't care: they lack that 'moral imagination'. What in Britain really interests them? The bright answers come: people talk of 'serviettes' instead of 'napkins'; they don't know the second law of thermodynamics; they are too sentimental about the Royal Family and/or the working classes; or, to quote the latest issue, they haven't made up their minds on 'sexual morality and religion'. The image *Encounter* presents of British intellectual life is that of some endless High Table conversation: smart, quick, cultured, easy, a little complacent, while underneath runs the nagging anxiety about just who is where in the social-intellectual game.

The New Statesman, 1961

Sigmund Freud's Letters*

It is strange how rarely scientific genius goes with a genius for living, even when the science was, like Freud's, the science of human nature. Without the respectful preface by the editor, his son Ernst, an innocent reader might suppose that this selection of Freud's letters represented a mild attempt to explode the myth of the great man. For it presents Freud without psychoanalysis, Freud either *en pantoufles* or as an unwillingly famous man writing to other famous men. For various reasons Ernst Freud has left out all the technical letters: the crucial fifteen-years exchange with Wilhelm Fliess because much of it has already been printed in Kris's *The Origins of Psycho-analysis*; the correspondence with his early collaborators because it may, sooner or later, be used for a similar purpose; the letters to his patients because, says the editor, they 'are jealously guarded by them – and rightly so – as their private property'. Even so, there was no lack of material: the final 315 letters were chosen from some 4,000. And since Ernst Freud admits that he was not trying to produce from them a biography to supplement Ernest Jones's, the image he has created of his father – this effect as of Freudian slippers – is presumably deliberate.

In a truly Freudian way, it is an oedipally mutilated image: the betrothed medico rather than of the founder of psychoanalysis. The first half of the volume is given over to letters written during his four-and-a-half-year engagement to Martha Bernays; the fifty years of Freud's great achievement is crammed into the last half.

* *Letters of Sigmund Freud*, edited by Ernst L. Freud (London: Hogarth Press, 1961).

Of course, there is a fascination in watching Freud go through the usual fatigue-drill of courtship: depressed by poverty and separation, elated as his meetings with his fiancée come and go, at times jealous, at others heavily playful ('With 100,000 kisses, all of which are to be cashed'). But reassuring though it may be to think 'Love made him weep his pints like you and me', it is not quite true. Even as a writer of love-letters, Freud was remarkable less for the intensity of his feelings than for his sanity. He rephrased the standard romantic anxiety – 'Ah love, let us be true to one another' – into something calmer and more domestic: 'Let us love one another and work.' His love-letters show, at least, that the guiding principles of his character – balance, devotion and tenacity – were present from the start, like the twin strengths of his intellect: his extraordinary ability to remember details and to relate one to another.

Nevertheless, despite the occasional insights into his character, Freud's life during his engagement was monotonous and his work relatively unimportant. He was simply another good doctor, making discoveries in histology, adding to his reputation as a neurologist, up to his ears in work, hospital politics and routine, ambitious, delighted to be taken up socially by senior doctors, worried about his career, the correctness of his dress and the impression he made. His real work did not begin until he was securely married. Before that the enforced tedium of his life was something he felt he must justify:

> I remember something that occurred to me while watching a performance of *Carmen*: The mob gives vent to its appetites, and we deprive ourselves. We deprive ourselves in order to maintain our integrity, we economize in our health, our capacity for enjoyment, our emotions; we save ourselves for something, not knowing what. And this habit of constant suppression of natural instincts gives us the quality of refinement.

It was only after he had become wholly at one with Viennese respectability that he was free to explore the chaos beneath the placid surface of middle-class refinement.

His discoveries were the outcome of a personal crisis which lasted all through the nineties, a decade in which, according to Ernest Jones, 'he suffered from a very considerable psycho-neurosis'. It was a period of great loneliness and disturbance: his old professor Meynert had denounced him, his close friend Breuer would no longer collaborate in his researches, and his only confidant was Fliess, the cranky mathematical-physiologist for whom Freud developed a passionate obsession. The way out of this waste land of ten years was his self-analysis, and the result was his masterpiece, *The Interpretation of Dreams.* His genius, in short, was precipitated by an extended, intense and unconventional anxiety. And it took all his genius finally to attain an inner calm to match the unruffled surface of his routine life. One would scarcely suspect it from this collection of letters. For the whole period, 1890–1900, Ernst Freud – who, perhaps significantly, was born in 1892 – prints only eleven of his father's letters; and they barely hint at the urgency and power of the intellectual effort he was making and the anguish that accompanied it.

No doubt the editor had his reasons for this censorship by omission. It imposes, for instance, a remarkable continuity on Freud's life and habits. The detailed accounts of hospital life which he sent daily to Martha Bernays become, twenty years later, the rather impersonal family letters of a dutifully thorough traveller, remorselessly reporting the sights, theatres and operas on his annual holiday; the conventionally anxious lover is transformed into the conventionally domesticated man: 'The weather is getting more and more glorious, the city [Rome] more and more marvellous. Yesterday I handed in my linen to be washed.' The politics change from the more or less petty hospital tensions to the grander manoeuvres of the Psychoanalytical Congresses. What Freud early described as his capacity for 'hating someone on intellectual grounds, just because he is a fool' grows impressively stronger as his own work matures: in this collection there is only one really savage denunciation of a colleague (Stekel), but a good deal of ruthless disagreement. His honesty was overwhelming, but I have the impression that Freud as a critic may not quite have known the power of his own punch. On the other hand, his generosity and unsentimental warmth when he is assured of a colleague's support remain as constant as his devotion to hard work. One can even see method in his very lack of madness: perhaps the endless patience with which he endured his protracted engagement became, in his professional life, part of the informing discipline of psychoanalysis.

What the editor has created, in fact, is an image of Freud not as a genius but as a kind of psychoanalytic ideal. There are some analysts who suggest, with the faint complacency of those who have come through, that their rarest, strongest word of praise is 'adjusted'. So by skimming over the Fliess episode and presenting his father first as a family man, then as a famous public figure, very little as a scientist and scarcely at all as the neurotic who once wrote 'I have been very lazy, because the moderate misery necessary for intensive work refuses to appear', Ernst Freud seems to insist that the founder of psychoanalysis was also a living example of the discipline's final aim: an adjusted, harmonious, hard-working citizen.

Perhaps this became necessary directly Freud's work ceased to be the exclusive domain of the professionals and emerged to influence the life of everyone, literate or otherwise, this side of the Iron Curtain. Today one need not have opened one of Freud's books to pronounce on slips and symbolism, the death-wish, Oedipus and the rest. Even a Western is no longer thought chic unless, in the final reel, the gunman stutters out his childhood trauma. So, on the popular level, Freud's name is associated with an infinite amount of half-baked mystification. To make matters worse, he was a genius; and the fantasy figure of the Genius has not yet been cut free from the Romantics who invented it. A Genius, that is, moves in utterly mysterious ways as Inspiration dictates. On these terms, Freud is transformed from a highly trained specialist to a kind of William Blake of the science of the unconscious. Nothing could be less true. After their first meeting, he wrote to Ferenczi:

> You were disappointed because you probably expected to swim in constant intellectual stimulation, whereas I hate nothing more than striking up attitudes and out of contrariness frequently let myself go. As a result I was probably most of the time a quite ordinary elderly gentleman, and you in astonishment kept measuring the distance between me and your phantasy ideal.

Yet, for all his assertions of conventionality, Freud managed to revolutionize our whole understanding of human nature. So it seems odd at first that his personal letters are such heavy-going and, compared with those of Keats or Lawrence, seem to show relatively little insight. The truth, however, is not simply that Freud was a great man but, despite the excellent translations of Tania and James Stern, a rather dull letter-writer. It entails, instead, an attention to the particular way his genius worked. The clue lies in a letter to a writer whom he enormously admired, Romain Rolland:

> Our terms such as regression, narcissism, pleasure-principle are of a purely descriptive nature and don't carry within themselves any valuation.

Scientific and artistic genius work, in fact, in precisely opposite ways. The artist's method is normative: that is, he uses his art to impose a unity on his chaotic experience, he tries to create standards out of his knowledge of his lack of them (which is, I suppose, much like Freud's own view of art as compensation). The scientist's method, on the other hand, is the product of norms, a matter of clear thinking, tenacity and a kind of logical courage – and courage, Freud insisted, was his most important Jewish characteristic. This is presumably what he meant when he described his hero Charcot as 'a man whose common sense borders on genius', why he constantly asserted that he himself was not 'brilliant' and that the writers he admired 'know through intuition – or rather from detailed self-observation – everything I have discovered by laborious work on other people'.

Where the artist's work is an attempt to create sanity, the scientist's is a product of it. Perhaps this is why so many scientists are such boring men: a certain level of tedium is an essential condition for their work. So though the original impulse which set Freud's genius in motion may have been neurotic, his final achievement was the result of the opposite: of assurance and method. 'It was', he wrote to Stefan Zweig, after reading Zweig's essay on him, 'less the result of intellect than of character.' 'On the other hand', Freud continued, 'I feel inclined to object to the emphasis you put on the element of *petit-bourgeois* correctness in my person.' But object to it or not, correctness was as necessary to Freud's work as hysterical epilepsy was to Dostoevsky's: it was an outward and visible sign of the strength on which his talent relied.

So, in the end, perhaps the editor is justified in producing a portrait of his father as a conventional middle-class man. The trouble is that it is liable to seem so much less than the truth. For Freud was a scientific genius and a genius only when he was being scientific, when he was talking shop. In the whole of this bulky volume there are only a few examples of his unique mode of insight at work: brief, incisive analyses of Napoleon, Dostoevsky and Charlie Chaplin, a letter to a mother on her son's homosexuality and a marvellous pre-analytical case-history of the suicide of a colleague at his Neurological Clinic. For the rest, Ernst Freud has produced a tribute less to his father's achievement than to the plain, solid foundations on which it rested.

The New Statesman, 1961

A Library of Poetry*

The Lockwood Library is a solid building in the college Greek manner, sitting on the windy campus of the University of Buffalo. And Buffalo itself is a big, ramshackle, ugly provincial city: Wyndham Lewis nicknamed it Nineveh. It was in the news recently when the Federal Bureau of Investigation began a new attack on gangsterism. All in all, it is an unlikely setting for the world's finest collection of twentieth-century English and American poetry.

Yet the Lockwood Library is unique. Other universities haphazardly gather a few random volumes of modern poetry as the whim takes them; some will even invest in twentieth-century manuscripts, provided of course the author is eminent and dead. But the Lockwood Library, apart from the usual working texts for students, is devoted wholly to modern poetry. It has, on a rough count, 16,000 printed books: first and variant editions of the poets, anthologies, biographies, memoirs and criticism. It also has about 450 files of magazines, particularly the little magazines where so much of the best verse of our time first appeared. This, by itself, would make a fine enough library; but what really makes the Lockwood Library important is its collection of manuscripts. Sorted away in the stacks are some 5,000 sets of poets' worksheets, the notes, drafts, revisions and completed texts of every kind of poem, masterpieces and doggerel. They come in all shapes and sizes, from a massive note book of W. H. Auden's, which looks rather like a company ledger, down to William Carlos Williams's prescription blanks, with fragments of verse scribbled on their backs. To reinforce all this are some

* From a talk in the Third Programme.

4,500 letters, a good many directly from the poets themselves, explaining their methods of composition.

The collection represents a brilliant idea and a prodigious amount of hard work by the librarian, Mr Charles Abbott. Simply to devote a university library to contemporary poetry was daring enough in 1935. After all, that was long before every American college worth its salt had its resident poet and its courses in Creative Writing. But Mr Abbott was not content to provide what he has called a 'bibliographer's paradise'. He was fascinated by the creative processes themselves. And so he visited or wrote to every poet with any kind of reputation, and begged them all to send in their worksheets. The idea was to provide not just the finished products but the whole assembly line of as many modern poems as possible. So the Lockwood Library is unique not merely for the material it has but for the principle behind it. It is devoted both to poetry and to what would, I suppose, be called the psychology of creation. It is wholly a product of the age of analysis.

Nevertheless, on the way to this psychological goal the Lockwood Library has become extraordinarily valuable for understanding modern poetry in more humdrum ways. First, it will preserve the poets from the whims of their editors and the vagaries of their printers. Think of the battalions of fighting footnotes that would never have been loosed upon us if Shakespeare's manuscripts had survived or if the only copy of 'Beowulf' had not been slightly charred. And then think of the often deliberate obscurity of so much modern verse. The best poets have so resolutely set out to change things, to avoid the obvious word, the obvious thumping metre and the obvious rhymes, that they have, in a way, played into the hands of the editors and emenders of the future. By showing not only what the poets wrote but also what they almost wrote and then thought better of, the Lockwood worksheets may ensure that the poets have the last word on at least some of their own poems.

Second, the collection may be a help in interpreting obscure poems. Seeing the drafts of a poem will not, of course, make the final version less complete in itself or less difficult. For often the real difficulty comes late: at the precise moment when the author sees how he can gather into one complex phrase all the stray feelings that had been scattered haphazardly through the poem. But though the cancellations will not improve the finished poem, they may help the reader on to the right track. For example, the library's showpiece is a collection of Dylan Thomas's drafts for 'The Ballad of the Long-Legged Bait'. The cases that display them run, as I remember, round three sides of a very large room. I do not think that any amount of poring over the dozens of sheets and thousands of emendations will necessarily make the poem clearer. It is not the kind of poem that has much truck with clarity or the precise definition of experience. It is, instead, a poem of texture, a great monument of surrealist rhetoric; and as such the criterion is the poet's inventiveness with language and metaphor. But pure invention, like pure sound, takes the reader only so far; one needs a few other signposts along the way.

What, for example, is one to make of a line like this: 'The anchor dives through the floors of a church'? In context, it seems like just another way, among many, of saying that the sailor has come home to the land, presumably to die – the 'floors of a church' tell one that; and this has something, obscurely enough, to do with a submerged village. But the drafts of the poem add quite another dimension. Apparently, the line began life with a heavy-handed manipulation of the usual unconscious symbols. It began as 'The mast-high anchor dives through a cleft'. But the poet steadily set himself to refine away that initial crudity. First he tried to introduce the idea of journey's end, so he wrote: 'The anchor dives through closing paths.' Then came a contrast between the sea and the fecundity of the land: but unfortunately it was just fantasy. It was: 'The anchor dives among hayricks.' Then finally the symbols, journey's end and death, all came together in his last version: 'The anchor dives through the floors of a church.' The drafts, in fact, show where the thing started – the direction in which it is moving and the kind of effort the poet was willing to make in order not to be obvious. They show, in short, that there is care and a kind of rhetorical brainwork behind what appears at first to be a haphazard piling on of effects.

And this is the third use of a collection of worksheets: it shows the kind of poet a man is: how much he revises and what he revises for; whether, like Pope, his work comes easily and then has to be cut down, or whether he accretes a poem slowly, painfully, from dull beginnings. There is much to be learned by comparing, say, Mozart's lucid manuscripts, where the corrections are occasional and confident, with Beethoven's illegible, tortured mare's nests. Or consider William Carlos Williams, who has presented a great stack of worksheets to the Lockwood Library. His poems often appear to me to be less poetry, in the strong sense, than Americana, random jottings on interesting but haphazard bits of American city life, unformed and inconclusive. Yet all of them have gone through endless elaborate revisions. So one begins to realize that the vividness of his little scenes, when they are vivid, depends on the actual shape of the poems on the page, or, as Karl Shapiro suggested, that the metre itself is, in a way, visual. In short, the early drafts will not make a poem better in itself but they will help one understand the kind of effect a poet is after, the kind of work he can and cannot do.

Finally, there is the matter of self-criticism. Crashaw, for example, Wordsworth, Keats, Tennyson, Yeats all revised or even completely rewrote a number of their poems, often a long time after they first appeared in print. So the later versions are, as it were, criticisms of the early poems by their own authors; they are ways of showing where the earlier versions failed and what the poet in his maturity thinks he was really after.

The Lockwood Library, then, is, in a sense, a feat of imagination in a realm where that kind of daring is about as rare as a good summer in England. Why, then, does one have certain misgivings about it? And I, for one, do have misgivings. The reason, I suppose, is that although the collection has none of the ponderous conservatism of most university libraries, it is still part of an institution. And so there is a danger of institutionalizing the very material that it is trying to preserve in all its original freshness. I do not mean that once a poet is invited to send his worksheets to Buffalo he can then sit back and imagine that he is safely fixed in his niche in literature, already part of the university syllabus. On the contrary, I doubt if an invitation will do any more than cheer him up and make him think that *someone*, at least, has read and liked his work. Nevertheless, however much the Lockwood collection owes to one man's bright idea and one man's hard work, it is not a private collection. It is there for the benefit of researchers. And there are, in America at least, far more Ph.D.s than genuine subjects for them. It is as though a man writes a poem in Connecticut and, almost before the ink is dry, a graduate student in Nebraska has started to write a thesis about it. Yet this does not make a poet's work more important or unique. The writer becomes just another thesis topic, and the manuscripts over which he has sweated, with all their mess, impatience, excitement and boredom, have become just so much useful evidence for an academic theory.

The institutionalizing of the living, however, is a minor evil, inevitable whenever scholarship grows larger than what it feeds on. But the Lockwood collection originally had behind it, as I mentioned at the beginning, a more ominous idea: that by studying a poet's worksheets one might eventually be able to understand the nature of the creative act itself. Whether or not this will ever happen none of us is likely to know; psychology will have to become a good deal more delicate and complex before the library's materials can be used for much except rough generalizations. But there is still the question of whether or not one wants it to happen. Psychology may eventually tell us a great deal about poets, but will it ever say very much about poems? Will knowing how a poet writes ever make much difference to what he writes? Or, to put it yet another way, is one interested in the inspiration or in what the poet has done with it?

Personally, I think the answer is clear: the worksheets show how the first loose approximations are tightened up until they are brought to the lucid inevitability of real poetry; but what started it all off seems to me almost entirely beside the point. For the process has little or nothing to do with the psychopathology of inspiration, or whatever you want to call it, and it has everything to do with the poetic intelligence. A poet is a man with a special gift for a special medium, language and insight; he is able to think in terms of his medium, just as a musician thinks in sounds, a sculptor thinks in physical masses, a mathematician in symbols, or a philosopher in abstractions or logical forms. Obviously, this kind of thinking has nothing to do with reaching certain general conclusions and then translating these into stone or notes or metaphor. It is a matter of exploring the potentialities of the medium itself. In recent years, for example, one major philosophical poem at least has been written: Eliot's 'Four Quartets'. But there is no question of Eliot's being an original philosopher. Instead, he experiences philosophical ideas; that is, he shows the relevance and dignity ideas assume when they impinge on a poet's sensibility. The revisions and corrections, the false starts of a poet's worksheets, reveal, then, far more about the calibre of his artistic intelligence, about his ability to deal responsibly with his material, than they reveal about its nature and origins. In short, the interest is critical, not psychological.

I suggest, then, that bothering too much about the making of a poem is a substitute for bothering about poetry itself. One of the gloomier aspects of modern verse is the steady decline in the interest in poetry and the steady rise in the interest in poets. It is as though the standards of the popular press – what they call the 'human interest angle' – were taking over even in the arts. It is no longer enough that someone writes good poems; in order to be read, he must also have a personal myth: he must have walked off with his professor's wife, drunk himself to death or given public lectures on his personal weaknesses (preferably, of course, to American universities). In short, he is expected to go through his poetic act for the benefit of those whose idea of art derives from *The Moon and Sixpence* and *The Outsider*. Perhaps this new fashion in curiosity may make it easier for one or two writers to make a living. But it will not improve the value of their work by one single jot.

Neither will their confessions about their ways of writing. It does not really help much to know that one poet could write only when locked in a soundproof box, or another needed a background of jazz records, or a third always chewed opium or coughdrops or gum. If a poet is continually harping on how he writes, the chances are that he is unsure of the value of what he writes, as though he felt it needed something more to make it interesting. For 'how' and 'what' in art have normally little to do with each other. There is, for example, a powerful passage in *Death in Venice* when Aschenbach, the ageing literary giant, composes his masterpiece while gloating over the sight of the Polish boy with whom he has become infatuated. 'Verily', comments Thomas Mann, 'it is well for the world that it sees only the beauty of the completed work and not its origins nor the conditions whence it sprang; since the knowledge of the artist's inspiration might often but confuse and alarm and so prevent the full effect of its excellence.' As though to prove how much the artist spoils the work of art, Robert Graves recently tried, in his book *The Crowning Privilege*, to judge English poetry by his personal opinions of the poets. And he found himself left, of course, with almost no poetry at all.

I wonder, in fact, if the desire to probe into how a poem came to be written is not an implicit denial of the nature of the completed work. Ten years ago there appeared a collection of essays on the Lockwood manuscripts; it was called *Poets at Work* and it showed that the worksheets have, at least, one thing in common: what one of the contributors, Professor Stauffer, called 'the drive towards impersonality'. The poet, that is, often begins with some trivial personal event – a walk, a squabble, the sack, a parting – but, after a little, ideas and images turn up that are often only tenuously connected with his original personal situation. It is when these take over that the real business of poetry begins: the business of using the personal disturbance to give to the objective theme its own vivid life. When the poet has done this he has created an independent object in the public world. Like a child grown up, it has to fend for itself as best it may. He has nothing more to do with it – its beginnings are, at best, only case history. This, presumably, is why Coleridge said that 'a second promise of genius is the choice of subjects very remote from the private interests and circumstances of the writer himself'. Coleridge went on to describe Shakespeare at work in this way, stressing the impersonality, 'himself, meanwhile, unparticipating in the passions, and actuated only by that pleasurable excitement, which had resulted from the energetic fervour of his own spirit, in so vividly exhibiting what it had so accurately and profoundly contemplated'. If Coleridge is right, then the attempt to understand the nature of poetry by working backwards from the finished poem to its scrappy sources is essentially a lack of respect for the whole creative effort.

The Lockwood Library at Buffalo has, then, the finest and most extraordinary collection of modern poetry in the world. But there is quite simply the question of how it is to be used: to serve the poems or the poets? Will it be used to provide the clearest understanding of the best versions of twentieth-century poems? Or will it be used as a museum of psychological curiosities, devoted not to poems but to the mystique of being a poet? Poetry is the profoundest and most moving expression of everything that most concerns us. But poets are, for the most part, a conceited, jealous, unpleasant lot. The more, I suggest, we know about their work and the less we know about them, the better for everyone.

The Listener, 1958

Shiprock

I suppose the first sight of a mountain is always the best. Later, when you are waiting to start, you may grow to hate the brute, because you are afraid. And when, finally, you are climbing, you are never aware of the mountain as a mountain: it is merely so many little areas of rock to be worked out in terms of hand-holds, foot-holds and effort, like so many chess problems. But when you first see it in the distance, remote and beautiful and unknown, then there seems some reason for climbing. That, perhaps, is what Mallory meant by his 'Because it's there'.

I first saw Shiprock on a midsummer day. I was exhausted, having driven the two-and-a-half-thousand miles from New Jersey to New Mexico in relatively few days. Moreover, I was unfit; I had not climbed for several weeks and I looked forward without much pleasure to what would probably be thirty-six hours on a vertical face. Finally, I had that morning left my wife and baby son in Taos; and going off for a big climb is always a wretched business; it leaves you tense and sick at heart. I think now that serious climbs are for bachelors; they become so much more difficult when you leave anything behind.

I was feeling, in short, just a bit sorry for myself as I drove across the rolling Apache country and into the wastes of the Navajo reservation. The area set aside by the U.S. Government for the Navajo Indians is the most desolate land in the world, flat, dried-up, harsh, stony. But, recently, oil and uranium have been found and a little wealth is beginning to creep in. In places the desolation seems almost busy – though no less desolate. It was a few miles south of one of these little centres, a new boom town called Farmington, that I first saw Shiprock. I had come out, imperceptibly, on top of a huge flat hill. To the north and west the desert dropped away to a lower level. A long way north rose the blue tiers of the Mesa Verde, where the prehistoric cave cities are. Sweeping round to the south, the desert was ringed with smaller mesas, the queer, flat-topped hills, looking like bits of plain set up on vertical cliffs. But in the west, about fifty miles away, below the sinking sun, where the desert seemed blank and endless, was Shiprock. Its bluish, hazy mass swam sheer out of the desert, rising eighteen hundred feet to the huge twin east and south towers. Between them peered the north tower, farther away and seeming smaller: then the bulk of the mountain bending a little towards the western desert.

I had never even seen a photograph of it before. Perhaps that is why I had agreed to join the climbing party. But in the late afternoon sun it looked very beautiful. No wonder it is the sacred mountain of the Navajos. It dominates the whole landscape continuously and effortlessly. As I drove towards it, it was hidden at times by corners and edges of sandstone, but it controlled, always, my whole sense of direction. According to the picture post-cards, Shiprock got its name because at sunset it looks like a great ship floating forwards across the desert. Perhaps it does. But in Navajo myth it stretches towards heaven and the souls of men descend to earth from it. It dominates their cosmology as it dominates the landscape.

There is a tiny Indian town of Shiprock, about twenty miles from the mountain. I had arranged to meet my Princeton climbing companions there. 'O, we'll meet at the main restaurant,' we had said. 'If we're not there, we'll be camping under the climb.' It was vague, of course, but then none of us knew what the town – or the mountain, for that matter – would be like. Mercifully, there were only a couple of restaurants, a couple of gas stations, a school and a couple of trading posts. There were mule carts in the street, which made it look more like Mexico than I had ever seen before in the States, and Indians were cramming into the usual pick-up trucks to return to their villages for the night. The men, small, thickish and rather saturnine, wore the regulation denims, except for a few wrapped in their blankets like dark, heavy Della Robbia infants. But the women were splendid, skirted to their feet and shawled in vivid reds, purples and oranges. In the huge golden sunset they looked oddly unreal – or at least, unexpected – as if I'd walked into the middle of some vast play, and didn't know the plot.

There is a big motel and restaurant run by the Navajos. One of the Princeton cars was outside it, but there was no sign of my friends in the café. They had left half an hour before, the proprietress told me. They would be under the mountain. It was almost dark now, so, with nothing to lose, I ordered a meal. If we were to climb the next day, heaven knew when I'd next eat properly.

Then I set about finding my way out to the rock. The directions were simple enough: go south on the main road until the gravelled turn-off to Lukachukai. Follow that for eight miles over the desert. When you come to the ridge, go right on a track straight towards the mountain. It was quite dark by the time I started, but the full moon was up, my headlights were good and the others would probably have lit a fire. I wasn't worried.

At first, the driving was easy enough. But it was darker than I thought and the eight miles bumping along the gravel road across the desert seemed long and slow. Finally, a great black wall of rock loomed up on either side of the road: the ridge. My headlights made strange, impertinent shadows on it. There was a track off to the right just before the ridge, but it seemed improbably vague. So I went past the thing and saw another. There seemed nothing to do but take it. As I swung the car off the road, it was like walking unexpectedly into the deep-end of a swimming pool. The car jerked and heaved and wallowed. The track was hardish sand, full of pot-holes and strewn with rocks. Sometimes it would go round the little dunes, sometimes it went over them. Then I usually had to back the car and take a run at the rise, careering over the top, headlights flailing in the air, not knowing if the track went straight on over or turned on the top.

It took me about an hour to drive two miles. Finally, of course, I went wrong. I found myself with the car stuck in the sand on the top of a dune, the track entirely vanished and what appeared to be a vertical drop on three sides. The only way off was to back down the steep slope I had just come up. Without a reversing light, it seemed impossible. The great black ridge rose sheer above me, its darkness jagged and menacing against the sky. I could just make out the peak of Shiprock heaving up darkly behind it. There was no sign of the others' fire, only that great black, menacing ridge looming up in front, and the desert, eerie and shimmering and vague under the moon. The wind blew soft but insistent sand into my eyes and mouth. I began to shout in the hope that the others were just the far side of the ridge. My yells echoed back to me and faded away. So I gave up and went back to the car. Being outside in the moonlit desert made me feel terribly exposed and isolated. The place is too vast and indifferent to be bearable at night. I stretched out in the back of the car, drank some whisky and settled down to sleep. A huge grasshopper which had settled on the ledge of the rear window creaked heavily from time to time, like a pair of ancient corsets. The moon shone in on me and all around was the vast, rustling silence of the desert. Oddly enough, I slept very well.

At dawn, I climbed the ridge, one of three thin, curving tentacles spreading out from Shiprock. The path I should have taken ran, quite distinct, along the other side. At the end of it, tiny against the desert, was the other car and my friends lying around it in their sleeping-bags.

The rest of that day was like a bad dream. We had three things to do: find the start of the route; get some more food and liquid from the town; wait for the fifth member of the party to arrive. We were to be in all four Englishmen and an American, all from Princeton. One Englishman was still missing. Simple enough. But what happened in fact was that we were systematically demoralized. First, there was the rock itself: the bulk of the mountain is sheer sandstone, whilst the back is shattered basalt. All of it is utterly rotten. It came away as you touched it, hardly waiting to be pulled. Most of the ordinary holds were useless; the only safe ones were cracks to jam your toes and fingers into. Second, there was the thirst. All day the wind blew steadily; our mouths and eyes and ears were full of sand; we were parched whenever we were not actually drinking. It was a permanent condition, like the beating of your blood, or the pain of someone with cancer. It seemed impossible that we should ever have enough to drink again. Third, was the heat. Shiprock had never been climbed later than May. This was the end of June. To move into the sun was like swinging open some great furnace door. The whole landscape shimmered and swayed and faded in the heat. The rocks became almost too hot to touch. In the village the temperature was about 110° F. in the shade. Heaven alone knows what it was out in the desert. Fourth, was the Accident. On the last ascent a man had been killed. When we went to get our stores in the village, we heard of nothing else. 'He was a young guy, just like you-all.

Say,' one would turn to the other, 'he looked just like this guy, didn't he?' 'Sure. And he bought the same candies. You should have seen him when they brought him in. Gee.' And so on. We fled from the place as soon as we could. But by the time we drove back across the desert we were sick to death of the whole miserable business: the rotten rock, the thirst, the heat, the shopkeepers' gloating over that poor wretch's death, and the mountain looming there impassively against another unbelievable sunset. It seemed a silly, pointless way of getting oneself killed.

Dick Sykes, the missing Englishman, had still not arrived, so we decided to go up without him. We had our excuses, of course: I had to get back to my family; the others were expected in the Tetons in two days; and so on. But the truth was none of us could bear the thought of another day of tension, heat and waiting like this one. If we didn't climb the mountain the next day, we wouldn't climb it at all. So we loaded ourselves up, like so many mules, with climbing equipment, food, drink and sleeping-bags, and groped in the fading light painfully up to the start of the climb.

The west wall of Shiprock is basalt. It drops down to a huge, curving overhang. The climb begins on the left side of this, where the lip of the rock sticks out less angrily. Underneath the overhang is a shallow, level, sandy cave shaped like a scimitar. We built a fire, heated some of the precious water for tea and lay down to sleep in the cave. Again I slept surprisingly well, but I was woken a couple of times by faint rustlings. For such a dead lunar landscape, the place seemed strangely unquiet.

I suppose it goes without saying that the climb, after all the horrors of thinking about it, was perfectly straightforward. We were up before the sun, had a miserable breakfast of cornflakes and tepid baked beans, and were off. It is a violent beginning. You go straight from the ground on to stirrups on the overhang. But this is mercifully short; four heaves, a little awkward straddling with the feet and we were up. And most important, once we began to climb all the worries and fears and tensions left us. Fear is always a matter of the future tense; the present is too blessedly factual.

You come over the overhang into a vast amphitheatre of shattered basalt. At the back of it the head-wall goes up a thousand feet in four giant steps. At the bottom, facing you as you pull over the lip, is a plaque to mark the spot where the poor devil had landed last year. He had fallen on the way back from the second ascent of the north tower. Still, we had our own work to do. We started to climb the head-wall.

It was surprisingly easy, just another rock climb, most of it not more than about grade IV. And provided you jammed in the cracks instead of pulling on the crumbling face, it was quite safe. Towards the top of the head-wall the climbing was harder for a little; but climbing, doing something, was such a blessed relief from thinking about it, that we were going well and quickly. John Wharton, the young leader of the climb, and I were at the top of the head-wall in a couple of hours.

The others were still two hundred feet down when there was a shout from below. It was Dick Sykes. He had arrived late in the night, and like me, had got stuck in the desert. Now he was angry, roaring at us from far below because we hadn't waited for him. Urged by his annoyance, he climbed the overhang and the first eight hundred feet of the head-wall on his own and unroped. But he had said his say and tied on to a rope before the real difficulties began.

Once we got to the top of the head-wall we lost the route. There were two ways on: the ordinary route and the north tower which went up vertically in front of us. The latter had been climbed only twice before and was technically harder than the ordinary route, but also much shorter. As for the ordinary: according to the description we had unearthed, we were supposed to rope down a smooth, vertical hundred-and-twenty-foot wall to a ledge, leaving the rope in position for the return. From the ledge the crux of the climb began: a hundred-and-twenty-foot friction traverse. Wharton had seen some horrifying photographs of it at the American Alpine Club. Mercifully, he had not shown the rest of us. After the traverse, there were only two small overhangs between you and the summit of the south tower. From where we perched we could see plenty of smooth vertical walls, but no ledges at the bottom of them. It took a long time to find the right one. It was far below and strewn with cans, as though too many people had waited there far too long a time. But there was no way of fixing a rope to get down there. The walls were quite smooth, without the smallest crack for a piton. Finally, we found two little holes drilled in the rock, where the bolts, of which the Americans are so fond, had been screwed. But being four Englishmen to one American, it had never occurred to us to bring bolts. Only Wharton, in fact, had ever used them. So there we were. It was the north tower or nothing.

It was, of course, the north tower. The route goes straight up from the platform at the top of the head-wall in two pitches of VI. It is not strenuous, but very thin and very rotten. It took a great deal of juggling with stirrups and pitons. But Wharton and Sykes led it beautifully between them. There was never any question but that we would get up. Only in the last fifty feet did the rottenness of the rock reach a point of lunacy. You could stick your fingers into the stuff, almost like mud. But the Colorado guide who had first climbed it must have known a great deal about rock structure; there was a string of pitons going straight up this putty, and they were as solid as the rock should have been. We had to climb from one to the other, ignoring the face itself contemptuously.

We sat on the summit and took the usual photographs. We opened the little steel canister bolted to the top and added our names to the list; we were the third party to get there. Then, since we knew we wouldn't be spending the night on the mountain after all, we passed our water-bottles round with wanton generosity. But the sun was high and the wind still blew parchingly. We could see trees and the San Juan River glinting twenty miles away in the town of Shiprock. Way to the north the Mesa Verde rose cool and blue. So we didn't stay long on the summit. We began to rope down the rotten vertical face at four p.m. By six-thirty we were back at our camp under the overhang, thirteen hours after we left it.

And that was that. The climb had been hard and was a brilliant lead by Wharton, who was, incidentally, only eighteen. But it was just a climb. It was not, oddly enough, the climbing that made the ascent of Shiprock so difficult. It was the place itself; the eerie, untouched lunar desert, the almost unbearable thirst and heat, the strange sense of threat in its continual rustling sounds. I understood better now why to the Navajos the mountain is sacred. You are often scared climbing, but scare is local: a move out of balance, a loose hold, too much exposure. You climb better when you are scared. But fear is generalized, like superstition. It clings to a place like its shadow. It is when you have to sit still under the shadow, wait and do nothing, that fear goes over you.

But it could have been worse. The following day I was in one of the trading posts buying a Navajo rug. The shopkeeper had asked me about the climb. Then, just as I was leaving, he added casually: 'Say, how many rattlers did you see?' 'Rattlers?' I asked. 'Sure, rattlers. Rattlesnakes. The place is full of them.' And I thought of that rustling, empty cave where we had slept and the deep cracks in the rocks we had so carefully climbed in. Full of rattlesnakes. But, mercifully, we had never known.

The Climbers' Club Journal, 1960

Everest*

When Hillary got down from the summit of Everest in 1953 he announced the victory in classic style: 'We knocked the bastard off', he said. Unromantic, disrespectful, and aggressive in a practical way, his statement was not only typical of the tone of modern climbing, it was also essential to it. The few remaining big peaks and vertical faces which are the present goals of mountaineers are too difficult, too technical and very much too serious to allow room for what the boys in the business used to call 'The Spirit of the Hills'. Mountain mysticism – the belief that slogging up a route or seeing a nice view from the top will promote a Vision of Truth – is a luxury for which there is precious little time on the hard climbs. (When a young English mountaineering mystic went on to the Eiger Wand two years ago, his partner was killed and he himself was saved only by the efforts of two of the toughest realists in British climbing.) Romanticism will never get you up a really serious mountain, and mysticism may well be the death of you. What counts is physical skill, power and stamina, good organization, and a driving desire to get the job done. The psychologists call the best climbers 'highly motivated'; among climbers themselves the approving trade name is 'hard men'.

The American Everest Expedition 1963 included some very hard men indeed. It was also, as you would expect, immensely well organized. But it did the job: four climbers reached the summit by

* James Ramsey Ullman and others, *Americans on Everest* (Philadelphia: Lippincott, 1964); Woodrow Wilson Sayre, *Four Against Everest* (Englewood Cliffs: Prentice-Hall, 1964).

the traditional South Col route; two others, Willi Unsoeld and Tom Hornbein, pioneered a brand new route by the West Ridge, reached the summit by it, and then traversed on down to the South Col – a major triple achievement in the Himalaya. Four of them also spent a night out without bivouac equipment at more than 28,000 feet, another Himalayan first which no one, I imagine, will be in a rush to repeat. Early on, the expedition's official scribe, James Ramsey Ullman, remarks that 'the raising of money for an Everest expedition proved only slightly less difficult than, say, soliciting funds for a statue of Karl Marx on the White House lawn'. As it turned out, the members of the expedition had their brilliant success and finished on the White House lawn, with President Kennedy giving them a medal.

They also raised a vast sum of money. The American expedition was the most expensive (it cost, in all, over $400,000), the best equipped (they had, for example, eleven walkie-talkies), and the largest Himalayan show ever mounted; twenty American climbers – including, heaven help us, a psychologist and a sociologist – more than two football squads of high altitude Sherpas, and 900 porters. As someone wrote to me afterwards: 'With all that lot, they could have run a super highway up the thing.' Had it failed it would have been, I suppose, another joke at the expense of the American passion for over-organization and over-equipment; but, the logic of these things being what it is, the achievement more than justified the fuss and expense.

Team-work, reserves and organization are, in fact, essential to climbing the really big peaks. The British had realized this by 1953 when they gave their expedition into the charge not of Eric Shipton, a fine mountaineer with great experience on Everest, but of Sir John Hunt, a man of great determination and guts but less climbing ability than Shipton. The difference was that Shipton was a mountaineering purist in favour of tiny, do-it-yourself expeditions, whereas Hunt was a professional soldier who knew all about the organization and co-ordination of complicated troop movements. This was precisely the kind of problem which faced Norman Dyhrenfurth, the American leader. In Ullman's account, the word 'logistics' turns up with great frequency; and, according to Webster's dictionary, it is a military term. So many cylinders of oxygen, so much food and climbing gear have to be at such and such a point on the mountain by such and such a date; so many climbers, Sherpas and porters have to be moved from here to there and back at specific times; X is resting while Y climbs; then Y rests and X climbs; and so on. At times it sounds less like a climb than a battle, or a big business take-over bid.

Yet when it came to the push, all that meticulous planning and smooth equipment counted for much less than the human effort: first from Jim Whittaker and the Sherpa Gombu, then from Lute Jerstad and Barry Bishop, finally the superlative push by Unsoeld and Hornbein. A computer might have been able to cope with all those logistics, and Corporation might have kept the whole affair running, but mercifully it is still individuals who do the climbing.

The effort is, after all, a good part of what the game is about. Climbing is not a matter of conquering a mountain – whatever that may mean – and sticking a flag on top; it is, instead, a question of testing the limits of your endurance, physical and mental. For that, the drive there and back to a summit is as good a gauge as any. (There are, incidentally, other gauges even in climbing: for example, the vertical or overhanging rock-faces in the Dolomites, Yosemite and Wales which, as often as not, reach no summit at all.) The competition is with yourself, however nationalistic the press makes the sport seem, and however tense the top climbers become about their colleagues' achievements. The point is to see how far you can push your own boat out, not for risks or for kicks – since practically no sane, or living, climber courts death voluntarily, or even takes unnecessary risks – but as a curiously objective test of personal skill and resilience. Some people test these qualities against the bottle, or with pen and paper, or paint, or with women. A mountain is as good a means as any to an end, and less socially destructive than most. And by translating aggression into straight physical action, it does help wonderfully to clear the head.

The expedition's sociologist observes interestingly that much climbing talk around Base Camp was devoted to one end: maintaining, by a canny vacillation between pessimism and optimism, a condition of continual uncertainty. This, he feels, somehow increased the climbers' 'motivation'. More simply, uncertainty has another end: it's so nice when you stop. Action is a great relief as well as a release. However odd it may sound to the non-climber, it is unusual to be frightened when actually climbing a mountain; but nearly everybody is scared when waiting to start. This may be nothing very peculiar to mountaineering, but it is important. For, despite the aggressive nonsense talked about it, climbing is not a maverick sport, nor even particularly dangerous. On the contrary, provided you are fit and not worried by heights, it is just like any other form of rather violent, skilful exercise. With this difference: you have to be very careful where you put your hands and feet.

It is a pity, then, that Ullman's account encourages the operatic, outsider's view of the job. There is, for example, almost no technically difficult climbing on Everest, compared, say, with Himalayan peaks like the Mustagh Tower, Gasherbrum IV or Nuptse. It is, rather, a racking snow and ice grind on a huge scale. Yet whenever Ullman's heroes touch rock he describes them as 'clawing' their way up. Now, anyone who has ever been on a rope knows that once you start 'clawing' you're off. The whole art of rock climbing is to play it cool.

It is the same with the expedition's one tragedy: Jake Breitenbach was killed when an ice-wall collapsed on him without warning – a gratuitous, wanton, wholly unpredictable death. Ullman records it all in detail, using the team's diaries and reminiscences. Yet there is something lush and over-stated in his account which strikes me as false. It was a terrible and shocking accident, but I know from my own experience that death in the mountains occurs in a context much more like that of *Catch 22* than of *The White Tower* – in a context, that is, which is distracting, even absurd, and where the inevitable insights the tragedy brings into loss, guilt and uneasy grief take a long time to be understood, or even registered. But the public demands that death be given to them as they expect it: played out with the major chords and grand choral swoop of high drama, yet with nothing haphazard, indifferent or final about it.

Ullman, however, has written his book with all the big magazine appeal he can muster: a combination of melodrama, joshing, rhetorical questions and continued-in-our-next fade-outs. Perhaps the reason is that, because of leg trouble, he was unable to go farther than the Hotel Royal, Katmandu. So he was never properly in tune with the grim practicality of the experience itself. There is something hard, factual and demanding about serious action which, to be reproduced in prose, needs a certain tenseness of line and sharpness of definition. It is not often found. Cherry Apsley Garrard had it in *The Worst Journey in the World*; but that book took years not just to write but to arrive emotionally at the point where he was able to write it. Hemingway had it, too, less because he was a man of action than because he had the genius and discipline to imagine himself into being one.

But if Ullman is no Cherry Garrard, it is scarcely his fault. Perhaps he has given the American public what it wants: an easily readable, not very technical story (the detailed information is in appendices by the team experts); it exudes good will, human interest and undemanding drama. The French and Italians seem to ask something still more high-pitched and choric from their mountaineers. The British prefer Hunt's blank, putty prose. For the moment, all that matters is that the Americans should be made aware of the superb achievements of their climbers on Everest. In time maybe someone will produce a real piece of literature about it. Certainly, the expedition deserves it.

Style is just one of the problems Woodrow Wilson Sayre has failed to solve in *Four Against Everest*, an account of a trip he and three companions made to Everest the year before the official American attempt. The main problem is to know what they were doing there at all, since they were totally without experience. They learnt to cut ice-steps by imitating their Sherpas on the ice fall above the Ngo Jumbo glacier – which is rather like learning to drive in a Ferrari; it's not only silly, it's an awful waste of opportunity. Still, they had stamina and great optimism, which helped them to push their way up to a little beyond the North Col. It was a respectable effort, though not quite as stunning as Sayre suggests; after all, the Mustagh Tower, technically one of the hardest routes ever done in the Himalaya, was also climbed by a party of four.

I suspect that the main purpose of this jaunt was to prove that all the epithets used by the detractors of mountaineering are true: irresponsible, dangerous, a bit stupid, a sport neurotically linked with the cult of the superman. All the qualities are there in Sayre's account. *Irresponsible*: to get to the North Col they spent a month in Communist Tibet; had they been found, no further expeditions might have been allowed to the area, and some kind of international 'incident' might have been provoked. A great deal of time and money was also wasted by search parties, who are scarcely mentioned by Sayre. *Dangerous*: Sayre himself seems to have come back down much of the mountain in the quickest possible way – that is, by falling. *Stupid and neurotic*: the style of the book is in keeping with the exploit; it vacillates between the Romantic joke and a constant, anxious, muscle-flexing one-upmanship. Perhaps it does provide a touch of light, farcical relief to all those painstaking logistics. It may even be a notable contribution to the history of the psychopathology of mountaineering. But the only certain achievement of Sayre's circus was, by some miracle, to have survived. When I think of the numbers of skilled and experienced climbers who each year, making no obvious mistakes, manage even so to get themselves killed, the only appropriate response is Adlai Stevenson's: 'I'm too old to weep, and it hurts too much to laugh.'

The New York Review of Books, 1964

About the Author

A. ALVAREZ was born in London in 1929 and educated at Oundle School and Corpus Christi College, Oxford, where he took a first in English. For a time he researched and taught in Oxford and America. Out of this came a critical study of modern poetry, *The Shaping Spirit* (1958). Since 1956 he has lived as a free-lance writer in London, traveling a good deal and making occasional academic forays to the States—most recently as a Visiting Professor of English at the State University of New York. His seminars on criticism at Princeton University in 1958 resulted in another book, *The School of Donne* (1961).

Mr. Alvarez has been poetry editor and critic of *The Observer*. He contributed to the *New Statesman* for ten years and was its drama critic from 1958 to 1960, and he has written for *The Spectator*. In 1961 he received the Vachel Lindsay Prize for poetry from *Poetry* (Chicago), and in the following year he edited and introduced for Penguin a best-selling anthology, *The New Poetry*. Mr. Alvarez has also written *Under Pressure: the Writer in Society: Eastern Europe and the U.S.A.*, and contributes articles to *Commentary* and *The New York Review of Books*.

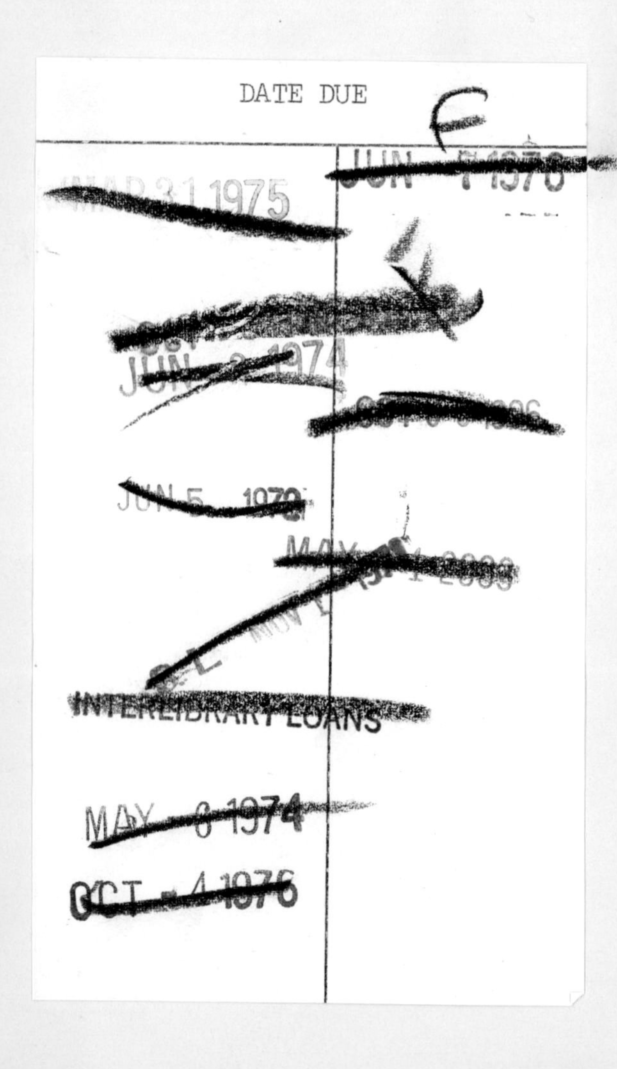
DATE DUE
MAR 31 1975
INTERLIBRARY LOANS
OCT - 4 1976